Therapeutic Communities

GW01086849

Therapeutic Communities for Psychosis offers a uniquely global insight into the renewed interest in the use of therapeutic communities for the treatment of psychosis, as complementary to pharmacological treatment. Within this edited volume contributors from around the world look at the range of treatment programmes on offer in therapeutic communities for those suffering from psychosis.

Divided into three parts, the book covers:

- The historical and philosophical background of therapeutic communities and the treatment of psychosis in this context.
- Treatment settings and clinical models.
- Alternative therapies and extended applications

This book will be essential reading for all mental health professionals, targeting readers from a number of disciplines including psychiatry, psychology, social work, psychotherapy and group analysis.

John Gale is CEO of Community Housing and Therapy, a mental health charity specialising in therapeutic communities. He is a board member of ISPS UK, and was development editor and deputy editor of the journal *Therapeutic Communities*.

Alba Realpe is the deputy manager at Mount Lodge, a therapeutic community in Eastbourne, run by Community Housing and Therapy.

Enrico Pedriali is a physician, clinical psychologist, psychoanalytic psychotherapist and consultant in mental health institutions. He is a group analyst and past President of the Italian Association of Therapeutic Communities.

The International Society for the Psychological Treatments of the Schizophrenias and Other Psychoses Book Series

Series editor: Brian Martindale

The ISPS (the International Society for the Psychological Treatments of the Schizophrenias and other Psychoses) has a history stretching back some 50 years during which it has witnessed the relentless pursuit of biological explanations for psychosis. The tide is now turning again. There is a welcome international resurgence of interest in a range of psychological factors in psychosis that have considerable explanatory power and also distinct therapeutic possibilities. Governments, professional groups, users and carers are increasingly expecting interventions that involve talking and listening as well as skilled practitioners in the main psychotherapeutic modalities as important components of the care of the seriously mentally ill.

The ISPS is a global society. It is composed of an increasing number of groups of professionals organised at national, regional and more local levels around the world. The society has started a range of activities intended to support professionals, users and carers. Such persons recognise the potential humanitarian and therapeutic potential of skilled psychological understanding and therapy in the field of psychosis. Our members cover a wide spectrum of interests from psychodynamic, systemic, cognitive and arts therapies to the need-adaptive approaches and to therapeutic institutions. We are most interested in establishing meaningful dialogue with those practitioners and researchers who are more familiar with biological-based approaches. Our activities include regular international and national conferences, newsletters and email discussion groups in many countries across the world.

One of these activities is to facilitate the publication of quality books that cover the wide terrain which interests ISPS members and a large number of other mental health professionals and policymakers and implementers. We are delighted that Routledge Mental Health has seen the importance and potential of such an endeavour and have agreed to publish an ISPS series of books.

We anticipate that some of the books will be controversial and will challenge certain aspects of current practice in some countries. Other books will promote ideas and authors well known in some countries but not familiar to others. Our overall aim is to encourage the dissemination of existing knowledge and ideas, promote healthy debate and encourage more research in a most important field whose secrets almost certainly do not all reside in the neurosciences.

For more information about the ISPS, email isps@isps.org or visit our website www.isps.org.

Other titles in the series

Models of Madness: Psychological, Social and Biological Approaches to Schizophrenia
Edited by John Read, Loren R. Mosher & Richard P. Bentall

Psychoses: An Integrative Perspective
Johan Cullberg

Evolving Psychosis: Different Stages, Different Treatments
Edited by Jan Olav Johanessen, Brian V. Martindale & Johan Cullberg

Family and Multi-Family work with Psychosis
Gerd-Ragna Bloch Thorsen, Trond Gronnestad & Anne Lise Oxenvad

Experiences of Mental Health In-Patient Care: Narratives from Service
Users, Carers and Professionals
Edited by Mark Hardcastle, David Kennard, Sheila Grandison & Leonard Fagin

Psychotherapies for Psychoses: Theoretical, Cultural, and Clinical Integration
Edited by John Gleeson, Eión Killackey & Helen Krstev

Therapeutic Communities for Psychosis

Philosophy, History and Clinical Practice

Edited by John Gale, Alba Realpe
& Enrico Pedriali

Foreword by Professor
R.D. Hinshelwood

LONDON AND NEW YORK

First published 2008 by Routledge
27 Church Road, Hove, East Sussex BN3 2FA

Simultaneously published in the USA and Canada
by Routledge
270 Madison Avenue, New York, NY10016

Routledge is an imprint of the Taylor & Francis Group, an Informa business

Typeset in Times by Garfield Morgan, Swansea, West Glamorgan
Printed and bound in Great Britain by T J International Ltd
Paperback cover design by Hybert Design

This publication has been produced with paper manufactured to strict
environmental standards and with pulp derived from sustainable forests.

British Library Cataloguing in Publication Data
A catalogue record for this book is available from the British Library

Library of Congress Cataloging in Publication Data
Therapeutic communities for psychosis : philosophy, history, and clinical
practice / edited by John Gale, Alba Realpe & Enrico Pedriali.
    p. ; cm. – (International Society for the Psychological Treatments of
the Schizophrenias and other Psychoses)
    Includes bibliographical references.
    ISBN 978-0-415-44053-0 (hbk.) – ISBN 978-0-415-44054-7 (pbk.) 1.
Psychoses–Treatment. 2. Therapeutic communities. I. Gale, John, 1953- II.
Realpe, Alba. III. Pedriali, Enrico. IV. Series: ISPS book series.
    [DNLM: 1. Psychotic Disorders–therapy. 2. Cross-Cultural Comparison.
3. Milieu Therapy. 4. Residential Treatment. 5. Schizophrenia–therapy. WM
200 T398 2008]
    RC512.T49 2008
    616.89–dc22

                                                                2007041466

ISBN: 978-0-415-44053-0 (hbk)
ISBN: 978-0-415-44054-7 (pbk)

Contents

PART 3
Alternative therapies and extended applications   185

Editors' biographies

John Gale is CEO of Community Housing and Therapy (CHT) a mental health charity specialising in therapeutic communities. Formerly a Benedictine monk, he was director of studies and lectured in philosophy and church history, specialising in late antiquity. After leaving the priesthood he trained as a psychotherapist and has worked in therapeutic communities in the voluntary sector for over 20 years. He was the clinical director of CHT before being appointed to his present post in 1999. He is a board member of ISPS UK and of the Association of Therapeutic Communities (ATC). He was development editor and deputy editor of the journal *Therapeutic Communities* for 7 years and is currently a member of its international editorial advisory group. He regularly speaks at conferences and has contributed to books and published articles in academic journals. He is particularly interested in the interface between philosophy, spirituality and psychotherapy.

Alba Realpe is a psychologist who trained at the Andes University in Colombia. She is a member of the Board of Directors of FUNGRATA where she was trained in accompanied self-rehabilitation working with Dr Alberto Fergusson. She has long experience working in therapeutic communities and was the deputy manager at Mount Lodge, a therapeutic community in Eastbourne run by CHT. Currently Alba is undertaking post graduate studies in research methods in psychology at the University of Southampton.

Enrico Pedriali is a physician, clinical psychologist, psychoanalytic psychotherapist and consultant in mental health institutions. He started his career at the Omega Therapeutic Community, under the direction of Dr Diego Napolitani. This was one of the first therapeutic communities in Italy. He is a group analyst and past President of the Italian Association of Therapeutic Communities. He is the author of a number of books and numerous articles on therapeutic communities.

Editors and contributors

Dr Anna Bielańska
Head of Day Treatment Centre, Community Psychiatry Unit, Collegium Medicum, Jagiellonian University, Krakow, Poland. Email: abielanska@interia.pl

Dr Alistair Black
Training Manager, Community Housing and Therapy, 24 / 5–6 The Coda Centre, 189 Munster Road, London SW6 6AW, United Kingdom. Email: training@cht.org.uk

Dr Andrzej Cechnicki
Director of the Medical Department, Community Psychiatry Unit and Chair of Psychiatry, Jagiellonian University, Krakow, Poland. Email: acechnicki@interia.pl

Professor Haroon Rashid Chaudhry
Head of the Department of Psychiatry, Fatima Jinnah Medical College, Lahore, Pakistan. Email: pprc@wol.net.pk

Dr Sarah Davenport
Consultant Psychiatrist and Psychotherapist, Women's Secure Services, Lancashire Care Trust, Guild Lodge, Preston PR3 2AZ, United Kingdom. Email: SarahDvnpt@aol.com

Professor Alberto Fergusson
President, the Institute of Accompanied Self-rehabilitation, Bogotá, Colombia. Email: afergusson@selfrehabilitation.org

John Gale
Chief Executive, Community Housing and Therapy, 24 / 5–6 The Coda Centre, 189 Munster Road, London SW6 6AW, United Kingdom. Email: jg@cht.org.uk

Raúl Gómez
Deputy Director, Department of Social Care, Fundación Manantial, Avda. Arroyo del Santo 12, 28042 Madrid, Spain. Email: rgomez@ fundacionmanantial.org

Teodora Groshkova
Researcher, National Addiction Centre, Institute of Psychiatry, Kings College London, Addiction Sciences Building, Windsor Walk, London SE5 8AF, United Kingdom. Email: teodora.groshkova@iop.kcl.ac.uk

Dr Vassil Jenkov
Psychiatrist, 1113 Sofia, Blvd Tzarigradsko shoes, Specialized Hospital For Active Treatment in Neurology and Psychiatry 'St Naum', Bulgaria. Email: vassal_j@abv.bg

Dr Raman Kapur
Chief Executive, Threshold, 432 Antrim Road, Belfast BT15 5GB, Northern Ireland. Email: loretta@thresholdservices.com

David Kennard
c/o The Retreat, Heslington Road, York YO10 5BN, United Kingdom. Email: david@dkennard.net

Dr Julie Kipp
Coordinator of a continuing day treatment programme for adults with mental illness, 18 Nepperhan Avenue, Hastings-on-Hudson, New York 10706, USA. Email: julie_kipp@psychoanalysis.net

Dr José Mannu
Director of the Therapeutic Community ASLRMB, Via Alberto Cadlolo 28, 00136, Rome, Italy. Email: jomannu@hotmail.com

Dr Christina Moutsou
Psychoanalytic psychotherapist, The Philadelphia Association, 4 Marty's Yard, 17 Hampstead High Street, London NW3 1QW, United Kingdom. Email: cmoutsou@googlemail.com

Dr Andrea Narracci
Consultant psychiatrist in the Mental Health Department, Via degli Scipioni 295, 00192 Rome, Italy. Email: andrea_narracci@hotmail.com

Kannan Navaratnem
Team Leader, The Arbours Crisis Centre, 41 Weston Park, London N8 9SY, United Kingdom. Email: navaratnem@yahoo.co.uk

Dr Saima Niaz
Consultant Psychiatrist, Fountain House, Lahore, Pakistan. Email: niazpsych@yahoo.com

Dr Andreas von Wallenberg Pachaly
Psychoanalyst and group analyst, Ehrenstr. 3, 40479 Düsseldorf, Germany. Email: andreas.vonwallenberg@t-online.de

Dr Diego Nin Pratt
Member of the École Lacanienne de Psychanalyse and Lecturer, Universidad de la Republica de Uruguay, Tristan Narvaja, 1674 Montevideo, Uruguay. Email: nindiego@adinet.com.uy

Dr Enrico Prediali
President of the Italian Association of Therapeutic Communities, Largo Settimio Severo 3, 20144 Milan, Italy. Email: epedrial@tin.it

Dr Kleopatra Psarraki
Group Analyst, 18 Nicosthenous Street, 11635 Athens, Greece. Email: kleopsar@hotmail.com

Alba Realpe
School of Psychology, University of Southampton, Southampton, United Kingdom. Email: albareal@hotmail.com

Beatriz Sánchez España
Deputy Director Clinical Services, Community Housing and Therapy, 24 / 5–6 The Coda Centre, 189 Munster Road, London SW6 6AW, United Kingdom. Email: bs@cht.org.uk

Dr Marcel Sassolas
President of the Association Santé Mentale et Communautés, 11 Place Antonin Poncet, 69002, Lyon, France. Email: marcel.sassolas@chello.fr

Tamar Schonfield
Team Leader, The Arbours Crisis Centre, 41 Weston Park, London N8 9SY, United Kingdom. Email: tschon@blueyonder.co.uk

Dr Federica Soscia
Psychiatrist, Mental Health Department VT2, Tarquinia, Viterbo, Italy. Email: fedesoscia@libero.it

María Sánchez Suárez
Psychologist, Policlínica Oviedo, C/Quintana 11, 33009 Oviedo, Asturias, Spain. Email: mariasan@cop.es

Dr Tahir Suleman
Consultant Psychiatrist, Cumbria Partnership NHS Foundation Trust, c/o Carleton Clinic, Cumwhinton Drive, Carlisle, Cumbria CA1 3SX, United Kingdom. Email: drtahir@tsuleman.freeserve.co.uk

Dr Peter Vassilev
Director Therapeutic Community Phoenix, 1407 Sofia, 16 Rilski Ezera Street, Bulgaria. Email: peter.vassilev@contact.bg

Foreword

It may be that the experience of psychosis is the very worst of all human suffering, worse than any state of bodily pain. And yet how would I know? I have been subjected neither to the extremes of physical privation and pain nor to the extremes of psychotic suffering. Who can know apart from those who have been there? Well, there is a kind of faith that some account of what it is like can be given and can be received. This book is homage to that faith. The book keeps faith too with another belief. Not just that the perfect act of listening can reveal what we have never experienced, but such a *tour de force* of listening can be institutionalised as the therapeutic community. This book celebrates that listening and does so in the standard therapeutic community posture – opposition. It has always been confrontational. The old mental hospitals were sadly dismal places that over a century of stagnation had declined into places of great inhumanity, doing considerable harm to vulnerable people. The arrival of therapeutic communities was a regenerative moment in standard psychiatry in the post-World War 2 years. Interestingly, therapeutic communities have come to stay and have discovered there is a continuing 'alternative' role to play.

The therapeutic community was spawned by two parents. More glamorously, the great names of Maxwell Jones, Tom Main and W.R. Bion worked with the casualties of war (Harrison 2000) and later with the borderline personalities (Whiteley, Briggs and Turner 1972). A different, perhaps quieter note was struck by those equally great names, Denis Martin, David Clark (1964) and Bertram Mandelbrote who tackled the problem of those with psychotic disorders incarcerated in the overwhelmed and degenerating mental hospitals. Those two parental inheritances have never merged fully and remain as distinct strands in today's therapeutic communities. Remarkably, the therapeutic community remains dependent on these two specific kinds of problem – severe personality disorders and people with chronic schizophrenia. They demand different kinds of organisation run on different principles connected with the different problems. In the 1960s a third kind of problem was added, with a third kind of organisational principle, needed by a third kind of clientele – namely, those addicted to substance misuse.

This rich book is about one of these three strands, the therapeutic communities for people with psychosis; they need to be strictly demarcated from other therapeutic communities. They need a book of their own and now they have got it.

The therapeutic community idea was a particularly productive one, embodying not just an approach to distressed and suffering individual persons, but an approach to malfunctioning institutions. It is more than just one or other form of individual therapy in an institutional setting, the therapeutic community embodies the idea that the institution itself has a role to play in therapeutic change – for the good or for the bad. There must, we used to say, be some different and better way to look after people. That was the oppositional stance we sought from therapeutic communities.

A while ago I tried to sort out how, in schematic and typical form, the SPD clients of the Cassel and Henderson hospitals and the chronic psychotic clients of the long-stay mental institutions set up different emotional eddies. They lead to characteristic dynamics in standard psychiatry, which does nobody any good (Hinshelwood 1999). I pointed to those especial dynamic problems with each category of client. As far as people who suffer schizophrenia are concerned it seemed to me there is a particularly pernicious collusion between persons and their institution which leads to a chronic state developing – on either side, patients and staff. It often seems that it is weird to seek an approach to the social institution that helps people who are characterised by their general ineptitude with social relations. However, it is their very social relatedness that is the agent that cripples them. I will briefly lay out the collusive dynamic that I thought leads to intractable chronicity. Although those persons are very often crippled in social relations with others, the underlying problem is their relation with themselves. It is an existential problem of identity, and their own inability to recognise their experiences as theirs (Hinshelwood 2004); it is a disorder of being-in-the-world, to turn to Heidegger, as do some of the more philosophically minded authors in this book. Separated from their own experiences, these people lose their sense of identity and even of being a person at all. In the psychiatric institution there is a comparable institutional dynamic, known as 'depersonalisation', in which the 'patient' is no longer a person, but an illness. A collusive process is there ready to get going between the vulnerable individual and his institution.

This is also interestingly described by Barratt (1996), who points out that the patient suffering psychosis is not held responsible in a court of law or in a psychiatric ward. His bizarre ideas and behaviour are attributed to his illness, he 'has schizophrenia', and thereby loses, in the minds of psychiatric staff, his capacity to have his own thoughts and be responsible for his own behaviour. He is no longer a moral agent in the sense of making his own decisions and thus not any more a person. It would appear that this depersonalisation is supported and enhanced by the contemporary attitudes of science which hunt down the biochemistry and brain functioning responsible, instead of the person of the patient. This psychiatric emphasis on an alien agent combines with the patient who foregoes the possibility of seeing himself as a person either. My argument is that this two-sided pincer movement that attacks the person's own personhood, becomes a stable system and leads to an enduring condition we call chronic schizophrenia.

Thus the institution can actively enhance the very specific problem the person brings to it, that problem being the essential gap in his ability to feel himself a responsible person making his own choices. Barratt also makes the fascinating point that within the psychiatric system at a later phase in the treatment a successfully treated case will begin to be held responsible again by the staff. He is thus restored bit by bit to a person. Barratt is describing a phasic process of first stripping the person of his agency and then restoring it again. What, however, happens when this psychiatric process gets stuck and the person (or the staff) cannot move on to the second phase, restoration. It is just those institutions that become stuck in the first phase, which the therapeutic community challenges.

Whereas I have ponderously spelled out detailed steps by which the institutional processes happen, they are never explicitly recognised. So much of this goes on in implicit ways via the intuitions of the staff (and the patients). Neither is the therapeutic community's challenge explicit, rather people intuitively challenge these implicit institutional ways in which a patient is separated from his experiences, his agency and his personhood.

What is so interesting to see in this collection is how over and over again in so many different settings in vastly different cultures the challenge goes on being made – made implicitly and creatively and without the need of explicit and ponderous psychoanalytic explanations. As we used to say, the therapeutic community stands for the healthy side of the patient, which we seek to rescue and support. But we never saw exactly how the healthy side is separated and lost. We only sensed that to dwell on the unhealthy symptoms and ignore the already ignored person is a self-fulfilling prophecy in which our patients become non-persons for our institutions.

That recovery of personhood is conceived technically in myriad ways in all this book's fascinating accounts of communities and approaches and theorisations. What appeals to me so much is the common strand of serious endeavour to put the institutions to right. That is a dogged endeavour that has lasted many decades and it excites me that it is still alive and well and puts me back in touch with my youthful enthusiasms and endeavours again.

Bob Hinshelwood
July 2007

References

Barratt, R. (1996). *The Psychiatric Team and the Social Redefinition of Psychiatry.* Cambridge: Cambridge University Press.

Clark, D. (1964). *Administrative Therapy.* London: Tavistock.

Harrison, T. (2000). *Bion, Rickman, Foulkes, and the Northfield Experiments: Advancing on a different front.* London: Jessica Kingsley.

Hinshelwood, R.D. (1999). The difficult patient: the role of 'scientific' psychiatry in understanding patients with chronic schizophrenia or severe personality disorder. *British Journal of Psychiatry* 174: 187–190.

Hinshelwood, R.D. (2004). *Suffering Insanity: Psychoanalytic essays on psychosis.* Hove: Routledge.

Whiteley, S., Briggs, D. and Turner, M. (1972). *Dealing with Deviants.* London: Hogarth.

Preface

Some miles to the north of Lahore, in the magnificent countryside of western Pakistan, reminiscent, perhaps, of the rural landscapes evoked by the Bengali poet Tagore, a group of around 10 young men are moving half a dozen beehives. It is spring and the apple trees are in blossom and this will provide plenty of work for the bee colony over the coming months. But this is not a team of professional bee keepers or farmers. They are a mixed group of psychiatric patients and psychiatrists from the Farm House therapeutic community. If we are to believe Virgil, the task is fitting, for according to him bees are the image of human life – orderly, public spirited and devoted to the community (*Georgics*, Book X).

Meanwhile, in the centre of Krakow about 20 men and women are rehearsing for a production of Aristophanes' *The Clouds*. The bawdy irreverence with which the gods and men are treated amuses the cast. Yet this is not a just a theatre company and none of the actors went to drama school. The cast, director, costume designer and the whole team is made up of psychologists from the day treatment centre of the Krakow psychiatry department and their patients, all of whom are suffering from schizophrenia. Coincidentally Aristophanes is a good choice, as the playwright was a passionate defender of democracy, one of the principles of therapeutic community practice.

This book records many similar examples of innovative and creative community treatment of the psychoses from around the world. Twenty nine authors from 14 different countries describe their work. The book is divided into three sections. Part 1 deals with the history of therapeutic communities for the severely mentally ill and opens up some philosophical questions in relation to the foundations of this approach. Part 2 describes how this approach works in practice in different situations, while in Part 3 the use of alternative therapies and extended models is discussed. Here we see practitioners working with people suffering from psychosis or with a dual diagnosis, where there is an addiction, with multifamily groups and with people in prison. In addition to using the environment as a therapeutic tool, art, drama and agro-therapy are discussed and we also read about the problems surrounding setting up a new therapeutic community. In each section, there are some outstanding contributions from senior practitioners and experts in the field. Notably, Julie Kipp tells the fascinating and neglected history of democratic therapeutic communities in the United States and, in an original and learned chapter, my colleague Alistair Black discusses some philosophical questions as they relate to the training of therapeutic community staff.

In the last 10 years there has been a revival of interest in therapeutic communities in general, including communities that treat and care for people with a psychosis. In part, this is one of the fruits of the user movement, which has resulted in commissioners and practitioners having to listen to the demands of users for talking therapies and psychological treatments for psychosis, as well as psychopharmacological interventions. Indirectly, this has brought with it a flattening of the hierarchical relationship between professional and patient and increased democracy, two notions central to therapeutic community practice. Additionally, the closure of the large psychiatric hospitals, and the subsequent relocation of services for the mentally ill into the community, has contributed to a greater appreciation of the importance of the social and environmental aspects of community itself in the recovery process. In the UK, this has resulted in the establishment of the Community of Communities at the Royal College of Psychiatrists Centre for Quality Improvement, which has developed specialist service standards for therapeutic communities.

The new generation of therapeutic communities run as efficient businesses. Many are located in the community, rather than in hospitals. Others are dispersed services, whose definition of community does not rely on shared accommodation and comprise of flats or day centres. Andreas von Wallenberg Pachaly gives a very detailed and thoughtful account of one such scheme in Germany. Many, in keeping with governmental trends that encourage charities to take a greater role in public service delivery, are run by voluntary sector organisations.[1] As a result, therapeutic communities are rapidly becoming an integral and integrated part of the delivery of mainstream psychiatric services. This is illustrated, from the Italian perspective, in a fascinating chapter by José Mannu and Federica Soscia. They illustrate clearly the future role of therapeutic communities in providing an environment in which the new antipsychotic medication can be used more effectively. The context for this is research evidence, which we survey in the final chapter. This needs to be seen in the light of an article published by Cameron in a recent edition of the journal *Therapeutic Communities*. Here a clear case is made that demonstrates that therapeutic communities are increasingly taking up the challenge of evidenced-based practice (Cameron, 2006). This mirrors another chapter in this volume, from Bulgaria, in which considerable evidence is presented to show the effectiveness of therapeutic communities in the treatment of drug addicts who have a primary diagnosis of psychosis.

Note

1 The increasing role of the voluntary and community sector in the delivery of public services has translated into an increasing transfer of resources from the statutory to the voluntary sector. In the UK, the sector now generates £15.5 billion of earned income and £11.8 billion of voluntary income and is now a major employer. The sector employed 611,000 people in 2005, an increase of 26 per cent in ten years.

References

Cameron, D. (2006). I am arresting you, therapeutic community, on suspicion of ineffectiveness; you are not obliged to say anything, but anything you do say may be used in evidence against you. *Therapeutic Communities* 27(4): 453–476.

Virgil (1916). *Georgics*, Book X, Eclogues, Georgics, Aeneid Books 1–6 (trans.) H. Rushton Fairclough revised by G.P. Goold. Loeb Classical Library. Harvard: Harvard University Press.

Acknowledgements

I should like to express my sincere gratitude to my fellow editors and to all who have contributed to this volume. I should also like to thank Lilias Gillies, chair of CHT's board of directors, for her support throughout this project and to Dr Brian Martindale, the series editor, and David Kennard, chair of ISPS UK, for their encouragement. I am indebted to my former colleague Yasmine Haimovici. Had it not been for her swift responses to my innumerable queries regarding the French manuscript, it would have been very difficult to include Chapter 14. I would like to thank Geruza Paula Agustini, my secretary. Her efficiency and patience, in the role of unofficial editorial assistant, in the midst of manifold duties, was invaluable. Finally, I would like to thank Inmaculada Vidaña Marquez, Chief Operating Officer of CHT, for helping me to free up my time, at what turned out to be a very busy period for the organisation, thus enabling me to complete this task. Needless to say, any errors are entirely my own.

John Gale
Senior Editor

Part 1

Historical background and philosophical context

What has made it possible here to speak of reasonable madness, of the preservation of clarity, order, and will, is the feeling that, however far into the phenomenon we go, we remain in the realm of the understandable. Even when what one understands can't even be articulated, named, or inserted by the subject into a context that makes it clear, it's already situated at the level of understanding.

Jacques Lacan 1993

A view of the evolution of therapeutic communities for people suffering from psychosis

David Kennard

The use of supportive living environments for people experiencing psychosis goes back several centuries. This chapter describes four phases in the evolution of therapeutic community principles and their adaptation to meet the needs of people with severe mental illness.

Phase 1: the emergence (and submergence) of a humane approach to the mentally ill

The earliest example of a humane, social approach to mental illness is often given as Geel (also spelt Gheel) in Belgium beginning in the 14th century, where the mentally ill were brought to the shrine of St Dymphna, an early Christian martyr. Many recovered, and for those who did not a tradition was established of having a lunatic living in the home (Clark 1967). In Geel, it was said that lunatics could walk the streets, engage in commerce, deliver food, carry milk and were incorporated into the society and respected.

Although Geel demonstrated that a humane approach to mental illness was possible, in the 17th century the prevailing view of the human mind, associated with the mind–body dualism of Descartes, separated the concept of the rational human from irrational beings, classing the mentally ill with animals. This view allowed society to tolerate appalling treatment of the mentally ill until it began to be challenged by the Quakers who set up the York Retreat. The development at the beginning of the 19th century of what came to be called moral treatment introduced and disseminated a humane approach that has since become a key reference point for contemporary mental health services. I cannot better the following passage as an account of its development:

> Any review of moral treatment as it was first practised at The Retreat needs to take into account the Quaker background of its founders. Early Quakerism, with its emphasis on the individual's responsibility to cultivate a lifestyle which would encourage and nurture the 'Inner

Light', brought its followers into many situations of personal and collective suffering. Quakers were vigorously persecuted for their beliefs and actions, often imprisoned, and regarded as deviant and troublesome. Quaker insistence on the spiritual equality of all human beings, regardless of race, education, gender, or age, offended many of the cultural mores of the period, and the sight of Quaker women preaching in public led to accusations of witchcraft. The relentless persecution suffered by the early Quakers led them to form a system of mutual solidarity. Those who had lost property or who had suffered injury or imprisonment could always count upon other Friends to provide money, shelter and other forms of practical and spiritual support. These two strands of thinking, that each individual is responsible for his or her own spiritual integrity and conduct before God, and that those who espouse these principles have a duty to serve, support, encourage and inspire each other towards a common spiritual goal, formed the basis for the practical expression of moral treatment as it was first practised at The Retreat.

Although the persecution of Quakers ceased by the late 18th century, the tradition of empathy with marginalized members of society was likely to have been a factor in the founding of The Retreat. In the 18th century 'madhouses' and asylums were brutal places. The justification for the treatment of the mad as if they were animals came largely from the Cartesian ideal that Reason and Logic formed the basis of all nature and that this was glorified and exemplified in the human being, God's supreme creation. A human being devoid of reason and logic was therefore a contradiction in terms, and in fact, must then be regarded as more like a beast than a person.

Quakers did not share this mainstream idea of humanity. Although they believed strongly in the desirability of clear and logical thought, this was not as an end in itself or a definition of personhood, but rather a means to focus on a greater truth, that of the Inner Light, a positive, life-affirming experience, beyond words or logic. The Retreat's founder William Tuke set about establishing an environment where people in mental distress could begin to take responsibility for their own emotions and conduct, in order that they might come into clearer focus with their own personal truth and their responsibility towards others.

(Borthwick et al. 2001: 428)

Borthwick et al. (2001) summarised moral treatment in terms of seven basic principles.

1   *A concern for the human rights of people with severe and disabling mental health problems.* There is a deep-seated belief that all men and women

are created equal and are equally deserving of care. Each individual is unique and of value.

2   *Personal respect for people with severe mental health problems.* More than a recognition of rights, this implies tolerance of odd behaviour, recognition of the need for privacy and dignity, respect for the meaningfulness to the individual of their subjective experiences, respect for individual and cultural differences.

3   *An emphasis on the healing power of everyday relationships.* Kindness, acceptance, encouragement, affection, friendship, the opportunity to give as well as receive and an expectation of responsible behaviour, are all seen as powerful forces in helping an individual to recover his or her mental health.

4   *The importance of useful occupation.* Structured activity can have a calming influence, occupation can be a basis for relating to others and being part of a group and a sense of achievement and purpose are sources of self-respect.

5   *Emphasis on the social and physical environment.* The Retreat aimed to create a 'quiet haven in which the shattered bark might find the means of reparation or of safety' (Tuke 1813). Moral treatment stressed both the physical and social environment: the setting and the views should be pleasing, staff were to be employed for their personal qualities of tolerance, intelligence and integrity and numbers should be small enough to create a family like atmosphere.

6   *A commonsense approach rather than reliance on technology or ideology.* There was a mistrust of professions, with their tendency to seek power through claims of specialist knowledge and techniques. At the same time a commonsense approach accepted a need for supervision to prevent harm or exploitation and set limits to the tolerance of anti-social behaviour.

7   *A spiritual perspective.* For Quakers this was expressed in the belief that there is 'that of God' in everyone, an inner light in every individual, no matter how disturbed or withdrawn.

The Retreat, which opened in 1796, helped to spark a revolution in care of the mentally ill. In the early and mid-19th century there was great optimism and idealism in England, and also in the United States,[1] that a calm, well-ordered environment would restore mental health and well-being to the 'shattered bark'. Sadly, the pressure of numbers combined with the growing belief that mental disorders resulted from biological rather than social factors, meant that the unintended legacy of moral treatment was the building of institutions of ever increasing size for 1000 or more patients. By the beginning of the 20th century they had became little more than ware-houses. In the 1950s an American psychiatrist J.S. Bockoven described the scene in a typical mental hospital as, 'the heavy atmosphere of hundreds of people doing nothing and showing interest in nothing, with endless lines of people sat on benches along the walls'. In a faint, poignant echo of moral treatment he adds that:

> The visitor learns that the attendant is proud of the ward because it is quiet and no mishaps have occurred while he was on duty; because the floor is clean, because the patients are prompt and orderly in going to and from meals. The visitor finds that the scene which appals him with the emptiness and pointlessness of human life is regarded by the attendant as good behaviour on the part of the patients.
>
> (Bockoven 1956: 168)

Phase 2: the impact of psychoanalytic ideas and democratisation on institutional psychiatry: the therapeutic community approach

While psychiatric patients languished in ward warehouses in the first half of the 20th century, elsewhere two ideas were having a major impact on therapeutic approaches to emotional and behavioural problems: psychoanalysis and democratisation. To put these two ideas at their simplest, Freud's psychoanalysis offered the intriguing possibility that irrational behaviour and utterances had meaning if you could decipher the code. Respect for someone with a mental illness was no longer only a matter of concern for their dignity and well-being. It also meant listening to what they said as meaningful communication.

Democratisation as a method of treatment was first and famously tried in England by Homer Lane with delinquent children and adolescents at the time of World War 1. Lane modelled his Little Commonwealth on junior republics in the USA that used the American constitution as a model for therapeutic living, with community members as citizens. Lane also tried out psychoanalytic techniques with individuals at the Little Commonwealth, with more enthusiasm than expertise and this led to allegations of inappropriate behaviour with a female resident and to the closure of the place. Despite this unfortunate end, Lane inspired a number of pioneers who set up residential schools for maladjusted children in the early decades of 20th century using similar principles (Bridgeland 1971; Kasinski 2003). The 1920s and 30s was a fertile period for many experiments in social living (Pines 1999), influenced by a mixture of social idealism, psychoanalysis and new ideas in the social sciences.

It was during the years of World War 2 that psychoanalysts, psychiatrists and social psychologists first applied the recipe of psychoanalysis and democratisation to the problems presented by service men who were emotional casualties of the frontlines and had been transferred to the military hospitals at Northfield in Birmingham and Mill Hill in north London.

Although there is no explicit evidence that they were directly influenced by the pioneering work with children,[2] it may be argued that they were influenced by a Zeitgeist that included the discoveries of psychoanalysis and a willingness – and freedom – to experiment with new approaches to emotional and behavioural problems. Bion, Bridger, Main and Foulkes at Northfield brought their interest in unconscious motivation and group and organizational dynamics, while Maxwell Jones, a research psychiatrist, brought to Mill Hill an enthusiasm for sharing explanatory models of stress symptoms (called effort syndrome) and encouraging patients to become teachers to one another – an early example of user involvement. Between them they created a new model of mental healthcare. While it was Jones whose unit established its core principles (see later), it was Main who is widely credited with giving it its name: 'a therapeutic community' (Main 1946).

In the 1950s and 60s, following the creation of the National Health Service in 1948, the impact of psychoanalytic ideas and democratisation also began to be felt in the mental hospitals that housed those with severe and enduring mental illness. The NHS brought all the county asylums in England into one service and also brought a new wave of resourceful and determined young hospital superintendents who were aware of the work and ideas of Main, Foulkes and Jones. Following the end of the war Foulkes went to the Maudsley Hospital to teach group psychotherapy, Main became director of the Cassel Hospital and Jones took charge of the social rehabilitation unit at Belmont Hospital – later renamed Henderson Hospital. At mental hospitals like Fulbourn, Littlemore and Claybury the new ideas began to be put into practice, with admission or rehabilitation wards that had been run in traditional fashion being made over with regular community meetings and patients sharing responsibility for the day-to-day life of the ward. In the United States these ideas were also introduced into psychiatric wards by Wilmer, who visited Great Britain after the war and was keen to challenge Maxwell Jones' view that psychotic patients could not be treated in a therapeutic community. In addition to attempts to set up ward-based therapeutic communities within a hospital, there was also what came to be called the 'therapeutic community approach' to the hospital as a whole (Clark 1965).

This, according to Clark, was 'in some degree a revival of the old principles of moral treatment' (Clark 1965: 948), and was supported by a report of the World Health Organisation in 1953 which said: 'Too many psychiatric hospitals give the impression of being an uneasy compromise between a general hospital and a prison. In fact the role they have to play is different from either: it is that of a therapeutic community' (WHO 1953: 17–18). The report spelled out the five constituent parts of this as:

- Preservation of the patient's individuality.
- The assumption that patients are trustworthy.

- That good behaviour must be encouraged.
- Patients must be assumed to retain the capacity for a considerable degree of responsibility and initiative
- The need for activity and a proper working day for all patients.

Two parallel developments gave a considerable boost to the development both of ward-based therapeutic communities and of a therapeutic community approach to the whole hospital. One was the extensive use from 1955 of tranquillisers that 'made possible contact with many patients who were previously unreachable' (Clark 1965: 948). The other was a spate of sociological studies of mental hospitals in the United States. The most famous of these, *Asylums*, published by Goffman in 1961, introduced the phrase total institution to describe the way inmates were treated in collective identical batches (Goffman 1961). Other key studies included *The Mental Hospital* (Stanton and Schwartz 1954), which demonstrated how unexpressed conflict between ward staff could lead to disturbed behaviour among patients, *The Psychiatric Hospital as a Small Society* (Caudill 1958) and *Institutional Neurosis* (Barton 1959). Between them these and other studies underpinned and supported the efforts of reformers to do something about the effects of the large institutional mental hospitals.

In adapting the therapeutic community from the methods developed at Northfield and Mill Hill Hospitals during World War 2, the mental hospital pioneers looked in particular to the model developed by Maxwell Jones at the social rehabilitation unit at Belmont Hospital. The four treatment principles that emerged in a seminal study by Rapoport of working practices at the unit (Rapoport 1960) became the touchstone for anyone wanting to establish a therapeutic community.

1   *Democratization.* Every member of the community should share equally in the exercise of power in decision making about community affairs.
2   *Permissiveness.* All members should tolerate from one another a wide degree of behavior that might be distressing or seem deviant by ordinary standards.
3   *Communalism.* There should be tight-knit intimate sets of relationships, with sharing of amenities (dining room etc.), use of first names, and free communication.
4   *Reality confrontation.* Residents should be continuously presented with interpretations of their behaviour as it is seen by others in order to counteract their tendency to distort, deny or withdraw from their difficulties in getting on with others.

These principles emerged in a setting for people with personality disorders and to some extent require modification for patients with other problems. For example the principle of reality confrontation is intended for people who are inclined to ignore social cues and would be counterproductive for those who are over-sensitive to social situations as may be the case for those experiencing psychosis, especially paranoid delusions. Nevertheless the therapeutic community at the Henderson has been inspirational to clinicians in many settings and countries. The inspiration has come from the demonstration that a hospital *can* be a therapeutic environment, that patients can be empowered to takes responsibility for their lives and that they can become a positive influence in their own and one another's treatment.

More recently John Cox identified how therapeutic community principles also apply to community mental health care and the work of community mental health teams, which to a large extent have taken over the role of the mental hospitals in caring for people with long-term severe mental disorders (Cox 1998):

- Respect for persons.
- Recognition that staff and users have in common their ability to be therapeutic.
- Realisation that a containing environment is essential and that leadership – multiple or single – is evident and acknowledged.
- Understanding the sociology of large and small groups, the culture of enquiry and the reflection on living and learning, which is transmitted and maintained by core staff.

We can see these as an updated version of the 'therapeutic community approach', with a greater awareness of group and organisational dynamics.

Phase 3: anti-psychiatry and alternative asylum

This can be described as the third phase in evolution of therapeutic community principles for the treatment of people experiencing psychosis. It could also be described as the antithesis of the therapeutic community approach which accepted the mental hospital as the necessary setting for the treatment and rehabilitation of those with severe mental disorders – and aimed to make the hospital environment as therapeutic as possible. The anti-psychiatry movement challenged this acceptance, rejecting both hospitals and a medical approach to psychosis. The alternative was to be a place where someone experiencing a psychotic breakdown could be cared for until they emerged from their psychosis without resort to medication and without any medical or professional intervention. The hypothesis was that natural healing would occur with sufficient tolerance and emotional and practical support.

The founder of the anti-psychiatry movement, R.D. Laing, and some colleagues set out to implement this vision at Kingsley Hall, in London's East End, which they ran from 1965 till 1970:

People who were psychotic were given space, they were given company if they wished, and they were given a great deal of physical support . . . people were not considered ill so they did not have to be treated. No drugs were given. There were no staff and no patients, and there was no formal structure of doing things around the Hall, yet things got done.

(Berke 1980: 99)

This encapsulates the key elements of the model:

- There is no such thing as mental illness (it is a social construct), therefore no need for people to be designated as staff and patients – everyone is equal in this respect.
- People experiencing a psychosis need a lot of support, but they also need space just to be, without any pressures.
- Everyone shares responsibility for running the household, doing what they feel able to.

Kingsley Hall and Laing's ideas were a key source of inspiration for small therapeutic households set up in the 1970s in England and California and also played a part in the emergence of the Democratic Psychiatry movement in Italy and the development of 'intermediate communities' following the closure of the country's mental hospitals (Pedriali 1997).

The two best-known examples of anti-psychiatry alternative communities are probably the Arbours Crisis Centre, opened in London in 1974 and still going (Berke et al. 1995) and the Soteria House project in California, which ran from 1971 to 1983 (Mosher 2004). The requirements described by Mosher were close to those of moral treatment. They included that those in the environment should:

- Treat everyone, and expect to be treated, with dignity and respect.
- Guarantee sanctuary, quiet, safety, support, protection, containment and interpersonal validation.
- Ensure food and shelter.
- Most importantly, the atmosphere must be imbued with hope – that recovery from psychosis is to be expected, *without* resort to anti-psychotic drugs.

Phase 4: synthesis of the therapeutic community and anti-psychiatry

Since the 1980s there have been some attempts to achieve a synthesis of the therapeutic community approach and the anti-psychiatry alternative community. In the UK, this has taken place mainly in the voluntary or charitable sector, through organizations like Community Housing and Therapy (CHT) in London and Threshold in Northern Ireland. In Switzerland and Germany, it has happened in the context of the state's mental healthcare provision. How and where it happens may depend on the chance elements of key individuals and the opportunities that present themselves.

The Soteria model was (re)imported into Europe in the 1980s by Luc Ciompi at Soteria Berne and subsequently taken up at a number of other centres, mainly in Germany. Ciompi was less anti-psychiatry than Mosher and wrote that, 'our primary goal was not to develop an almost drug free treatment strategy, but to implement as comprehensive treatment of acute schizophrenia patients as possible by combining all available psycho-social-biological knowledge on therapeutic factors in innovative ways' (Ciompi and Hoffmann 2004: 141). Ciompi formulated eight therapeutic principles as practical guidelines. The following is a summary of Ciompi and Hoffmann (2004):

1   *Small, relaxing, stimulus-protecting and as normal as possible therapeutic setting.* Instead of a traditional hospital setting, acute psychotic patients are admitted to a small, open, friendly and family-like house with a nice garden located in the middle of the community.

2   *Continual personalized being-with the psychotic patient.* During the acute psychotic stage (phase 1), the patient is never left alone, but given round the clock company in a pleasant so-called soft room. The main task of the accompanying person is to calm the individual by silent or talking, being-with or by simple activities like as drawing, playing, foot massages, walking or jogging together. Gradually the patient is integrated in the daily life of the therapeutic community (phase 2).

3   *Personal and conceptual continuity.* This is assured by a small, closely collaborating therapeutic team supported by a part-time psychiatrist. Team members are carefully selected for their personal qualities and life experiences, with a balance of gender, age and psychiatric versus other professional backgrounds. Two team members (usually a man and a woman) are assigned to each patient.

4   *Close collaboration with family members and other important persons of reference.* From the first day close and collaborative relations are systematically built up with family members and other important persons, with extensive sharing of information, liberal visiting policies and monthly educational discussions.

5   *Clear and concordant information for patients, family and staff.* To minimize tension-creating confusions and misunderstandings, as clear, complete and concordant information as possible on the illness itself, its prognostic risks and chances, the methods of treatment and relapse prevention etc. is given on every possible occasion to patients, family members and to the team members.

6   *Elaboration of common realistic goals and expectations.* From an early
     phase of treatment, concrete therapeutic aims and priorities concerning
     future housing and work are systematically elaborated with each
     patient and family, on the basis of realistic expectations of risks and
     opportunities.
7   *Consensual low-dose antipsychotic strategies.* Medication is used to
     reduce otherwise uncontrollable states of tension, in close collaboration
     with patient and family, with the final aim of controlled self-medication.
8   *Aftercare and relapse prevention for at least 2 years.* This is systematic-
     ally prepared for by extensive education on personal relapse indicators
     and relapse prevention procedures, and by making contact with
     external therapists and follow-up services.

Ciompi commented that these principles overlap with Mosher's initial
practice, but that they have 'integrated educational techniques, a systemic
family approach and modern rehabilitation and relapse prevention strategies' (Ciompi and Hoffmann 2004: 142), together with a more flexible
medication strategy that tends to resemble current low-dose medication
techniques with atypical antipsychotic medication. It could be argued, and
no doubt Ciompi would agree, that Soteria Berne represents an attempt to
synthesise the best bits of all the different approaches to psychosis: moral
treatment, therapeutic community, anti-psychiatry, family involvement and
judicious use of medication.

While the Soteria House model was established for people experiencing a
first psychotic episode, Community Housing and Therapy (CHT) grew out
of the Richmond Fellowship, a network of supportive therapeutic communities started in the 1960s by Elly Jansen to help patients coming out of
psychiatric hospital to reintegrate back into society. As such, the model
developed by CHT was focused more than Soteria on the longer term
problems following a psychotic breakdown. Launched in the late 1980s,
CHT brought together elements of the pragmatic TC approach with the
existential and socio-political philosophy that inspired Laing when he set
up Kingsley Hall and the Philadelphia Association.

The CHT model is underpinned by four key concepts – care, dialogue,
dwelling and community – that combine psychoanalytic and philosophical
concepts with the everyday realities of life and relationships in the therapeutic community (Tucker 2000). These expand one of Ciompi's key
principles: continual personalized being-with the psychotic patient. Thus
someone's avoidance of involvement, eruption of anger, panic attack or
paranoid delusion, is responded to as expressing an underlying question the
person is asking about themselves or others. The task of the staff member
working with them is to try to translate this question into ordinary language.
Dialogue occurs when the person feels they are really being seen, understood
and acknowledged by the other. Similarly the role of the staff is to help an

individual to fully dwell, not merely exist, in their room: to choose colours, furnishings, decorations, arrange things etc. They try to do this by working alongside the person, doing things with them rather than to them.

Tucker (1999) gives the example of a new staff member working with a client with a diagnosis of schizophrenia and proneness to panic attacks when he believes he is being chased by insects. The staff member has the task of working with the client on cleaning the sitting room:

> The client stops hoovering after about three minutes and sits down on the sofa reporting that he is having a panic attack. The member of staff feels anxious and worried . . . she feels she should not disturb him but rather comfort him and do his cleaning chore for him.
>
> (Tucker 1999: 152)

Tucker points out that the kind of care that results in doing the job for the client promotes dependency and passivity and leaves the client stuck where he is. It is the antithesis of CHT's approach and of the therapeutic community principles outlined by Rapoport: undemocratic in that it promotes hierarchy, non-permissive in that staff take control, avoiding reality rather than confronting it and preventing communalism by keeping a barrier between staff and clients.

Conclusion

The account presented here includes several different sets of principles developed at different stages in the evolution of therapeutic communities for people going through or recovering from a psychotic experience. I will conclude by suggesting what appear to me to be three continuing threads:

1   *Personal respect.* This has been expressed as the protection of personal privacy and dignity, preservation of individuality, tolerance of unusual behaviour, the assumption of trustworthiness and a capacity for responsibility and initiative. Treating the individual as a person – as one would like to be treated oneself – is a thread that goes right through from moral treatment to the therapeutic community principles enumerated by Rapoport (1960) and Clark (1965) to their adaptation for community mental healthcare of Cox (1998).

2   *The healing power of everyday relationships.* Recognising the capacity that all staff and patents/clients have to be therapeutic emerges as one of the core features of this type of therapeutic community, in which a certain kind of calm, responsive, being-with or working alongside, without any particular therapeutic technique, is seen as a key to enabling the psychotic individual to cope with their experience and gradually re-connect with the world around them.

3   *The containing quality of the environment.* This extends from William Tuke who sought to create a 'quiet haven in which the shattered bark might find the means of reparation or of safety' (Tuke 1813/Jones 1996 foreword) to Ciompi's recognition that in the light of research on the impact of high expressed emotion 'the creation of a therapeutic setting that consistently reduces emotional tension appeared as crucial' (Ciompi and Hoffmann 2004: 141). Cox extended the importance of this into care in the community, noting that 'some community services are like sieves with no containment and no clear leadership' (Cox 1998: 5).

At the risk over oversimplification, we may conclude that this review of the history of therapeutic communities for people suffering from psychosis has found the following to be their simple yet powerful commonality: personal respect and everyday relationships in calm, emotionally containing environment.

Notes

1 See the fascinating account by Rothman, D. (1971). *The Discovery of the Asylum.* Boston, MA: Little, Brown & Co.
2 Pines (1999) has suggested that the psychoanalytic adviser to the Hawkspur Camp for maladjusted youths, Dennis Carroll, passed this experience on when he became a commanding officer at Northfield Hospital during the war.

Bibliography

Barton, R. (1959). *Institutional Neurosis.* Bristol: Wright.
Berke, J.H. (1980). Therapeutic community models: II Kingsley Hall, in E. Jansen (ed.) *The Therapeutic Community.* London: Croom-Helm.
Berke, J.H., Masoliver, C. and Ryan, T.J. (1995). *Sanctuary: The Arbours experience of alternative community care.* London: Process Press.
Bockoven, J.S. (1956). Moral treatment in American society. *Journal of Nervous and Mental Disease* 124: 167–194.
Borthwick, A., Holman, C., Kennard, D., McFetridge, M., Messruther, K. and Wilkes, J. (2001). The relevance of moral treatment to contemporary mental health care. *Journal of Mental Health* 10(4): 427–439.
Bridgeland, M. (1971). *Pioneer Work with Maladjusted Children.* London: Staples Press.
Caudill, W.A. (1958). *The Psychiatric Hospital as a Small Society.* Cambridge, MA: Harvard University Press.
Ciompi, L. and Hoffmann, H. (2004). Soteria Berne: an innovative milieu therapeutic approach to acute schizophrenia based on the concept of affect-logic. *World Psychiatry* 3(3):140–146.
Clark, D.H. (1965). The therapeutic community – concept, practice and future. *British Journal of Psychiatry* 131: 553–564.
Clark, D.H. (1967). Psychiatric halfway house. Thesis for the degree of Doctor of

Medicine of Edinburgh University. Published at http://www.pettarchiv.org.uk/survey-dhclark-mdthesis.htm#historical

Cox, J. (1998). Reflections on contemporary psychiatry: where is the therapy? *Therapeutic Communities* 19(1): 3–10.

Goffman, E. (1961). *Asylums*. New York: Doubleday.

Kasinski, K. (2003). The roots of the work: definitions, origins and influences, in A. Ward, K. Kasinski, J. Pooley and A. Worthington (eds) *Therapeutic Communities for Children and Young People*. London: Jessica Kingsley.

Main, T. (1946). The hospital as a therapeutic institution. *Bulletin of the Menninger Clinic* 10: 66–70.

Mosher, L.R. (2004). Non-hospital, non-drug intervention with first-episode psychosis, in J. Read, L.R. Mosher and R.P. Bentall (eds) *Models of Madness*. London: Brunner-Routledge.

Pedriali, E. (1997). Italian therapeutic communities: from historical analysis to hypotheses for change. *Therapeutic Communities* 18(1): 3–13.

Pines, M. (1999). Forgotten pioneers: the unwritten history of the therapeutic community movement. *Therapeutic Communities* 20(1): 23–42.

Rapoport, R.N. (1960). *Community as Doctor*. London: Tavistock.

Stanton, A. and Schwartz, H. (1954). *The Mental Hospital*. New York: Basic Books.

Tucker, S. (1999). Community care: the therapeutic approach and learning to care, in P. Campling and R. Haigh (eds) *Therapeutic Communities: Past, present and future*. London: Jessica Kingsley.

Tucker, S. (ed.) (2000). *A Therapeutic Community Approach to Care in the Community*. London: Jessica Kingsley.

Tuke, S. (1813/1996). *Description of the Retreat*. London: Process Press.

World Health Organization (1953). *Expert Committee on Mental Health: 3rd Report*. Geneva: WHO.

Chapter 2

The American contribution to therapeutic community for people with psychosis and a reflection on current milieu treatment in the United States

Julie Kipp

> All real living is meeting
> (Buber 1958)

I preface this chapter with this quote from Martin Buber, in honour of my own community, Bronx REAL, a continuing day treatment programme for adults with serious mental illness. Although REAL stands for Rehabilitation and Education in the Art of Living, I like even better the implications of 'all REAL living is meeting', as a lovely and funky wall hanging at the REAL proclaims.

As a result of my experience working at the REAL, I wanted to know to what extent therapeutic community continues in American milieu programmes for people with serious mental illness. I conducted a small research study for a dissertation in social work, in which I interviewed directors throughout the United States with a view to assessing the extent to which their programmes were like or unlike the therapeutic community (Kipp 2005).

It should be noted that milieu programmes of all sorts in the United States have tended to focus mostly on patients with psychosis or a mixture of psychotic and personality disorders. It is true that in the United States in the absence of national healthcare, every one of the 50 states has a different mental health system. However, the criteria for such programmes throughout the States usually focus on disability related to a serious Axis I disorder. People with disabling Axis II disorders are often included in American milieu programmes along with Axis I patients, as they often share functional disabilities which are just as severe and usually merit some Axis I diagnosis, for example, major depression, which can be used to make them eligible for services.

In this chapter, I will summarise some of the contributions of the United States to the therapeutic community movement, especially in the treatment of psychosis. I will end with a discussion of what has happened to the therapeutic community for treatment of psychosis in the United States.[1]

The therapeutic community began in besieged Great Britain as a response to the challenges of treating military personnel during war time. It was an auspicious new expression of several cultural trends of the time: social psychiatry, psychoanalysis and group psychotherapy. Some of the threads which were knitted into this new treatment were American in origin and some were the result of a great deal of cross-fertilisation between the United Kingdom and the United States.[2]

The grandfather of the therapeutic community could be said to be the American, Homer Lane. He was part of a movement in the early 20th century in the United States of Boys' Republics or Junior Republics, which were self-governing children's communities. After achieving success in running such a community in Detroit, Michigan, Lane was invited to Great Britain as the superintendent of the Little Commonwealth in Dorset, a community of about 50 children. With a more psychological bent than some others of his time, he believed in every child's innate goodness, the importance of the children making their own rules and taking responsibility for their own community and in the power of the community to effect change in their lives.

That Lane was influential in subsequent British therapeutic community phenomena has been recognised, especially by David Wills (1964), Lane's biographer, an American-trained British social worker, who went on to found Hawkspur, the first of the Q-Camps, with Marjorie Franklin.

In addition, Malcolm Pines (1999) has noted the intriguing connection between Hawkspur, influenced by Lane, and wartime Northfield Hospital, the birthplace of therapeutic community, in the person of psychiatrist Dennis Carroll. Carroll was at both Hawkspur and Northfield and had contact with Wilfred Bion of the first Northfield Experiment, when they worked together at the London Psychopathic Clinic before the war.

Social psychology was one of the influences on the early therapeutic community innovators at Northfield Hospital. In this sense, Kurt Lewin, a Prussian immigrant to the United States and the father of social psychology, could be said to be one of the muses of the therapeutic community. His concepts of field theory, group dynamics and action research were known to the early therapeutic community innovators. Field theory focuses on the whole psychological field as crucial to the understanding of human behavior, an important basis for the therapeutic community. Lewin's group research resulted in the basic skill training group or T-group as it came to be known and included feedback, especially in the here-and-now; participant observation; and the creation of a group environment in which the member's belief system could be challenged. His concept of action research bears a close resemblance to Tom Main's culture of enquiry, in which all aspects of the milieu experience are open to examination and subsequent change and development, a crucial factor in the work of the therapeutic community.

Harry Stack Sullivan's ward at a small private Quaker hospital, Sheppard Pratt in Maryland in the late 1920s, is an intriguing therapeutic community precursor, although it was evidently not in any direct line of influence to the later therapeutic community movement in the United States. Harrison (2000) believes that Sullivan was the first to use the phrase therapeutic camp or community in 1939, some years before Tom Main applied the term to the Northfield Experiments.

The Sheppard Pratt experiment was a very small six-bed male unit, which Sullivan staffed exclusively with male workers. Sullivan believed that the patients' schizophrenic illness resulted from arrested development at a homophillic[3] stage which he believed was a normal part of human development. The hospital unit encouraged close relationships between male patients and staff in order to provide a new developmental opportunity for patients to find a chum, as Sullivan referred to the crucial task of this life stage.

The unit embodied Sullivan's so-called one genus hypothesis, that 'everyone is much more simply human than otherwise' (1953: 32), and treated schizophrenic patients as people, not as a separate class of humanity. There was a flattened hierarchy, a relaxing of medical authority and a living-learning situation, as Maxwell Jones called it, in terms of patients having an opportunity to re-experience a failed stage of development.

Although the unit was evidently successful, it did not continue and it was not replicated. However, later American practitioners of therapeutic community often referred to Sullivan's unit as an inspiring forerunner of their work.

During the later months of World War 2, Karl Menninger, an American psychiatrist of the influential Menninger Clinic in Topeka, Kansas, toured Europe, along with a commission of American military psychiatrists, studying psychiatric problems of the US Army there. They visited Northfield in Great Britain and were extremely impressed. On return to the States, Menninger devoted an entire issue of the *Bulletin of the Menninger Clinic* to papers by the Northfield innovators, thankfully republished in 1996 in a special issue of *Therapeutic Communities* journal (Menninger 1946/1996). The issue included papers by Wilfred Bion on the leaderless group project of the War Office Selection Board, Tom Main on the hospital as a therapeutic institution, Harold Bridger's description of the daily life of the patients at Northfield and Foulkes, along with two lesser known female officers, Millicent Dewar and Susan Davidson, on group work at Northfield. These articles were important in introducing the therapeutic community modality to American psychiatry.

The first important research done on the therapeutic community was by the American anthropologist Robert Rapoport and his team, at Maxwell Jones' Belmont Hospital Social Rehabilitation Unit in the mid-1950s and presented in the 1960 book, *Community as Doctor: New Perspectives on a Therapeutic Community*. As is well known, Rapoport identified three principles of the Belmont Unit: 'Everything is treatment . . . All treatment is rehabilitation . . . [and] All patients (once admitted) should get the same treatment' (Rapoport 1960: 52).

In addition, four themes, which guided concrete policies and everyday decision making, were identified: democratisation, permissiveness, communalism and reality confrontation. These themes have become defining features of the therapeutic community.

Rapoport pointed out that the themes, while all considered to be important, do not work together comfortably at all times. In fact, they may be in conflict in any given actual milieu situation. Particularly important for contemporary programmes, is the treatment–rehabilitation dilemma, which Rapoport considered to be a central dilemma for the Belmont community, but also for the field of modern psychiatry as a whole. Treatment requires some shelter from the world-at-large in order that healing may take place: the patient has become too ill to remain in the world. Rehabilitation, however, involves a return to the real world. In practice, the therapeutic community may foster behaviours which may contribute to psychological healing (e.g. free expression of feelings or honestly addressing those higher in a hierarchy) which may be detrimental to integration in the world-at-large. By the same token, in this time of shortened length of stay in hospitals and time limits on many outpatient settings, contemporary programmes may err on the side of pushing patients too quickly back into responsibility for which they are not ready.

Rapoport's work was crucial in beginning to define the characteristics of therapeutic community, at a time when this mode of treatment was becoming the 'best practice' of the mid-20th century.

Other American anthropologists and sociologists, as well as psychiatrists and psychologists, produced work on the effects of the environment in mental illness in the 1950s and the 60s. Especially influential was *The Mental Hospital* by Alfred Stanton and Morris Schwartz (1954).[4] Even at an excellent private hospital like Chestnut Lodge, Stanton and Schwartz found that staff conflict negatively affected the patients. These works gave weight to the therapeutic community finding that the whole environment of the hospital affects the treatment given, and therefore attention to the workings of the milieu is crucial.

The first therapeutic communities in the United States, as in Great Britain, were initiated in military hospitals. According to Dennie Briggs, a Navy psychologist who served with Harry Wilmer, the first therapeutic community in North America was created by Wilmer at the US Naval Hospital in Oakland, California in July of 1955, and continued until April of 1956 (Briggs 2000).

Wilmer had gone to Great Britain after the war to see Maxwell Jones, Tom Main, Joshua Bierer and T.P. Rees, all of whom were continuing their work with therapeutic communities (Wilmer 1977). He was inspired to try this modality himself at the admissions unit of the Naval Hospital in Oakland, California, where all the psychiatric casualties from the Pacific and Korea were sent.

Wilmer brought back from Great Britain a conviction that psychiatric patients could be treated without the use of restraints, seclusion rooms and intimidation. He found that when seclusion and restraints were not part of the picture and when community meetings and staff review meetings were used on a daily basis violence was, in fact, controlled by the patients themselves.

Wilmer expanded the limits of what the therapeutic community innovators thought was possible. Craig Fees interviewed Wilmer in 1999:

> At that time Max[well Jones] didn't think you could treat psychotic patients in a therapeutic community, and he never did understand that until he came to Stanford and worked with me there. And Tom Main also felt you couldn't have an effective therapeutic community with a mixture of neurotics, psychotics, character disorders.
>
> (Fees 1999: 5)

Wilmer was pragmatic about the ability of the entire hospital system to embrace the therapeutic community, but seems to have had enough support from his superiors to maintain the autonomy of his unit. However, he noted that his efforts were sabotaged at times, when in his absence a covering psychiatrist would overuse medication or put a patient in seclusion.

Wilmer went on to publish *Social Psychiatry in Action* in 1958, which described the Oakland community. He collaborated with Maxwell Jones on a comprehensive mental health service in San Mateo county in California which served as a prototype for the community mental health centre proposed by President John F. Kennedy's Community Mental Health Act of 1963 (Briggs 2002). He also set up therapeutic communities at San Quentin Prison, in San Francisco, for young drug abusers and on a ward for schizophrenic Vietnam veterans. His work deserves to be better known by contemporary American programmes.

Austen Riggs Centre is a small psychiatric hospital in Massachusetts, still in operation, founded by Austen Fox Riggs, a New York medical doctor, who himself had recovered from tuberculosis in the Berkshire mountains there. Based on his own emotional experiences, he became interested in mental problems, leading to the founding of the hospital. Over the years, Austen Riggs Centre has especially focused on treatment of young people with psychosis and personality disorder.

Austen Riggs continues to this day, as one of the very few American institutions which embraces the therapeutic community as an important element of treatment, along with two other modalities: individual psychodynamic psychotherapy and various arts programmes which are interpretation free. Winnicott's concept of the holding environment is important, as is the idea that the whole community can be used as a transitional object:

> The community itself can be a perfect example of a transitional object, one that hovers in the potential space between the real and the created. Each patient creates the community for himself, and yet it exists waiting to be created. It is born anew with each encounter, being endowed with whatever attributes the patient needs to project at the time.
>
> (Smith 1989: 518–519)

The American psychiatrist Loren Mosher was a regular visitor to Laing's anarchistic community at Kingsley Hall during his year of study in Great Britain in the mid-1960s. While also training at Tavistock and the Maudsley, Mosher was fascinated by what he saw going on at Laing's experimental community of mental patients and mental health professionals. Back in the USA, Mosher experimented with these new ideas on an inpatient ward and then went on to become the director of the newly formed Centre for Studies of Schizophrenia of the National Institute of Mental Health (NIMH) in 1968. From this position, although not without opposition from the increasingly pharmaceutically oriented agency, he was able to get some funding to continue his exploration of the effectiveness of milieu settings to ameliorate serious mental illness.

In 1971, Soteria (from the Greek word for *salvation* or *deliverance*) (Mosher 1996: 45) House opened in a working-class neighbourhood in San José, California. It was located in a two-storey home, with room for about six residents, as they were called. There were few rules, neuroleptic medication was not usually used for the first 6 weeks and residents stayed for an average of 5 months.[5]

Mosher felt that the therapeutic ingredients were that the settings were small and in homes in normal neighbourhoods. The young, non-professional, but well supervised staff had the task of understanding the background and precipitants for the resident's breakdown. The residents were encouraged to make their own decisions, keep contact with whatever outside social and treatment networks they chose and to have easy access and departure to the community as they got better (Mosher 1999).

Mosher's research showed that the original Soterians did as well as hospitalised and medicated controls and were in better shape 2 years' post-admission, working at higher levels, more often living independently and experiencing fewer re-admissions to hospital. In addition, Soteria-type treatment was much less costly than comparable hospital and psycho-pharmaceutical treatment.

Mosher's work challenged the need for professionally trained staff and neuroleptic medications to successfully treat the mentally ill, but his work has not been as influential as might be expected. He himself was confrontational and did not try to sugar coat the bitter aspects of this message for professionals and pharmaceutical companies invested in their approaches to mental illness. Even the aspect of Soteria which might be seen as easiest for the current psychiatric establishment to swallow, its cost effectiveness, was out of step with today's climate, as there is little incentive for managed care to consider a patient's long-term needs. Many of the seriously mentally ill will be dropped from insurance plans, as they lose jobs and family connections or the benefits run out. The cost will be shifted elsewhere (Sharfstein 1999), to the widely varying state Medicaid plans. Without a national healthcare plan in the United States, no one entity has long-term responsibility for the health of the country.

Sandra Bloom is an American psychiatrist who has developed an approach to short-term inpatient treatment of psychiatric patients which she calls Sanctuary. Her work, which has also been applied to other treatment settings, brings together the therapeutic community with the contemporary trauma research.

Bloom had been a psychiatric aide before training as a psychiatrist and so was perhaps more attuned to the issues of workers in often violent, chaotic and inhuman psychiatric wards. She trained as a psychiatrist at a time when therapeutic milieu was still part of the climate of psychiatric education. By 1985, she had established a psychiatric unit using a feminist approach to leadership which dovetailed well with the therapeutic community modality. Then Bloom experienced an epiphany when she was exposed to the work of Bessel Van der Kolk and Judith Herman on trauma. She realized that the patients who she treated had more substantial histories of abuse than had been recognised and that their traumas and the repetitive attempts to relive them actually constituted their psychiatric illnesses. She began to work to create an environment which would focus on healing the effects of trauma, particularly by emphasising safety.

Sanctuary posits a four-stage recovery model, summarised in the acronym SAGE: safety, affect management, grief and emancipation:

> This model is meant to provide a structure and framework for the evaluation and treatment of people who have been traumatized as children and/or adults. SAGE represents aspects of recovery, and although Safety is always the first step, and Emancipation usually the last, in actual life, these aspects tend to intertwine, interconnect, and present ongoing challenges at each life stage. Future episodes of danger or grief are likely to reawaken old wounds. Therefore, the goal of recovery is to provide the tools necessary to guarantee that a person will be equipped to deal with future experiences without turning to behaviour that is destructive to self or others.
>
> (Bloom 2000a: 84)

As well as being inspired by trauma research, the work is equally grounded in the therapeutic community. The summer 2000 issue of the journal *Therapeutic Communities* was devoted to the Sanctuary model. Bloom is well aware of her therapeutic community predecessors: Main, Wilmer and Jones. Her inpatient units made use of twice daily community meetings, open communication, reality confrontation, patients being part of each others' treatment and the living–learning situation. 'Creating Sanctuary' was their aphorism for working on the community to create more safety and emphasising that it does not just involve a place but is also a process.

Unfortunately, the work of Bloom and her colleagues has not been widely replicated and they have found it daunting to keep it going. It seems that even less argumentative, more diplomatic innovators than Mosher are swimming against the tide when trying to promote therapeutic community approaches in contemporary American psychiatry. Bloom wrote:

> This, perhaps, is our largest area of failure so far: that our challenge to the existing paradigm is like a cry in the wilderness. Clearly we are going against the flow of events in health care. We want to succeed and cannot do so without a great deal more help and support from the social systems within which we are embedded. Just as our patients need safe environments, compassion, encouragement, and social support, so do we.
>
> (Bloom 1997: 188)

She wrote that she felt like a scholar entering the Dark Ages, trying to 'keep the knowledge alive in the hope that somewhere, someday, the ground will be more fertile for the development of institutions that truly are conducive to human health, creativity, and well being' (Bloom 2000b: 134).

There was a time, before the current Dark Ages, from the 1950s through the 1980s when therapeutic community was a very influential concept in American psychiatry, although in practice the actual implementation was often watered down. Today in the United States, there are islands of therapeutic community, either still surviving from its heyday, like the Austen Riggs Centre or accidentally recreated without a conscious awareness of our heritage, as was my own programme, Bronx REAL. However, from my research it appears that therapeutic community in the United States is, as David Clark wrote as early as 1977, 'last generation's fad, the fashion of the 1950s, gone like the hula-hoop, Camelot, the Apollo missions and the snows of yesteryear' (Clark 1977: 555). What happened? I can only suggest some possible areas for further exploration in this brief account.

In the United States, it appears that the clubhouse model actually has been more influential, or at least more lastingly influential, than the therapeutic community. Fountain House, the first clubhouse was created by a group of ex-hospital patients in the early years after World War 2, in New

York City. The model was based on people helping each other and, as originally conceived, was strongly opposed to the medical model, which the patients greatly distrusted, given their state hospital experience. A recent textbook on psychiatric rehabilitation states:

> [U]sing a strategy similar to the mythical Johnny Appleseed, Fountain House and programs like it vigorously trained their staff members and then sent them out to develop new clubhouses around the country. Today literally hundreds of clubhouse programs can trace their roots back to either Fountain House or one of the other early clubhouse programs.
>
> (Pratt et al. 2002: 140)

The clubhouse model shares in several of the values of the therapeutic community, including a flattened hierarchy, the value of patients helping other patients, the use of community meetings and the provision of learning experiences. It differs in its rejection of the medical model, which the therapeutic community retains to some extent. That is, in the therapeutic community, some members of the community – the staff – carry the responsibility for treating other members of the community – the patients or clients. Clubhouse also emphatically does not share in the therapeutic community's psychoanalytic roots, with its culture of enquiry and use of staff process groups. One clubhouse director I interviewed held *no* staff-only meetings: clients were welcome at all meetings.

In addition to the influence of the clubhouse model, another explanation for the disappearance of the therapeutic community from the American scene may have to do with the decline of psychoanalysis. As I said, the therapeutic community took one of its lines of inspiration from psychoanalysis and, insofar as psychoanalysis has become less influential, the therapeutic community has also faded. Added to this has been the incredible upsurge of the importance of psychopharmacology, which is considered to be the main, and often only, treatment for psychotic and other mental illness. Psychosocial treatments of all kinds, including milieu treatments, are relegated to second class status, or in some parts of the United States, not offered at all.

Another issue in the decline of the therapeutic community in the United States is related to the treatment–rehabilitation dilemma, first described by Robert Rapoport. The therapeutic community embraces both sides of the dilemma, but may in the past have erred on the treatment side. Insofar as psychosocial approaches are used in the United States, the current emphasis appears to be on rehabilitation approaches, best represented by the psychosocial rehabilitation model of William Anthony (for example, Anthony and Liberman 1986). It seems that the treatment–rehabilitation dilemma is also a pendulum and it is currently swinging over to the rehab side. In many ways this is a welcome development for clients, when hope for recovery is a sanctioned value in available programmes. It can also backfire when applied without sophistication: one director told me of a recent time when a number of clients had been suddenly pushed out to work, resulting in a number of them de-compensating and the ensuing apathy and despair which overcame his milieu. Also of concern, however, is the fact that rehab approaches do not address the milieu setting in which they are often delivered and provide no theory of how best to use the milieu setting to deliver the services. Therapeutic community provides a seasoned theory of how best to make the milieu work, whether in a community emphasising the treatment or the rehab pole. Therapeutic community also recognises that any patient's recovery needs to include both treatment and rehabilitation.

It is my belief that milieu programmes in the United States would do well to remember the history of important American contributions to the therapeutic community and to reinstitute this effective way of thinking about and delivering milieu treatment.

Notes

1 The therapeutic community, or TC, for treatment of substance abuse is alive and thriving in the United States. However, as a somewhat different form of treatment, the success of the TC in the USA has not allowed the therapeutic community for treatment of serious mental illness to ride on its coat tails.
2 This paper is admittedly English language centric. I have not taken into account here the many contributions and elaborations on therapeutic community from other countries.
3 Homophillic refers to the characteristic of liking someone who is similar to you.
4 Such basically ethnographic research on issues of mental illness has been carried on into the present day, although not meeting the contemporary almighty gold standard of randomly controlled, quantitative research. See, for example, Sue Estroff's fascinating study of client life in a residential programme in Wisconsin, *Making It Crazy: An ethnography of psychiatric clients in an American community*, University of California Press, Berkeley,1981; Tanya Luhrmann's *Of Two Minds: The Growing Disorder in American Psychiatry*, Alfred A. Knopf, New York, 2000, on the conflicting pressures on psychiatrists in training and on the treatment of mental illness in general, with special attention to Austen Riggs Centre's longstanding therapeutic community approach.
5 In subsequent years other programmes were inaugurated based on Soteria ideas, but responding to tougher demands with more chronic patients of lower socioeconomic level and shorter length of stay. In these communities daily life was more structured, and use of neuroleptic medication more common.

Bibliography

Anthony, W.A. and Liberman, R.P. (1986). The practice of psychiatric rehabilitation: historical, conceptual, and research base. *Schizophrenia Bulletin*, 12(4): 542–559.

Bloom, S.L. (1997). *Creating Sanctuary: Toward the evolution of sane societies*. New York: Routledge.

Bloom, S.L. (2000a). Creating sanctuary: healing from systematic abuses of power. *Therapeutic Communities: The International Journal for Therapeutic and Supportive Organizations* 21(2): 67–91.

Bloom, S.L. (2000b). Epilogue. *Therapeutic Communities: The International Journal for Therapeutic and Supportive Organizations* 21(2): 133–134.

Briggs, D. (2000). In the navy: therapeutic community experiment at the U.S. Naval Hospital, Oakland, California. Retrieved 15 June 2002, from the website of Planned Environment Therapy Trust Archive and Study Centre, http://www.pettarchiv.org.uk/pubs-dbriggs-navy2pdf.pdf

Briggs, D. (2002). *A Life Well Lived: Maxwell Jones – a memoir*. London: Jessica Kingsley.

Buber, M. (1958). *I and Thou* (R.G. Smith, trans. 2nd edn). Edinburgh: T. & T. Clark.

Clark, D.H. (1977). The therapeutic community. *International Journal of Psychiatry* 131: 553–564.

Fees, C. (1999). *Dr. Harry Wilmer interviewed by Craig Fees*, 7 September 1999. Unpublished manuscript.

Harrison, T. (2000). *Bion, Rickman, Foulkes and the Northfield Experiments: Advancing on a different front*. Philadelphia, PA: Jessica Kingsley.

Kipp, J. (2005). *An Exploration of the Prevalence of Therapeutic Community as a Contemporary Treatment Modality for People with Psychiatric Illness in the United States*. New York: New York University.

Menninger, K. (1946/1996). Foreword. *Therapeutic Communities: The International Journal for Therapeutic and Supportive Organizations* 17(2): 75–76.

Mosher, L.R. (1996). Soteria: a therapeutic community for psychotic persons, in P.R. Breggin and E.M. Stern (eds) *Psychosocial Approaches to Deeply Disturbed Persons*. New York: Hawarth.

Mosher, L.R. (1999). Soteria and other alternatives to psychiatric hospitalization: a personal and professional review. *The Journal of Nervous and Mental Disease* 187: 142–149. Retrieved 12 August 2004 from http://www.moshersoteria.com/

Pines, M. (1999). Forgotten pioneers: the unwritten history of the therapeutic community movement. *Therapeutic Communities* 20(1): 23–42.

Pratt, C.W., Gill, K.J., Barrett, N.M. and Roberts, M.M. (2002). *Psychiatric Rehabilitation*. New York: Academic Press.

Rapoport, R.N. (1960). *Community as Doctor: New perspectives on a therapeutic community*. Springfield, IL: Charles C. Thomas.

Sharfstein, S.S. (1999). Soteria and the medical marketplace. *Journal of Nervous and Mental Disease* 187(3): 120–130.

Smith, B.L. (1989). The community as object, in M.G. Fromm and B.L. Smith (eds) *The Facilitating Environment: Clinical applications of Winnicott's theory*. Madison, CT: International Universities Press.

Stanton, A.H. and Schwartz, M.S. (1954). *The Mental Hospital: A study of institutional participation in psychiatric illness and treatment*. New York: Basic Books.

Sullivan, H.S. (1953). *The Interpersonal Theory of Psychiatry*. New York: W.W. Norton.

Wills, W.D. (1964). *Homer Lane: A biography*. London: George Allen & Unwin.

Wilmer, H.A. (1958). *Social Psychiatry in Action*. Springfield, IL: Charles C. Thomas.

Wilmer, H.A. (1977). Therapeutic community: a symbol of transformation, in P.F. Ostwald (ed.) *Communication and Social Interaction: Clinical and therapeutic aspects of human behaviour*. New York: Grune & Stratton.

Chapter 3

The decline and rediscovery of the therapeutic community

Enrico Pedriali

The idea of the therapeutic community (TC) is the conception of a new healthcare system which originated from a wide range of cultural premises, some connected with the specific political, social and emotional situation issuing from World War 2 and others stemming from a fruitful integration of different disciplines, such as social psychology, psychoanalysis and systems theory.

An heroic origin

The TC spirit was imbued with an atmosphere of active participation, mutual commitment and the defence of freedom and communal interest that characterised that specific historical time. During the war years it seemed that there was a duty, which was unavoidable for the whole nation, to take an active part in defending the basic values of its cultural tradition against totalitarian dictatorships. Maybe it is not accidental that the first TC experiments were designed and carried out in a military hospital in the United Kingdom. Many have wondered how it was possible that within the context of the military – by definition an authoritarian and top-down institution – something opposite to that structure could develop. A possible answer to this question could be that it was a kind of revolution that took place in those years, within the hierarchical relationships in the British Army. One way to deal with the tension and the anxiety of those times was for the soldiers and the officers to discuss current events. In this way, an equality was established using thinking and investigation as a means of exploring (Rayner 1991). In other words, the army was open to new ways of thinking and was affected by the theories of Kurt Lewin and other Gestalt psychologists about the work on and with groups.

Beside that, in the 1940s and 1950s Great Britain was probably the country in which the most interesting cultural trends in the field of human sciences developed and were later carried out within psychiatry. The spirit of solidarity, social change and institutional innovation lasted throughout the years following the war and were an integral part of what was dubbed, probably for the first time in 1941, by the Archbishop of Canterbury, the Welfare State. By this formula he meant a broad social and community policy involving the entire population without any exclusions based on differences in status, function or income.

Myth and reality

An echo of the British experience was soon to be spread outside the United Kingdom as well. Almost everywhere in the west at the time was ripe for a meaningful cultural change that would affect social policy in many countries with greater or smaller repercussions on health and psychiatric care. Therefore, the notion of the therapeutic community became part of the vocabulary of mental health workers and others and it assumed a variety of meanings according to different national and historical situations and contexts in which it was applied. At times it was given a radically anti-institutional and almost revolutionary significance; on other occasions its solidarity and humanistic, religious or political value was emphasised; or else an exclusive feature concerning the specific activity of its followers was highlighted; or often it was characterised by a compromise between conflicting trends and pressures. The therapeutic community gradually underwent such a transformation in its original significance, that Tom Main wrote that the term itself was of such frequent use that it had lost its meaning. It had been used to describe so many different situations that the term had become confusing and imprecise (Main 1989).

After the exciting pioneering stage in the 1950s and 1960s therapeutic communities went through a long trial that toned down their emphasis and, in some cases, marked their end. However, many therapeutic communities have survived and in some countries they have even multiplied as a result of a high demand for residential treatment programmes to treat severe pathologies affecting adults, socially maladjusted adolescent patients and problems connected with substance abuse. As we want to consider both the decline and the survival of therapeutic communities it is remarkably interesting to examine the reasons for such a swing between success and failure. If we examine closely the history of the first years of the therapeutic community movement it is possible to find some problematic aspects that played an important role in causing its crisis.

A determinant factor at the beginning of many therapeutic communities was the overt inadequacy and anti-therapeutic nature of the asylums (Goffmann 1961). In this sense, we could say that the therapeutic community idea was informed by the notion of being the opposite of a total institution, that is to say, the opposite of the traditional mental hospital. As Maxwell Jones noted, therapeutic communities originally developed as a reaction to the closed and hierarchical systems characterizing the psychiatric units in the 1950s (Jones 1976). Therapeutic community basic concepts aimed to develop an open system in contrast with the closed system of the mental hospital, an egalitarian context instead of an hierarchical and vertical one, an experience of socialisation instead of isolation and institutional passivity, a transformation process facilitated by a group approach rather than just pharmacological treatments. Being able to describe positively what a therapeutic community is and show its specificity, methodology and limits was a much more complex task and not all therapeutic communities proved to be up to it.

Of course, there are also other examples that ran counter to this trend and, since their start, were able to define clearly their theoretical model and devise a consistent method. However, one can maintain, with Hinshelwood (1998), that a specific issue of therapeutic communities was their very inability to adjust to the environment.

Towards the decline

In other words, most of the time therapeutic communities paid attention almost only to their internal environment and ignored the fact that they lived in connection with what happened outside, i.e. a world in which social attitudes and values change on a large scale, both nationally and internationally (Hinshelwood 1998). From this standpoint the study made by Rapoport (1960) at the Henderson Hospital on Maxwell Jones' request was emblematic. The research did not aim to assess the treatment outcome but to identify the characteristics and the kind of culture permeating the environment in which the patients lived. As we know, Rapoport formulated the four renowned principles to which all the 'inhabitants' at the Henderson – patients and staff – referred: communalism, democratisation, permissiveness, reality confrontation (Rapoport 1960). At that time there was a cultural atmosphere which put some pressure on institutions to develop more egalitarian and democratic relationships. Therapeutic communities were involved and carried those values into the field of psychiatry, mental healthcare and the other helping professions. Permissiveness and democratisation, Hinshelwood claims (1998), were probably a driving force prompting the patients to actively participate in the decision-making process and share real power with their caregivers.

Internal factors

Paradoxically, here lay the unknown condition for what would become the main limitation of many therapeutic communities. Beyond the accomplishment of sophisticated treatment methods and ways of functioning, most – supported by the certainty of their own intentions and their confidence in being the only possible option to an obsolete and inhuman system such as the asylum – ended up losing sight of the increasingly changing context of which they were part. In some therapeutic communities, a sharp split between an internal world ruled by sound principles, good intentions, high skills and an external world replete with lack of understanding, hostility and persecutory intentions developed. In clinical terms, this turned sometimes into a symbiotic relationship between the community and the patients. These latter, despite some satisfactory progress, were not able to deal with the process of separation from the therapeutic community and were thwarted by a similar difficulty experienced by their caregivers. From a psychodynamic perspective we could say that often the TC countertransference strengthened the transference of the patients, resulting in a progressive chronicity on both sides. Thus the therapeutic community itself, originating in an anti-institutional urge, was institutionalised. Parallel to these critical internal factors, as we may call them, we need to take into account the external factors with which therapeutic communities were confronted.

External factors

The first arena was embodied in the asylum. While the start and development of individual therapeutic communities outside the hospital context was quick and relatively easy, the impact on mental hospitals was not as easy. Moreover, the developments were very different according to national contexts.

Developments in France

In France, the innovative seeds which developed immediately after World War 2, coincided with a societal renewal, sparked off by the movement of resistance against Nazi fascism that involved the entire country in an effort to rebuild a society in which the value of human life and desire for human freedom once again acquired significance. A variety of experiments thrived: in Fleury-les-Aubrais with Georges Daumezon, in Saint-Alban with Francois Tosquelles, in Ville-Evrard with Paul Sivadon.

The French experience evolved along several lines among which psychoanalysis was central. It applied individual working techniques to group settings and it basically consisted of the analysis of projective mechanisms and transference interpretation. Institutional psychotherapy (Oury 1972), a newly coined expression, synthesised this approach and this can be viewed as the French version of the culture of inquiry, peculiar to British therapeutic communities. In France a real therapeutic community movement never really developed and the extensive changes which occurred in the years following the war affected the psychiatric care system in a broad sense. They gave rise to so-called sector psychiatry (Bonnafé 1963) that had its best expression in the 13th arrondissement in Paris. There a group of psychiatrists and psychoanalysts set up a project in which they tried to export psychiatric practice to homogeneous and circumscribed areas out in the community, establishing direct contact with the real living conditions of their patients (Bleandonu and Despinoy 1974). The few therapeutic community experiences took place in Besançon with Paul Claude Racamier, probably the most prominent figure who applied psychoanalysis to institutions in France (Racamier 1970), in Villeurbane with Marcel Sassolas and Jaques Hochmann, and partly at the Clinique La Borde in Cour Cheverny with Jean Oury. Save the experience of Villeurbane, which is still operating (Sassolas 1997), the others gradually shifted to a state of painful isolation. After the enthusiasm in the 1960s and 1970s French psychiatry was overwhelmed by a reaction that has to some extent affected the whole of Europe, so that today in France the scene is characterised by traditional psychiatry, strongly anchored in the old mental institutions and with only a few scattered therapeutic communities here and there.

Developments in Italy

In Italy, innovation appeared with some delay compared to France and Great Britain. Only in the 1960s were there experiments with therapeutic communities and these were not common. Franco Basaglia (1968) carried out a project in psychiatric hospitals first in Gorizia and later in Trieste that could only be partially assimilated into a therapeutic community experience. His overt and well-defined goal was to close down the mental hospitals and for this reason Basaglia himself was always very critical of and hostile to the therapeutic community model as an alternative to the institution of the hospital. At that time the only Italian experiments that can be considered consistent with the definition of therapeutic community were set up by Diego Napolitani in Milan in the 1960s and 1970s, at first within the state and then in the private sector (Napolitani 1972). They were interesting though strongly idealised experiments that referred back to the famous British therapeutic communities, as well as to Racamier's thinking both theoretically and methodologically. Their ending was, however, determined by their progressive isolation and inability to integrate into a cultural context which was not ready to accept such innovative practices and which was, in fact, far more sensitive to the ideologically oriented anti-institutional atmosphere dominant at that time which led to closing down mental hospitals altogether in Italy 1978.

Following this event there was a gradual flourishing of services that filled in the gaps that had been created. These treatment units, all called therapeutic communities and informed by a wide range of theoretical models, are still operating today. They navigate several difficulties connected with a lack of financial sources, some political ideological distrust that views them as attempting to reintroduce a more acceptable and up-dated version of the old mental hospitals, but also because of their own cultural weakness due to their late appearance on the psychiatric scene.

Developments elsewhere and in North America

Other European countries have shown to varying extent some interest in the therapeutic community movement more or less successfully, but we cannot claim that outside the United Kingdom therapeutic communities managed to impose and strengthen their identity in terms of alternative models, or rather treatment systems with well-defined features, goals and boundaries (Kennard 1983). In the United States, some interest in what had happened in Great Britain during the war appeared for the first time in 1946 in a famous paper by Karl Menninger, (co-founder and director of the American psychiatric clinic that bears his name) published in the *Bulletin of the Menninger Clinic* (Menninger 1946). In the paper's introduction the author frankly outlined the reasons why some of his colleagues and himself had literally fallen in love with British psychiatry. He wrote that one of the most striking things was a competent use of group psychology and group dependence principles in different kinds of therapeutic programmes.

In the wake of the success psychoanalysis was having in the United States at that time, some interesting experiences developed where a strictly psycho-analytic approach was coupled with some of the therapeutic community principles and methods. Chestnut Lodge, Austen Riggs and the Menninger Clinic itself were the most significant examples of such an approach, which some called bifocal. Here the patients underwent individual treatment and lived in an environment that partially applied the therapeutic community model. At the same time there was a flourishing of centres also called therapeutic communities, that treated patients with problems of substance-abuse (drug, alcohol etc.), where staff members and residents formed an hierarchical continuum or chain of command. Synanon, Daytop and Phoenix House are the best known examples of this kind of therapeutic community. Similar initiatives were set up in some prisons following the English example at Grendon Underwood.

These units were also called concept houses or hierarchical therapeutic communities in contrast with the democratic model typical in Britain. Many of them differed because of a very rigid methodological approach often linked to authoritarian and charismatic leaders. Most of the popular treatment centres in the 1960s and 1970s were either overwhelmed by neo-positivist scientific culture or a neo-liberal oriented policy that dras-tically clamped down on welfare spending or disappeared when their leaders retired.

Certainly, there still exist therapeutic communities everywhere, but throughout the western world centres and services that are somehow inspired by this model are confronted with a very different cultural climate than in the heroic years. Since the 1970s the original driving force has failed to continue to impact the traditional psychiatric culture, as the ideal and social tensions from the time during and immediately after the war, dissipated. The few hospitals that tried to carry out a therapeutic community model within their structure were isolated. To synthesise the situation that developed let us refer to Stuart Whiteley (1979) who maintains that today the general ideas are vaguely exported into hospitals and society, but means and meanings have been separated. In most cases what was supposed to be a democratic community model is just a superficial gesture towards open communication and a partition of power, without any real understanding of the underlying principles (Whiteley 1979).

In Great Britain, the therapeutic community movement slowly found itself in a position of progressive weakness as well. The establishment has clung strongly onto traditional institutional culture and, with a few exceptions, the common trend has continued to be a biologically oriented approach.

The crisis of the welfare state, evidence-based culture and the consumer society

In the 1980s and 1990s the welfare state started to totter and the reduction in welfare spending was inevitable. At the same time the success of the neurosciences, statistical methods and pharmacological research all contributed to steering official psychiatry towards short-term therapy and outpatient treatments. Medications and physical therapies, especially to treat quite severe patients, were viewed as the main methods to be applied in order to decrease hospitalisations, even though they proved quite ineffective in terms of the long-term course of psychiatric illness. Therapeutic communities, in contrast, provided by their nature long-term perspectives and were therefore more expensive and incompatible with a purely financial approach aimed at short-term saving. The drastic cutback in resources allocated for social spending forced the entire psychiatric field to be confronted with a new reality test, just as much as the undeniable success of neuroscience has compelled it to be faced with a choice – either change or disappear – and has required it to give evidence of the validity of its methods as though these were just consumer goods. In the wake of these new conditions a new kind of faith has ubiquitously spread. It is faith in evidence-based practice. Behind the obviousness of such an axiom, there is the risk of overlooking or denying what can be concealed behind the evidence. In this perspective the therapeutic community has a remarkable advantage stemming from its familiarity with the culture of inquiry or institutional psychotherapy if one prefers, i.e. a particular attitude to look for the significance of what happens even beyond appearances.

Responding to the challenge

A new situation is taking shape. On the one hand, cultural, economic, and scientific stimuli require us to look for quick, cheap and self-evident solutions. On the other hand, the concept of the therapeutic community seems to be able to offer realistic responses because of the very use of a culture of inquiry. The latter can reveal the illusoriness of some evidence and confront us with the need for greater tolerance of diversity and consequent frustration.

While nowadays therapeutic communities are able to establish a different methodological framework in order to deal with extraordinary social and cultural pressures and ensure some possibility for their own survival, at the same time they have a chance to take up the challenge.

Therapeutic communities can deal with severe pathologies where it is only too evident that the idea of a quick, easy and economic solution would be a misleading and magical one. This is the reason why the kind of patients in therapeutic communities are gradually shifting towards severe personality disorders and psychosis and it also explains the survival and setting up of new therapeutic communities, as has been the case in Italy in recent years (Pedriali 1999). This implies an adjustment of the therapeutic community model to these kinds of patients and it requires us to differentiate therapeutic community methods according to different pathologies. The same kind of treatment cannot be identical for such a wide spectrum, ranging from patients with personality disorders or schizophrenic pathologies to maladjusted adolescents. Furthermore, the context in which a therapeutic community is placed and the relationship that needs to be developed with the outside have to be taken into account.

The need for a methodological differentiation had previously been highlighted by Tom Main. In a lecture he gave at the Richmond Fellowship International Conference in 1975 he said that to assess therapeutic communities by comparing them with one another would be a mistake. We should rather be able to assess it in terms of its ability to understand the specific kind of patients it accepts and to devise particular psychosocial processes that meet their specific needs (Main 1980).

Hinshelwood keenly describes the features of this transition. He states that from the 1970s the therapeutic community movement had to start to think about itself and acquire a higher degree of professionalism, by shifting from a social movement to a professional method (Hinshelwood 1997). In his view, to state that the development of the therapeutic community movement carries some signs of cultural change that occurred first in the post war period and then in the 1970s, is not a lack of respect toward that movement. We are all immersed in our historical context and our choices might have been different in another situation. The crucial point here is the transition from a model, in which a feeling of belonging and participating was the core of the therapy, to another one that looks at the therapeutic project designed differently for and suited to each patient. In the latter, it becomes a tailor-made treatment with timing and characteristics that can foster personal growth. Basically this means helping subjectivity, if only embryonic subjectivity, to be formed through the group setting. This implies a therapeutic alliance between the community and patient, characterised by a differentiated approach depending on how severe the pathology is. The four principles formulated by Rapoport cannot be rigidly interpreted as their application will depend on the consistency of the residual ego of each single patient (Pedriali 2003).

Conclusion

Just as the therapeutic community culture has gone through a diminution of its original emphasis, the culture of evidence-based practice and the logic of the consumer society seem to mark time as they are confronted with the most severe problems of psychic pain. In the 1940s, facing the dramatic trials of World War 2, British psychiatry was able to make a creative effort that resulted in the therapeutic community movement (Kennard 1983). Today, throughout the world, psychiatry needs to deal with economic globalisation and neo-liberalist policies. The re-launching of therapeutic communities and their culture of inquiry will depend on the ability of the mental health workers to make just as much creative use of this new and difficult situation. The learning context (the spirit of enquiry) and its concrete applications within institutional therapy is a method which has proved to be a valuable source of knowledge for generations of mental health workers.

It is difficult to find a context comparable to this where we can experiment with our relationship with patients, share everyday life, group dynamics, the practice of team work, the habit to think about events and grasp their overt and latent determinant factors, with the same intensity. In this way, the therapeutic community also represents a learning community, not only for the patients but also for the workers and in this respect it can become an effective model that can be exported into many other contexts.

Indeed, it is not by accident that the therapeutic community culture based on learning from experience is one of the inspirational sources of the group relations conferences promoted by the Tavistock Institute of Human Relations throughout the world as a training method for people working in the areas of business, education and helping professions.

Bibliography

Basaglia, F. (1968). *L'Istituzione negata*. Torino: Einaudi.
Bleandonu, G. and Despinoy, M. (1974). *Hôpitaux de jour et psichiatrie dans la communauté*. Paris: Payot.

Bonnafé, L. (1963). *Théses de 1963 sur la psychiatrie de secteur. Information Psychiatrique* 9: 507.

Goffmann, E. (1961). *Asylums. Essays on the Social Situation of Mental Patients and Other Inmates.* New York: Anchor Books.

Hinshelwood, R.D. (1997). Terapeutico e antiterapeutico, in M. Corulli (ed.) *Cosa accade nelle comunità terapeutiche?* Torino: Bollati Boringhieri.

Hinshelwood, R.D. (1998). Pressioni culturali sulla comunità terapeutica: fattori interni ed esterni, in A. Ferruta, G. Foresti and E. Pedriali (eds) *La Comunità Terapeutica. Tra Mito e Realtà.* Milano: Raffaello Cortina Editore.

Jones, M. (1976). *Maturation of the Therapeutic Community. An Organic Approach to Health and Mental Health.* New York: Human Sciences Press.

Kennard, D. (1983). *Introduction to Therapeutic Community.* London: Routledge.

Main, T. (1980). Some basic concepts in therapeutic community work, in E. Jansen (ed.) *The Therapeutic Community.* London: Croom Helm.

Main, T. (1989). *The Ailment and Other Psychoanalytic Essays.* London: Free Association Books.

Menninger, K. (1946). Foreword. *Bulletin of the Menninger Clinic* 10(3).

Napolitani, D. (1972). Un ensemble de communautés thérapeutiques: le processus de personnation des institutions communitaires, in C. Chiland and P. Bequart (eds) *Traitment au long cours des ètats psychotiques.* Toulouse: Eduard Privat Editeur.

Oury, J. (1972). Thérapeutique institutionelle, in *Encyclopédie medico-chirurgicale* Vol. 6. Paris: Edition Techniques.

Pedriali, E. (1999). *For a Therapeutic Community's Policy.* Unpublished paper given at the annual Windsor Conference of the Association of Therapeutic Communities.

Pedriali, E. (2003). *Therapeutic Community as a Theatre: Psychoses enter the stage.* Paper given at the annual Windsor Conference of the Association of Therapeutic Communities.

Racamier, P.-C. (1970). *Le Psychanaliste sans Divan.* Paris: Payot.

Rapoport, R.N. (1960). *Community as Doctor: New perspective on a therapeutic community.* London: Tavistock.

Rayner, E. (1991). *The Independent Mind in British Psychoanalysis.* London: Free Association Books.

Sassolas, M. (1997). *La Psychose à Rebrousse-poil.* Ramonville Saint-Agne: Editions Erès.

Whiteley, J.S. (1979). *Group Approaches in Psychiatry.* London: Routledge & Kegan Paul.

Chapter 4

Exegesis, truth and tradition: a hermeneutic approach to psychosis

John Gale

A hermeneutic approach to understanding is one shared by religion and psychoanalysis, the latter having indicated its exegetical programme in the composite title of Freud's first major work *Traumdeutung*. We can say that hermeneutics is a dynamic approach to meaning which points to the primacy of language (Grondin 1995; Lacan 1984) and thus of being[1] (Lacan 1988). That is to say, because language forms its substratum, understanding is fundamentally an ontological concern.[2] It is an event we undergo, rather than a subjective act of meaning (Kisiel 1985; Lammi 1991). The double signification of language (Ricoeur 1970), which is implicit here, demands in the case of religion that we get under the surface of texts, beliefs, rituals or myths or, in the case of psychoanalysis, of dreams, symptoms or behaviours to reveal another sense, the hidden signification of experience in its historical and cultural context. Recognition of the distorted nature of language opens both religion and psychoanalysis to the inherent dangers of dualism[3] (Lacan 2006). Coupled with this exegetical approach lies our understanding of religion or psychoanalysis itself, in which our ever changing evaluation forms a parallel hermeneutic. Thus we can divide research on texts or authors into various stages.

In this chapter, I discuss some philosophical ideas that are fundamental to the treatment of the psychoses. They revolve around the revelation of truth and the meaning of experience. In this context, the uncovering of truth is understood as an ontological event in which textual commentary functions in a way that makes it more than an analogy, because psychosis, like the unconscious, is structured like a language (Lacan 1977) in which allegory and interpretation already form a part. Thus Freud considered that dreams should be treated as texts akin to sacred scripture (*einen hieligen* Text SE V: 514). As such psychosis is always situated within a specific historical community or tradition.

Dislocation and disclosure

The interpretative treatment of texts has a long history. As a model for understanding it can be viewed as the way in which we come to see ourselves in the present, by making contact with historical truth. Hermeneutics in antiquity was exclusively the work of biblical scholars and characterised by rabbinical interpretations of the Old Testament – including the Dead Sea scrolls, other apocalyptic writings and psuedoepigrapha – and New Testament exegesis of the Old Testament. That is to say that many biblical texts are themselves commentaries or a reworking of ideas found in earlier texts. This included various patristic systems of exegesis, notably that of the Alexandrian school, represented by writers greatly influenced by the Platonic tradition,[4] and the school of Antioch (Wilkinson 1963).[5] Already with these two great patristic methodologies we can detect the emergence of a fundamental dislocation, a dislocation which, by the 4th century, St Augustine was already attempting to resolve (Pépin 1957; Pontet 1944).

The Alexandrian school developed an allegorical exegetical methodology, which answered principally to the quest for meaning, with the awareness that understanding is a necessary condition for knowledge and that speech always says something other than what is said (*allēgoria*) (Lear 1990). For language demands we rise above (*anagōgē*) the literal in order to grasp a more taciturn, underlying concealed sense (*hyponoia*) both in the text and as it moves beyond the text (Crouzel 1964, 1999; de Lubac 1947).[6] Interpretation involves, therefore, an uncovering. Thus Heidegger (1990) insists that interpretation always functions as a disclosure:

> In interpreting, we do not, so to speak, throw a 'signification' over some naked thing which is present-to-hand, we do not stick a value on it; but when something within-the-world is encountered as such, the thing in question already has an involvement which is disclosed in our understanding of the world, and this involvement is one which gets laid out by the interpretation.
>
> (Heidegger 1990: 190–191)

The silent, ambiguous structure of speech (Gale and Sanchez 2005a)[7] points to unclarified issues and enigmas and it is this concealed element that makes possible the emergence of *alētheia*, generating what Lacan referred to as *parole pleine*, true speech or full speech, speech impregnated with meaning (Lacan 1984).[8]

> Every discourse, as we have found with Augustine, goes back to an unsaid to which we must be able to listen if we want to understand what is said. Augustine speaks here of the internal world. If the internal world of a human thought is explained only in thought, the external world still never exhausts what wants to be said, the wishing-to-be-shouted of the internal word. This return of the said to the unsaid, of the finite order of the discourse to the infinity of wishing-to-say, corresponds to what Gadamer calls in *Truth and Method* the *speculative* achievement of language. '*Speculative*' according to Gadamer comes

from *speculum*, 'mirror', and evokes that 'truth of the word' that is able to allow the resonance of a meaning that goes beyond what is said.

(Grondin 2003: 146–147)

Lacan even went so far as to say that textual commentary is useful precisely because 'commenting on a text is like doing an analysis' (Lacan 1988: 73). This does not mean that through the interpretation of a text we are conducting an analysis of the author but that:

[I]f we understand how to approach, find meaning, and question this meaning within a text this may help us in our understanding of what it means to interpret with respect to our encounter with clients in the therapeutic relationship. In both instances we work with language, with meaning and with non-meaning, with confusion and ambiguity, with truth and error . . . In any text as with any client we encounter a surplus of meanings, a history and a future that cannot be reduced to a simplistic schema.

(Black 2006: 1)

The divergence between rationalism and phenomenological hermeneutics, which was foreshadowed in the dislocation between the approaches of patristic writers like Clement and Chrysostom, can be found in the divergence between the understanding of the psychoses found in biological psychiatry and psychoanalytic approaches to psychosis (Ross 2006). Furthermore, it is mirrored in various disagreements about the nature of psychoanalysis itself (Crews 1993; Freud 1900; Grünbaum 1986; Habermas 1971; Lacan 1984; Nagel 1994) which, in their turn, have fostered a climate of uncertainty that goes to the heart of any philosophical consideration of those approaches to the understanding and treatment of psychosis which rest on a psychoanalytic foundation (Bachmann, Resch and Mundt 2003; Birchwood and Spencer 1999; Fenton 2000; Gale and Sanchez 2005b; Jackson 1994; Lacan 1993; Paget 2000; Thornicroft and Susser 2000). Thus psychoanalytic approaches to psychosis like those of Bion (1967), Fromm-Reichmann (1960), Giovacchini (1979), Klein (1930, 1948, 1975), Lukas (1992, 1993), O'Shaughnessy (1992), Rosenfeld (1966), Segal (1957), Sohn (1985) and Yorke (1991),[9] need not be seen as part of the scientific project, as their concern is not with scientific truth but with understanding. Neither need they be seen merely as an alternative to a biological approach or in competition with scientific truth.[10] Biological psychiatry stands, as it were, in the place of critical, literal exegesis. And while much has been written of the ascendance of pharmacological treatments for the psychoses (e.g. Cullberg, 2006; Mosher, Gosden and Beder, 2004) and our understanding of the psychoses within the overall epistemological framework of a medical illness, it is well documented that biological and genetic explanations do not exclude the thesis that other factors may have a role to play (Andreasen

1999; De Waelhens and Ver Eecke 2001; Hartmann et al. 1984; Kendler and Diehl 1993; Mortensen et al. 1999; Tienari 1992). These other factors may be described, at least analogously, as allegorical in their overall approach to truth. Indeed, it is precisely within the context of double meaning that the language of psychoanalysis is set apart from empirical science (De Waelhens and Ver Eecke 2001).

The emergence of truth

Dialectic is the tactic that Plato ascribed to Socrates, who is shown beginning most dialogues by first reducing his interlocutor to a state of confusion and helplessness, bringing out the contradictions in his discourse (Gale 2007). Lacan compares this to the first stage of psychoanalytic treatment when the analyst forces the patient to confront the contradictions and gaps in his narrative. Just as Socrates tried to draw out *alētheia* from the confused statements of his interlocutor, so also the analyst proceeds to draw out truth from the patient's free associations.[11] But what kind of truth is revealed to hermeneutic thought? The Socratic dialogues, according to Gadamer, do not suggest the victory of logic and absolute truth but rather emphasise Socrates in the role of a midwife, there at the birth of *alētheia* and thus a bringing to birth of being. Truth, in this ontological sense, is what happens whenever dialogue is genuine:

> Not only does Socrates facilitate truth he facilitates dialogue . . . Here Socrates is only one voice in a larger conversation where all are participants rather than disputants; he provides the conditions for the emergence of truth from the collective voice of the conversation. Truth, whatever it is, can only emerge from dialogue (essentially a conversation with and within tradition). For this reason, the early works of Plato are written in dialogical form, not just because this makes for a stylish and dramatic literary presentation. The works are in dialogue because truth *is* dialogue.
>
> (Lawn 2006: 70–71)

Although in *Seminar II* he says that Plato would never have understood psychoanalysis, Lacan casts Socrates in the role of a psychoanalyst, revealing to his disciples a truth that escapes their own consciousness (Roudinesco 1997). In a style similar to the Socratic dialogues,[12] he describes the analyst undermining the patient's rational illusions of certainty and security that are based in the ego. The patient's ignorance is important because it is the direction that his error takes, that uncovers *alētheia* (Lacan 1988).[13]

Lacan shows how psychoanalytic treatment uncovers truth by a series of dialectical reversals (Lacan 2006). He argues that psychoanalysis is a dialectical experience, an art of conversation designed to teach the patient to give his own speech its *alētheia* and its meaning[14] (Lacan 1988) and that understanding the psychoanalytic process in these terms leads to a reappraisal of the notion of transference (Lacan 2006, 1988). *Alētheia* refers here to ontological truth and is not held up in opposition to falsehood or error, as empirical descriptions can be described as true but in opposition to emptiness (Crouzel 1961).[15] 'If the true work of art is the revelation of being, its opposite is an empty or hollow presentation, which raises up nothing' (Grondin 2003: 53).

> Freud progressed on a course of research which is not characterised by the same style as other scientific research. Its domain is that of the truth of the subject. The quest for truth is not entirely reducible to the objective, and objectifying, quest of ordinary scientific method. What is at stake is the realisation of the truth of the subject, like a dimension peculiar to it which must be detached in its distinctiveness [*originalité*] in relation to the very notion of reality.
>
> (Lacan 1984)

To describe psychoanalysis and by implication therapeutic community methodology, which is one of its derivatives, as directed at disclosing the *alētheia* of the subject implies that it is 'an action that goes right to the core of being (*Kern unseres Wesens*)' as Freud put it [SE IV: 4: 146–50, 151, 157–62 and 7: 603]. It is, therefore, only 'in relation to being' that the analyst operates (Lacan 2006: 491, 513). The drawing together and interconnectedness of language, interpretation, truth and being hangs on this notion that meaning is a function of being:

> [Meaning] is the revelation, the bringing to the fore of the true dimension of being. Therefore, meaning is dependent on being, though it is of course a peculiar kind of dependence, in the sense that it is rather a kind of reciprocity. Meaning is not something 'external to' or 'in relationship to' being, but rather the manifestation of the internal 'dynamism' of being itself. This means for man that he is essentially dependent on being which becomes accessible through meaning. Meaning therefore cannot be arbitrary, but is bound by an absolute criterion: the truth, the *alētheia* of being (*ens et verum convertuntur*).
>
> (D'hert 1978: 159)

Our hermeneutic concern is not, therefore, so much with the facts but with a meaning of a different kind. However, as the literal sense of the text, for the patristic exegete, was the source of the spiritual, mystical or allegorical sense (Crouzel) so too, double meaning (Ricoeur 1970) or the other sense (De Waelhens 2001), 'always has some relation to the patient' (De Waelhens and Ver Eecke 2001: 281). This means that the facts ground interpretations and so they are never arbitary or merely extrinsic. Consequently, this grounding relationship forms a dialectic in which the emergence of meaning occurs, yet at the same time the facts are never obvious because they are always an expression of another, deeper conflict.

Community and *paradosis*

One of the key differences between the interpretation of dreams as we find it in pagan antiquity and in psychoanalysis is that while the former was primarily concerned with finding out about the future, Freud's interest was in the past, in the sense of the unconscious origins of things.[16] However, paradoxically this historical focus is also a concern with the present, in that the present reaches back into the inescapable past with which we always remain intimately connected.[17] Thus we can speak of our sense of self and our self-understanding being fundamentally rooted in a specific historical tradition (Gadamer 1989),[18] in the sense of an inheritance (*paradosis*) rather than as something handed on. For understanding is, in itself, an immersion into the process of tradition:

> In understanding we are already part of history and subject to its continuity, which discloses itself more clearly to our eyes through hermeneutic activity. Since it is the background of the continuing influence of the past which in general enables us to make progress in understanding, our hermeneutically acquired insights remain also constantly limited and circumscribed.
>
> (Bubner 1990: 61)

Tradition and language stand together and here the human subject is embedded (Lacan 1988) for the past is part of our engagement with the *saeculum* and we can never be separated from that which is handed over to us (*paradosis*) and therefore 'the past and the future correspond precisely to one another' (Lacan 1988: 157). For this reason truth as *alētheia* can be described as historical in the sense that we can only understand ourselves from within a community.[19] Memory (*mnēmē*) and *anamnēsis* play a vital role here in the dynamic experience of historical being. For this reason we can describe the unconscious as a sort of 'register of memory' (Lacan 1993: 155). In fact, in the *Écrits*, Lacan goes so far as to say that 'what we teach the subject to recognise as his unconscious is his memory' (Lacan 2006: 52). Thus, memory, rather than being a mere storehouse of concepts and unconscious phantasies or reminiscence, bears an intimate relationship to the emotions and to interior experience in general. This perspective influenced a number of writers in late antiquity, both pagan and Christian, and contributed to the treatment of the unconscious we find in that epoch in a way which draws these writers closer to psychoanalysis than is generally recognised.[20] Thus, under the rubric of tradition history, memory and present recalling of the past are linked experientially with self-continuity and therefore with transcendence:

> History is always experienced by us, as it were, from the inside, in so far as we stand in it and become conscious of this unalterable fact of standing in a continually elapsing history. The experience of history normally implies the experience that one cannot detach oneself from this history since it is one's own. The dependence on something which already existed before I was conscious of it and which there is no prospect of escaping, since my being has already been marked by that which preceded, was characterized in Heidegger's analysis of existence as historicity. Gadamer recalls this when he conceives of interpretation as a process by means of which the past continues to exert its influence. He connects interpretation in this way very closely with the past.
>
> (Bubner 1990: 61)

Despite the centuries, ancient texts, however obscure, can speak to us in the present as they may still have something to say to our current experience. Yet this is not only the case for the written word. This hermeneutic principle applies equally to all thought and thus to all speech. Interpretation, that is, draws us into a dialogue with the past or to use Gadamer's phrase, it inserts us into a process of tradition, whether that past is the historical past, our childhood or merely yesterday (Gadamer 1989). Thus, past and present are experienced as continually adjusting themselves to one another. Likewise, the more we realise the continuing influence of the past, the greater our likelihood of understanding, as understanding itself is limited by its historical context (Bubner 1990).

The past is not a static object that can be viewed from afar but rather something (Gadamer 1989) which appears linguistically in our present experience. For this reason the past can never be viewed entirely from the outside, objectively, but is always experienced by us from within. It is, therefore, always in need of re-interpretation, for the meaning of our past does not remain fixed and constant. This is clearly the case in psychotherapy where the past under consideration is the patient's own history from which he cannot be detached. As the past lives on in the present of each one of us, that personal past always belongs to a specific context other than the individual. It is situated, that is, within a specific community.

Conclusion

Hermeneutics asserts the possibility to create a dialogue that generates a common idiom between hostile and apparently irreconcilable cultures. This principle is clearly applicable to the division between biological psychiatry and the various psychoanalytic approaches, of which the therapeutic community is one. In this sense, we can say that the divergence between these two models of understanding is founded on an inadequate conception of truth, something already noted by Gadamer in relation to psychiatry (Gadamer 1996).[21]

Through interpretation, progress towards the always incomplete truth can be made in a dialectic process in psychotherapy, within a community. What emerges transcends those engaged in the dialogue, while revealing something about them. The new perspective that appears allows for re-interpreting the patient's past, from the perspective of his present and has the effect of relocating him in relation to his history and thereby helping him form a new sense of self-continuity. Hermeneutics allows for the possibility of an integrated approach, which brings together phenomen-ological psychoanalysis and biological psychiatry.

Language, which is the foundation of community, as well as the only instrument of psychoanalysis, demands we rise above the literal manifes-tations found in psychosis, which are already an allegorical interpretation and grasp the concealed sense (*hyponoia*) beyond its text (de Lubac 1947; Crouzel 1964, 1999). Interpretation involves, therefore, an uncovering of the truth of the being of the subject. Language, interpretation, truth and being hang together on the notion of meaning and describe the process of psychotherapy. Within a therapeutic community we see this in terms of process and event, in which all participate in the birth of *alētheia* and consequently of being, in the dialogic history of a specific tradition. Tradi-tion inaugurates understanding and finding meaning within the spectrum of self-continuity – something characteristically dislocated in psychosis (Cullberg 2006) – and this brings with it the possibility of transcendence (De Waelhens and Ver Eecke 2001).[22] Thus one of the signs of progress in the psychotherapy for someone afflicted with psychosis is necessarily the flickering sense of an historical identity and a future self-project. This means that interpretations need to move between past and present realities, as well as between the literal and allegorical. The patient is already marked, of course, by that very history he is being helped to unravel, through inter-pretations, which are structurally dialogical. This amounts to a conversation within a tradition (Bubner 1990; Lawn 2006). This has particular relevance in the context of a therapeutic community, with its own history and development, its own 'permanence and temporality in meaning' (Gale and Sanchez, 2005 p.436). As the patient gradually becomes familiar with the routines and stories of community events and individuals often long gone, he takes on a new identity as a community member, and in so doing makes the community's past part of his own present experience and future self-project. This assuming of a community history, as it is reinterpreted in the present experience of the community and of the individual, helps situate the patient within a tradition. It is only by absorbing, in this way, a cultural past, that the present takes on meaning and significance.

Notes

1 Jean Grondin op. cit. p.154, (2003), suggests that Gadamer's view that being is incarnated in language may rely on St Augustine's commentary on Genesis.

2 Turgundhat has argued that this is where the phenomenology of Heidegger and linguistic analysis, represented by thinkers like Wittgenstein, converge. In fact, he demonstrates this reconciliation in reference to Aristotle's *Metaphysics* where what is expressed by *pollachōs legetai* is the basis on which the question about being as being is raised. Cf. Aristotle, *Metaphysics* iv, 1004b15; Tugendhat, *Wahrheit und Methode*, Tübingen 1960 p.53ff.; R. Bubner, *Modern German Philosophy*, Cambridge: Cambridge University Press, 1990, esp. pp. 69–103.

3 Although Lacan in his paper The Instance of the Letter in the Unconscious, *Écrits* op. cit. pp. 412–441 poses the question of whether or not the unconscious represents confirmation, at the level of psychological experience, of Manichaeism it seems unlikely that he was referring to anything other than the dualism found in Manichaean metaphysics in which the opposing good and evil principles are considered completely separate entities (A. Chavannes and P.Pelliot, Un traité manichéen retrouvé en Chine, *Journal Asiatique* 10: 18 (1911) 99–199 and 11: 1 (1913) 177–196). The reference to Manichaeism may, however, be yet another indication of Lacan's indebtedness to St Augustine whom he considered the precursor of psychoanalysis. Augustine, as he grew older, realised that Manichaeism despite its rhetoric about psychological liberation, offered a form of *gnōsis* that aimed to bypass the prolonged intellectual discipline of working through unconscious mental material essential for the achievement of any real psychological growth, inner healing or lasting personal renewal cf. Augustine, *De moribus Ecclesiae catholicae (1), xxv. 47, PL 70*. On the Manichaean background in Augustine see A. Solignac's intoduction to *Oeuvres de Saint Augustin 13 Les Confessions Livres I–VII* 9–266, esp. 118–132 Paris: Institut d'Études Augustiniennes, 1998; W.H.C. Frend, The Gnostic-Manichaean Tradition in Roman North Africa *The Journal of Ecclesiastical History* 4 (1953) pp. 3–25 and P. Brown, The Diffusion of Manichaeism in the Roman Empire *The Journal of Roman Studies* 59: 1/2 (1969), pp. 92–103.

4 Writers like Clement and Origen.

5 The main exponents included John Chrysostom and Theodore of Mopsuestia. Wilkinson not only reviews the history of exegesis in antiquity but also shows considerable familiarity with modern literature on the subject, including Freud. However, his book needs to be read in the light of the, mostly critical, review by Grant. See R.M. Grant, *Vigiliae Christianae* 18 (1964), p. 183.

6 *Allēgoria, anagōgē* and *hyponoia* are the key words used by Origen to describe the allegorical method. On the general patristic background to these terms see G.W.H. Lampe (ed.), *A Patristic Greek Lexicon*, Oxford, Clarendon Press, 1961, 1: 74–5, 101 and 2: 1452.

7 Recently, Elsa Ronningstam described the wide range of meanings and functions of silence by bringing together recent cultural and psychoanalytic thinking on silence. Despite significant omissions it is an interesting study. E. Ronningstam, Silence. Cultural function and psychological transformation in psychoanalysis and psychoanalytic psychotherapy, *International Journal of Psychoanalysis* 2006: 87: 1277–1295.

8 Lacan's distinction between *parole pleine* and *parole vide* is largely dependent on Heidegger's notions of *Rede* and *Gerede*. Evans points out that whereas the former 'articulates the symbolic dimension of language . . . [the latter] articulates the imaginary dimension of language, the speech from the ego to the counterpart' D. Evans, *An Introductory Dictionary of Lacanian Psychoanalysis*,

Routledge, London and New York, 1996, p. 191. Cf the interesting discussion of *Geschwätz* in Heidegger, Walter Benjamin and Paul Celan where it is understood as every day talk cut off from true being, or as empty speech after the fall, speech without Adam's power of naming, in J. Felstiner, *Paul Celan: Poet, Survivor, Jew*, New Haven and London: Yale University Press, 1995, pp. 144–145.

9 These approaches have been usefully summarised by R. Lukas, Managing psychotic patients in a day hospital setting, in *Psychosis (Madness)* (ed.) P. Williams, The Institute of Psycho-Analysis, London, 2001, pp. 65–77. See also A.-L. Silver, B. Koehler and B. Karon, Psychodynamic psychotherapy of schizophrenia. Its history and development, *Models of Madness* (eds) J. Read, L.R. Mosher and R. Bentall, Routledge, London and New York, pp. 209–222.

10 The hermeneutical approach to truth goes more to the heart of the question of knowledge (*scientia*) than these interpretations, many of which assume that psychoanalysis adheres to an empirical model of truth (cf. Grünbaum, 1986) by failing to address the more fundamental question of the possibility of certainty in everything. A more radically hermeneutic position is implicit in the thought of the early Lacan.

11 Lacan devoted eleven chapters of his Seminar VIII to discussion of Plato's Symposium. Cf. J. Lacan Transference 1960–61 *The Seminar of Jacques Lacan Book VIII* (trans. C. Gallagher from unedited MSS).

12 In his presentation of Socrates as a psychoanalyst Lacan echoes the views of Werner Jaeger who considered Plato the father of psychoanalysis. Lacan, however, was to reserve this ultimate epithet for Augustine. W. Jaeger, *Paideia: the Ideals of Greek Culture* (trans.) G. Highet Vol II, 1986, p. 343, New York/Oxford: Oxford University Press.

13 This bears some resemblance, not only to various ideas found in Zen Buddhism, but also to the spiritual goal of descending into a state of 'infinite ignorance' as we find it in a number of monastic writers in late antiquity, notably in Evagrius Ponticus. What is described here as a descent into the unlimited or infinite is, according to Wensinck, synonymous with the unconscious. See R. Graffin, *Les Six Centuries des 'Kephalaia Gnostica' d'Évagre Le Pontique* Patrologia Orientalis XXVIII: 1, 134, 1985; Wensinck, *Mystic Treatises by Isaac of Niniveh*, Amsterdam, 1923 and particularly I. Hausherr, Ignorance infinie, *Orientalia Christiana Periodica* XXXV, 1959, pp. 44–52. Also, H. Dumoulin, *A History of Zen Buddhism* (trans. P. Peachey), London: Faber & Faber, 1963.

14 Hobson, in his discussion of the therapeutic community also refers to psychotherapy as a special kind of conversation, cf. R.F. Hobson, The Messianic community, *Therapeutic Communities: Reflections and progress* pp. 231–244 (eds) R.D. Hinshelwood and N. Manning, London, Boston and Henley: Routledge and Kegan Paul, 1979.

15 In relation to the meaning of *alētheia* in Origen see particularly Crouzel's discussion of the relationship between *alētheia* and *ta mystēria* or *ta mystika* and their opposites *plasma* and *mythos* in the section entitled Ἀλήθεια *et mots de même racine* pp. 31–35. Cf. also the interesting, though partially critical comments by Quispel in G. Quispel (1974) Origen and the Valentinian Gnosis, *Vigiliae Christianae* 28: 29–42, esp. 29–30.

16 This is a perspective which Freud shared with a number of writers in late antiquity (Näf 2004). Although Professor Näf discusses the case of Gregory of Nyssa's *De Hominis Opificio*, where Gregory considers the genesis and validity of dreams, he fails to notice that observations concerning a therapeutic approach to psychological processes in dreams are found in a number of texts by Evagrius Ponticus, notably in his *Capita Cognoscitiva* and in other Christian writers in late

antiquity, including Augustine cf. Évagre le Pontique *Sur les Pensées* (ed.) P. Géhin and C. Guillaumont Source Chrétiennes 438, Les Éditions du Cerf (1998) esp. 249–257. Indeed Näf's mistaken assumption seems to be that Christian authors merely adopted a pagan perspective on dreams, a view which Refoulé in his discussion of the connection between Evagrius' position and that of Freud, shows holds no water. See F. Refoulé Rêves et vie spirituelle d'après Evagre le pontique *La Vie Spirituelle Supplément* 14 (1961), pp. 470–516. Cf. also W.V. Harris, Roman Opinions about the Truthfulness of Dreams *The Journal of Roman Studies* 93 (2003) pp. 18–43; E.R. Dodds, Theurgy and its relationship to Neoplatonism *Journal of Roman Studies* 37 (1947) pp. 55–69 and P. Athanassiadi, Dreams, Theurgy and Freelance Divination: The Testimony of Iamblichus *The Journal of Roman Studies* 83 (1993) pp. 115–130.

17 In view of Lacan's assessment of Augustine as the forerunner of psychoanalysis, it may be worth noting that in relation to the signification of dream images Augustine, like Freud, assumed that these arise from a precise event and bridge the mental divide between consciousness and the unconscious, the split between the two resulting, in Augustine's view, from the fall. Cf. P. Brown, *Augustine*, London: Faber & Faber, 1967; J. Pépin, *Mythe et Allégorie: les origins greque et les contestations judéo-chétienne*, Paris: Éditions Montaigne, 1958 pp. 69–71.

18 This is an example of the convergence between Gadamer's thought and that of Freud.

19 Interstingly, studies of Greek usage show *historia* and *theōria* often used in juxtaposition, with for example Origen referring to something not in its literal interpretation (*historia*) but in its deeper meaning (*theōria*). Cf. H.N. Bate, Some Technical Terms of Greek Exegesis *Journal of Theological Studies* 24: (1922), pp. 59–66.

20 Something that did not go unnoticed by Grün in his discussion of the similarity between Evagrius and Jung, cf. A. Grün, *Der Umgang mit dem Bösen*, Münsterschwarzach: Münsterschwarzacher Kleinschriften, 1980. In an interesting study Bamberger examined the notion of *mnēmē* in Basil of Caesarea (AD 330–79) with particular reference to the Greek text of his so called Long Rules or *Regulae Fusius Tractate* and of the Short Rules or *Regulae Breviter Tractate* (J.E. Bamberger, ΜΝΗΜΗ – ΔΙΑΘΕΣΙΣ: The Psychic Dynamisms in the Ascetical Theology of St. Basil *Orientalia Christiana Periodica* XXXIV: II (1968) pp. 233–251). Here he demonstrates the close connection between the thought of St Basil and that of Freud. On the wider context within Basil's overall scheme cf. J. Gribomont, Les Règles épistolaires de saint Basile: Lettres 173 et 22 *Antonianum* 54 (1979) pp. 255–287.

21 See specifically pp. 125–140 on treatment and dialogue and pp. 163–173 on hermeneutics and psychiatry.

22 Thus for De Waelhens the world of psychosis is one 'without transcendence or mystery [It is] a place where all meaning is spoken, and none is yet to come. It is also, as regards its truth, a world without risk. Likewise, the Other's transcendence is excluded from it, since the imaginary other has no background, no inaccessibility, and no consistency of his own' (op. cit. p. 239).

Bibliography

Andreasen, N.C. (1999). Understanding the causes of schizophrenia. *New England Journal of Medicine* 340(8): 645–647.

Bachmann, S., Resch, F. and Mundt, C. (2003). Psychological treatments for psychosis. *Journal of the American Academy of Psychoanalysis* 31: 155–176.

Bion, W. (1967). *Second Thoughts: Selected papers on psychoanalysis*. London: Maresfield Library.

Birchwood, M. and Spencer, E. (1999). Psychotherapies for schizophrenia, in M. Maj and N. Sartorius (eds) *Schizophrenia*. New York: John Wiley & Sons.

Black, A. (2006). Unpublished lecture notes.

Bubner, R. (1990). *Modern German Philosophy* (trans. E. Matthews). Cambridge: Cambridge University Press.

Crews, F. (1993). The unknown Freud. *New York Review of Books* 40(19): 55–66.

Crouzel, H. (1961). *Origène et la 'Connaissance Mystique'*. Paris: Desclée de Brouwer.

Crouzel, H. (1964). 'La distinction de la "typologie" et de l'allégorie'. *Bulletin de Littérature Ecclésiastique* 65: 161–174.

Crouzel, H. (1999). *Origen* (trans. A. Worrall). Edinburgh: T. & T. Clark.

Cullberg, J. (2006). *Psychoses*. London and New York: Routledge.

de Lubac, H. (1947). 'Typologie' and 'allégorisme'. *Recherches de Science Religieuse* 34: 180–226.

De Waelhens, A and Ver Eecke, W. (2001). *Phenomenology and Lacan on Schizophrenia, after the Decade of the Brain*. Leuven: Leuven University Press.

D'hert, I. (1978). *Wittgenstein's Relevance for Theology*. Bern: Peter Lang.

Fenton, W.S. (2000). Evolving perspectives on individual psychotherapy for schizophrenia. *Schizophrenia Bulletin* 26(1): 47–72.

Frend, W.H.C. (1953). The Gnostic-Manichaean Tradition in Roman North Africa. *The Journal of Ecclesiastical History* 4: 13–25.

Freud, S. (1900). *The Standard Edition of the Complete Psychological Works of Sigmund Freud* (trans. J. Strachey) (Vols. IV–V). London: Hogarth Press.

Fromm-Reichmann, F. (1960). *Principles of Intensive Psychotherapy*. Chicago: University of Chicago Press.

Gadamer, H.-G. (1989). *Truth and Method* (trans. J. Weinsheimer and D. Marshall). New York: Crossroad.

Gadamer, H.-G. (1996). *The Enigma of Health: The art of healing in a scientific age* (trans. J. Gaiger and N. Walker). Stanford, CA: Stanford University Press.

Gale, J. (2007). Xenophon and psychoanalysis: lessons in management. *Organisational and Social Dynamics* 7(1): 1–19.

Gale, J. and Sanchez, B. (2005a). The meaning and function of silence in psychotherapy with particular reference to a therapeutic community treatment programme. *Psychoanalytic Psychotherapy* 19(3): 205–220.

Gale, J. and Sanchez, B. (2005b). Reflections on the treatment of psychosis in therapeutic communities. *Therapeutic Communities* 26(4): 433–447.

Giovacchini, P.L. (1979). *The Treatment of Primitive Mental States*. New York and London: Jason Aronson.

Grondin, J. (1995). *Sources of Hermeneutics*. Albany, NY: SUNY Press.

Grünbaum, A. (1986). Précis of *The Foundations of Psychoanalysis: A Philosophical Critique*. *Behavioural and Brain Sciences* 9: 217–228.

Habermas, J. (1971). *Knowledge and Human Interests* (trans. J. Shapiro). London: Heinemann.

Hartmann, E., Milofsky, E., Vaillant, G., Oldfield, M., Falke, R. and Ducey, C.

(1984). Vulnerability to schizophrenia. *Archives of General Psychiatry* 41(11): 1050–1056.

Heidegger, M. (1990). *Being and Time* (trans. J. Macquarrie and E. Robinson). Oxford: Basil Blackwell.

Jackson, M. (1994). *Unimaginable Storms*. London: Karnac.

Kendler, K.S. and Diehl, S.R. (1993). The genetics of schizophrenia: a current genetic-epidemiological perspective. *Schizophrenia Bulletin* 19(2): 261–285.

Klein, M. (1930). The psychotherapy of the psychoses. *British Journal of Medical Psychology* 10: 242–244.

Klein, M. (1948). *Contributions to Psychoanalysis 1931–1945*. London: Hogarth Press.

Klein, M. (1975). *Envy and Gratitude*. New York: Free Press.

Kisiel, T. (1985). The happening of tradition: the hermeneutics of Gadamer and Heidegger, in R. Hollinger (ed.) *Hermeneutics and Praxis*. New York: Notre Dame.

Lacan, J. (1977). *The Four Fundamental Concepts of Psycho-analysis*, (ed.) J.-A. Miller. London: Vintage.

Lacan, J. (1984). *Speech and Language in Psychoanalysis* (trans. A. Wilden). Baltimore and London: Johns Hopkins University Press.

Lacan, J. (1988). *The Seminar of Jacques Lacan. Book I, Freud's Papers on Technique 1953–1954* (trans. J. Forrester). Cambridge: Cambridge University Press.

Lacan, J. (1993). *The Psychoses. The Seminar of Jacques Lacan Book III 1955–1956* (trans. R. Grigg). London: Routledge.

Lacan, J. (2006). *Écrits*. New York, London: W.W. Norton.

Lammi, W. (1991). Hans-Georg Gadamer's 'correction' of Heidegger. *Journal of the History of Ideas* 52(3): 487–507.

Lawn, C. (2006). *Gadamer. A guide for the perplexed*. New York and London: Continuum.

Lear, J. (1990). *Love and its Place in Nature. A philosophical interpretation of Freudian psychoanalysis*. New York: Farrar, Straus & Giroux.

Lukas, R. (1992). The psychotic personality: a psychoanalytical theory and its application in clinical practices. *Psychoanalytic Psychotherapy* 6(1): 3–17.

Lukas, R. (1993). The psychotic wavelength. *Psychoanalytic Psychotherapy* 7: 15–23.

Mortensen, P.B., Pedersen, C.B., Westergaard, T., Wohlfahrt, J., Ewald, H., Mors, O. et al. (1999). Effects of family history and place and season of birth on the risk of schizophrenia. *New England Journal of Medicine* 340(8): 603–608.

Mosher, L.R., Gosden, R. and Beder, S. (2004). Drug companies and schizophrenia: unbridled capitalism meets madness, in J. Read, L.R. Mosher and R.P. Bentall (eds) *Models of Madness*. London and New York: Routledge.

Näf, B. (2004). *Traum und Traumbedeutung im Altertum*. Darmstadt: Wissenschaftliche Buchgesellschaft.

Nagel, T. (1994). Freud's permanent revolution. *New York Review of Books* 41(9): 34–38.

O'Shaughnessy, E. (1992). Psychosis: not thinking in a bizarre world, in R. Anderson (ed.) *Clinical Lectures on Klein and Bion*. London: Routledge.

Paget, S. (2000). Delusions as discourse in a therapeutic community. *Therapeutic Communities* 21(4): 253–259.

Pépin, J. (1957). À propos de l'histoire de l'exégèse allégorique: l'absurdité, signe de l'allégorie. *Studia Patristica* 63: 397–400.

Pontet, M. (1944). *L'exégèse de S. Augustin prédicateur*. Paris: Aubier.

Ricoeur, P. (1970). *Freud and Philosophy*. New Haven and London: Yale University Press.

Rosenfeld, H. (1966). *Psychotic States: A psycho-analytical approach*. New York: International Universities Press.

Rosenfeld, H. (1971). A clinical approach to the psychoanalytic theory of the life and death instincts: an investigation into the aggressive aspects of narcissism. *Psychoanalytic Psychotherapy* 52: 169–178.

Ross, C.A. (2006). Dissociation and psychosis. The need for integration of theory and practice, in J.O. Johannessen, B.V. Martindale and J. Cullberg (eds) *Evolving Psychosis*. London and New York: Routledge.

Roudinesco, E. (1997). *Jacques Lacan* (trans. B. Bray). New York: Columbia University Press.

Segal, H. (1957). Notes on symbol formation. *International Journal of Psycho-Analysis* 38: 391–397.

Sohn, L. (1985). Narcissistic organisation, projective identifications and the formation of the identificate. *International Journal of Psycho-Analysis* 66. 201–214.

Thornicroft, G. and Susser, E. (2000). Evidence-based psychotherapeutic interventions in the community care of schizophrenia. *British Journal of Psychiatry* 178: 2–4.

Tienari, P. (1992). Interaction between genetic vulnerability and rearing environment, in A. Werbart and J. Cullberg (eds) *Psychotherapy of Schizophrenia: Facilitating and obstructive factors*. Oslo: Scandinavian University Press.

Wilkinson, J. (1963). *Interpretation and Community*. London: Macmillan.

Yorke, C. (1991). Freud's 'on narcissism': a teaching text, in J. Sandler (ed.) *Freud's 'On narcissism: an introduction'*. Yale: Yale University Press.

Chapter 5

Applying Bion's concept of psychotic personality to staff and patients

Raman Kapur

Introduction

> This is a complex study, but the main findings are quite simple. It appears that the most disabled patients were still being looked after in hospital in the worst conditions by the most institutionalised staff. Organisation and management practices were much more restrictive in hospital, compared with community settings and staff who had worked in hospital for several years were likely to show the highest levels of negative interactions with residents.
>
> (Shepherd et al. 1996: 454)

The intra-psychic and interpersonal characteristics of staff members are central to how the patient is looked after in residential and other settings. Unfortunately, over and above the routine and necessary training in the fundamental practices of good psychiatric care, most staff have little exposure to the effects of how they feel and think influences the well being of the patient. Even more so, organisational managers of mental health settings have little or no exposure to such knowledge and training and often leadership styles are adopted without taking cognisance of the effects on staff and, inevitably, patients. This chapter will apply a Kleinian and post-Kleinian psychoanalytic framework to understanding the management and organisation of mental health services and suggest that particular leadership styles could enhance the quality of the work environment and thus increase the possibility of staff having more positive interactions with patients.

Theoretical overview

> Requirements of only health for staff and only invalidation for patients are, however, neither socially inevitable nor truly practiceable, for human states are never absolute. Stable healthy people contain elements of instability and ill-health and unhealthy unstable people contain elements of health and stability. Indeed, there is something

strainfully collusive about those psychiatric hospitals that are managed so that one party comes to regard the other as being in an absolute state, either of health or ill health, and they offer us paradigmatic questions for all similar large groups.

(Main 1975: 52)

Main goes on to report a study with his colleague, Malcolm Pines, which highlighted how many staff in mental health settings reported traumatised childhoods with grossly inadequate nurturing, who had developed dysfunctional patterns of dealing with the needy or untended parts of themselves by disowning and projecting these parts into their patients. Through vicarious caretaking, they were able to have an experience of looking after their own needs through others, which, of course, becomes a maladaptive process potentially lending to burnout. It is this human frailty of staff as human beings that I think is best conceptualised both with Melanie Klein's concepts of paranoid-schizoid and depressive position functioning (Segal 1986a) and Bion's concept of psychotic and non-psychotic personalities. It is the latter that I shall particularly draw on while making reference to the former Kleinian theory.

Psychotic and non-psychotic personalities

The fundamental premise of this theoretical framework is that we all contain within our minds sane (non-psychotic) and mad (psychotic) parts to our personality. This original work was undertaken by Bion (1967) in his seminal paper on this issue which he describes as displaying four essential features:

> A preponderance of destructive impulses so great that even the impulse to love is suffused by them and turned to sadism; a hatred of reality, internal and external, which is extended to all that makes for awareness of it; a dread of imminent annihilation and, finally, a premature and precipitate formation of object relations, foremost amongst which is the transference, whose thinness is in marked contrast with the tenacity with which it is maintained.

(Bion 1967: 44)

Within a setting characterised by paranoid-schizoid functioning (Segal 1986b) where massive negative projections and projective identifications are present (Kapur 1991) unwitting members of staff are exposed to significant regressive processes. Here, well meaning staff who want to relate in a non-psychotic and compassionate way are often forced to act out roles (Sandler 1976) where they become persecuting and/or depriving. In many ways, these settings bring out the worst of staff where their own psychotic personalities are activated.

In identifying the psychotic personality of both staff and patients as active ingredients in creating an anti-therapeutic atmosphere, there then emerges the question as to how to maximise non-psychotic functioning? Within the traditional therapeutic community model this is carried out through the usual activities of communalism, flattening of hierarchies and democratisation with each style of therapeutic community having its own emphasis on reality confrontation. Through structured activities of individual and group work the atmosphere is humanised as much as is possible (Kelly et al. 2004). However, the suggestion within this chapter is that this may not be enough to contain the psychotic personality of the environment as manifested through the thoughts, feelings and behaviour of staff. Elsewhere (Kapur 2008) I have referred to this as managing or containing love and hate in organisations.

Containment of love and hate

One of Bion's most helpful concepts is that of therapeutic containment (Bion 1959) which describes the transformational capacity of the helper/therapist to receive the negative projections from the patient and return these in a digestible and non-persecutory way, similar to a nurturing mother containing the infantile neediness/demands of her baby. Similarly, staff have to contain the psychotic personalities of their patients with the organisational mother having to contain the psychotic personalities of both staff and patients. Consequently, the transformational capacity of the organisational parent has to be significant to ensure there is a minimum of acting out into day-to-day human relations. Essentially, this involves trying to create an atmosphere characterised by non-psychotic processes, the opposite of psychotic processes. These are:

- a preponderance of constructive impulses
- an acceptance of reality, internal and external
- fundamental trust in human relations
- stable authority figures.

Unfortunately, as described in this paper, this rarely occurs within organisations, particularly mental health settings. Often the organisational parent is asked to contain extreme hatred manifested through sibling and oedipal rivalry. This is usually managed by the traditional model of resolving disputes and can lead to numerous grievances and disciplinary hearings – without addressing the deeper hidden issues of where the conflict may belong i.e. either party acting out their psychotic personality.

Alternatively, extreme love is acted through idealisation and sexualisation of relationships which can lead to the perpetuation of destructive processes which inevitably impinge on patient care.

The essence of this chapter is to highlight the pressures on the organisational parent/leader to contain such psychotic anxieties and thus maximise the possibility of a positive atmosphere for patients. This is no easy task, as leadership brings with it many demands. So aptly summarised by Kernberg (2003):

> In earlier work, I proposed that, ideally, functional leadership combines the following characteristics
> 1. High intelligence, enabling the leader to apply long-range strategic thinking to diagnosing, formulating, communicating and implementing the requirements of the task within its constraints.
> 2. sufficient emotional maturity and depth to be able to assess the personality of others in selecting subordinate leaders and delegating appropriate authority to them.
> 3. a solid and deep moral integrity that protects the leaders from the unavoidable temptations intimately linked to the exercise of power and from the corrupting pressures of the leader's entourage.
> 4. sufficiently strong narcissistic tendencies to be able to maintain self-esteem in the face of the unavoidable criticism and attacks of the followers and to avoid depending upon the followers for fulfilment of excessive narcissistic needs.
> 5. sufficient paranoid features – in contrast to naiveté – to diagnose early the unavoidable ambivalent and hostile undercurrents in the organisation that express the resentful, rebellious and envious aspects of the aggression directed toward leadership.
>
> (Kernberg 2003: 683–689)

Organisational example

I will now describe an organisational experience which illustrates how I applied this theoretical understanding to resolve the eruption of the psychotic personality within the organisation of which I am chief executive.

Several years ago we opened a personality disorder residential project, the first of its kind in Northern Ireland, to provide a service for this particular patient population that often falls through the net of traditional mental health services. There was an acknowledged clinical need identified by professionals on the ground, but, in retrospect, the agency did not receive solid contractual agreements from the principal stakeholders to receive the funding streams. Nevertheless, I was persuaded that significant need and funding was in place for the project to be successful. Within the voluntary sector, our services operate as the agency functioning as a limited company and thus, we have to operate within the financial reality of breakeven or surplus budgets, otherwise jobs and the survival of the agency are at risk. It was within this context that the project was opened.

The early months of the project were fraught with the inevitable teething problems of new staff settling in to the culture of a therapeutic community and a shortage of referrals until existing services became aware of our regional facility. However, by the end of the first year and into the second, the unit was hitting an occupancy level of 50% whereas the breakeven was 80%. Slowly, the agency's reserves were being drained and other services (60 residential therapeutic community beds for severely mentally ill patients) were subsidising the project and, inevitably, putting their own funding at risk. After 2 years with a deficit of £100k I decided to close the unit, with a loss of six posts, inevitable damage to the reputation of the agency, discharge of three of the five patients into other statutory/prison facilities and the possession of a vacant new building with no services. Also within 1 year of the closing, one former patient took her own life. This is my psychoanalytic interpretation of events, particularly using Bion's concepts of psychotic personality and therapeutic containment.

The birth of a personality disordered 'baby' into mother Threshold was too much for the agency. Whatever the theoretical and clinical formulation of personality disorder, the existence of an aggressive psychotic personality is evident. Furthermore, if we take seriously Main and Pines' observation (Main 1975) then staff who have similar personality disorder features will be drawn to this service. Thus, the splitting off and disowning of aggressive impulses is massive. Furthermore, if we accept that this type of service activates the personality disorder in all of us, the agency then had all the key players inside and outside the agency projecting their most primitive impulses in the services, and inevitably, into me as the leader. My counter-transference via the relentless projective identifications was:

> I am containing a dying baby, if this project fails, someone, somewhere may die. If I don't close the project, the mother agency will potentially die as it cannot sustain the neediness of this project. No-one was helping to contain me – as with all personality disorder dynamics, there was a wish to see me fail and 'hit me when I'm down'. Closing the project, to protect the agency from closing down, will bring accusations of ruthlessness, murder and cruelty. People will use this opportunity to act out their oedipal and sibling rivalries to also murder me.

Inevitably, this experience stirred up my own psychotic personality where I had a choice either to act out my own aggressive impulses or try to contain, in a non-psychotic way, the burden of such pressures. Sinason (1993) describes this in respect of psychic pain as:

> Bion has described how the difficulty of dealing with psychic pain can
> give rise to the development of two parts of the personality, each with a
> very different way of coping. The psychotic part, intolerant of frustra-
> tion, gets rid of its perceptions and the part of the mind that registers
> them. The non-psychotic part of the personality which retains a capa-
> city for tolerating psychic pain is able to experience jealousy or envy or
> disappointment without denying the experience and without attempting
> to change his attitude to the object in order to avoid these experiences.
>
> (Sinason 1993: 209)

The latter proved the most difficult to do. Containment or ℓ – functioning of B – elements in Bionian terminology (Lopez-Corvo 2003) is an
extremely difficult task within the parameters of a consulting room when
you have a patient's mind in your hands. Alpha (α) processing refers to the
thinking and analysing that has to take place to convert primitive emotions,
or beta (β) elements into more understandable thoughts that can be
assimilated to promote knowledge and growth. Here it is crucial for the
organisational leader to maximise the alpha processing by applying thought
and meaning to events that will promote understanding and thus lessen the
possibility of primitive emotions being acted out.

However, as an organisational leader you do not have the luxury of a
private consulting room with a minimum of external impingements. The
financial, legal and organisational responsibility means that all decisions
have a consequence on services and patient care.

Thus the psychotic pressures were enormous, which included the wishes to
retaliate or collapse in a psychic heap. This of course, represents the internal
psychic reality of the patient and staff who have personality disorders. Their
own psychotic personality lives between the extremes of despair and manic
excitement. Alternative psychotic responses to the situation would have
been to deny the experience and respond in one of two ways:

- Closing the unit immediately without working through the experience
  of loss with a message of: 'Tough cookie, you had it, your chance is
  over, end of story *and* I am going to make staff pay dearly for setting
  me up with a project that had failed so badly.'
- Retreat into my own despair, paranoid functioning and 'siege
  mentality' and give up on the idea that therapeutic communities are
  of use to anyone and take sole blame for the 'dead baby'.

Several years on I am glad to say that the unit has reopened with secure
funding and provides a vital service for severely mentally ill people discharged from the local psychiatric unit. The agency is now a thriving baby
with strong referral and income flows and a sound cash base. We are an

established and significant provider of mental health/therapeutic services in Northern Ireland. So what where the key elements of my containment?

As I had learned in my clinical training as a psychoanalytic psycho-therapist I had to:

- Receive and not deny the disturbing projections and projective identi-fications and use my countertransference responses as a way of under-standing the state of mind of the 'Other'.
- Rely on, and remember, my own personal therapy/analysis in providing me with an experience of therapeutic containment; I knew how to ℓ process as I had an experience of this being done with me.
- Contain my massive impulses to go mad, i.e. retaliate and persecute.

Much of this work was done privately, in my own introspections. As stated in my 2008 paper, the containment of retaliatory impulses was undertaken by keeping the patient in mind. In other words, how would such an aggressive response affect the services provided by the agency? Inevit-ably, the answer was that any such response would lead to a deterioration of services rather than an improvement. I had to forfeit my own personal feelings of revenge and felt injustice for the greater good of the agency, which in the long term, of course, would lead to a positive effect on the agency and for me. A successful agency is a greater source of healthy narcissism than the feelings of narcissism associated with destructiveness. In processing all of these experiences I tried to follow the non-psychotic correlates of Bion's psychotic personality listed earlier. This was an onerous task, but one that has proved successful. Also, I realised that leadership of an organisation is a full-time psychic job and one that cannot be underestimated in terms of the non-psychotic experiences a leader requires to keep him/her from going mad.

Training and support processes

Containing the psychotic personality of an organisation also requires the establishment of a firm boundaried and structured training and support system. Not unlike the analytic frame, it is a set of parameters that brings order to the psychic chaos of organisational life that can help maximise non-psychotic processes. In particular, the traditional psychoanalytic setting emphasises the importance of:

- The analyst/therapist has a protected space to think about what the patient has said; these free associations are analysed with the patient on the couch, so maximising the opportunity for the patient to say what s/he really feels and thinks and for this to be thought about with a minimum of distraction.

- Order and regularity in the frequency of the sessions with good notice given of breaks.
- The analyst/therapist through their knowledge and training being maximally preoccupied with the state of mind of the patient.

I shall now describe three systems that have been purposely set up to apply this analytic frame to the day-to-day running of our agency.

Comprehensive in-service training programme

It is crucial that staff are equipped with the knowledge base and expertise to deal with the most severely mentally ill patients within the psychiatric system. It is often a paradox of the social care services, of which voluntary organisations operate, that the least trained staff are given the task of dealing with the most difficult and disturbed states of mind. So as equipping staff with the relevant knowledge and expertise, the agency operates a training system based on Maslow's (1954) hierarchy, ensuring that the basic and important needs of patients are met; from food hygiene and health and safety training and employment legislation to providing a psychoanalytic/ psychodynamic knowledge base from which to understand severely ill patients. Often staff will overvalue the 'top' of Maslow's hierarchy so forgetting about the basic needs of patients. Indeed, this would contradict much of the research in psychiatric rehabilitation which values these basic components of day-to-day living:

> The differences between hospital and community samples are very consistent and probably do reflect genuine differences in satisfaction (and quality of care). What gives rise to these differences appears to be apparently small items – access to the kitchen in the evenings, choice over mealtimes, locks on the bathroom door, one's own television, etc. These relatively small differences seem to have a large impact on residents' personal judgements regarding their quality of life.
>
> (Shepherd and Murray 2001: 316)

Alongside this in-service training, there exists the more traditional opportunities for professional development via our 'NVQ to PhD' route. This gives staff at all levels the opportunity to develop their careers consistent with their own professional roles and the aims and objectives of the agency as detailed in our corporate plan.

Through linking in with established centres for psychotherapy training in the UK (Tavistock Centre and Association for Therapeutic Communities) and with our partnership with colleagues from the USA (American Group Psychotherapy Association) we are able to ensure that staff are equipped with a knowledge base which has both depth and breadth to maximising the possibility of them relating to patients non-psychotically.

Staff dynamics

Containing the psychotic, disturbed and difficult object relations of staff and patients is helped by the regular, once-weekly opportunities that all staff have to explore their relationships with each other. All senior managers, including myself, are part of this process with a group that operates on a monthly basis. The aims of such groups are to:

- Provide a regular space where an outside consultant, trained in group dynamics, can comment on and understand the relations within the group.
- Provide an opportunity for staff to resolve differences, misunderstandings that correct (or confirm!) negative phantasies of those in authority.
- Offer an open channel of communication through the line management hierarchy so that staff have an opportunity to relate more positively to their supervisor/manager and lessen the chance of persecutory/ psychotic anxieties.

The group also acts as a setting for staff to share their day-to-day pressures of managing difficult and disturbed behaviour from severely ill patients. Often, allowing staff to 'feel retaliatory' towards patients can defuse a negative countertransference and so increase the possibility of non-psychotic functioning. Also, within any management structure there are ambivalent feelings about authority. If we take seriously the observation cited earlier by Main and Pines (1975), then staff will often bring to this work their own negative experiences of authority figures, thus increasing the possibility of managers being seen as persecuting or depriving objects via a distorted and negative transference.

Ideally, managers and I, as CEO, should be experienced as a benevolent authority figure with firm boundaries and as such, the existence of such groups gives staff a chance to work more effectively and closer with their leaders. Alderfer and Klein (1985) have commented on this in the context of A.K. Rice Group Relations Conferences:

> In general, the further away the group, the more negatively it was viewed: the more unlike management, the harsher the stereotype. The good groups were those who looked like them, were familiar and might even be considered part of a comfortable extended family, with shared values. These groups were also clearly defined in an equal or lower position in the authority structure and related with a greater sense of mutuality.
>
> (Alderfer and Klein 1985: 210)

Structured line management and clinical consultation

One of the major benefits of the analytic frame is the importance given to consistency, reliability, starting and finishing on time with the focus of the analytic interchange being the recipient of the work, i.e. the patient. Within the agency there is a clear order given to regularity of line management supervision of day-to-day organisational issues and alongside this, regular clinical consultations with qualified adult and child psychotherapists (for our children's services) Both are on a once-weekly basis. This maximises non-psychotic functioning with the organisation by letting staff know that the organisation takes seriously the importance of systematic support for the delivering of the primary task of the organisation. Furthermore, this establishes good role modelling for staff in how those in authority conduct their day-to-day professional work, so increasing the possibility of intro-jecting good experiences from the agency and thus putting staff in a better state of mind for their patients.

Conclusion

The spirit of the therapeutic community movement originates in the idea of creating an alternative to the asylum model of care and thus humanise psychiatric environments for patients with mental illness. This chapter suggests that the management of day-to-day relationships has a significant impact on the care patients receive. While clinical knowledge and expertise can improve patient care, the style and quality of how authority is discharged has a similar effect on the quality of care.

This chapter proposes a theoretical model that can help leaders of mental health settings think differently about their management style and hopefully produce better outcomes for their patients.

Bibliography

Alderfer, C.P. and Klein, E.B. (1985). Affect, leadership and organisational boundaries. *Group Relations* 2: 197–211.

Bion, W.R. (1959). Attacks on Linking. *International Journal of Psychoanalysis* 40: 308–315.

Bion, W.R. (1967). *Second Thoughts*. London: Karnac.

Kapur, R. (1991). Projective processes in psychiatric hospital settings. *Melanie Klein and Object Relations* 9(1): 16–25.

Kapur, R. (2008). Managing Love and Hate in Organisations. *Submission to Group Analysis* 2008.

Kelly, S., Hill, J., Boardman, H. and Overton, I. (2004). Therapeutic communities, in P. Campling, S. Davies and G. Farquarson (eds) *From Toxic Institutions to Therapeutic Environments: Residential settings in mental health services*. London: Gaskell.

Kernberg, O. (2003). Sanctioned social violence: a psychoanalytic view, part II. *International Journal of Psychoanalysis* 84(3): 683–689.

Lopez-Corvo, R. (2003). *The Dictionary of the Work of W.R. Bion*. London: Karnac.

Main, T. (1975). Some psychodynamics of large groups. *Group Relations* 2: 49–69.

Maslow, A. (1954). *Motivation and Personality*. New York: Harper & Row.

Pines, M. (1975) Personal communication cited in T. Main, Some psychodynamics of large groups. *Group Relations* 2: 52.

Sandler, J. (1976). Countertransference and role responsiveness. *International Review of Psychoanalysis* 3: 43–47.

Segal, H. (1986a). *Introduction to the Work of Melanie Klein*. London: Hogarth Press.

Segal, H. (1986b). *The Work of Hanna Segal: A Kleinian Approach to Clinical Practice*. London: Free Association and Maresfield Library.

Shepherd, G. and Murray, A. (2001). Residential care, in G. Thornicroft and G. Szmuckler (eds) *Textbook of Community Psychiatry*. Oxford: Oxford University Press.

Shepherd, G., Muijen, M., Dean, R. and Cooney, M. (1996). Residential care in hospital and in the community – quality of care and quality of life. *British Journal of Psychiatry* 168: 448–456.

Sinason, M. (1993). Who is the mad voice inside? *Psychoanalytic Psychotherapy* 7(3): 207–221.

Chapter 6

When philosophy meets practice: setting up a Philadelphia Association community household

Christina Moutsou

Introduction

This chapter is concerned with the philosophy behind the Philadelphia Association (PA) therapeutic community households with regard to the kind of intervention they offer to people experiencing emotional suffering. It attempts to reflect on the scope of therapeutic[1] intervention for people in acute mental distress. In order to do so, it focuses on the setting up of a therapeutic community household in 2003. It examines the place of the new house in relation to the history of the PA therapeutic community households and in relation to the current predominant political and sociocultural climate around mental health.

The PA community households have existed for the last 40 years and have provided a home for a number of people suffering from acute mental distress. The so-called PA houses have had a turbulent history. Many have had to survive on meagre resources and have often had to close down at short notice and were seen as short-life housing. However, in more recent years the PA houses became more comfortable and stable and the invitation for residents to feel at home was literally put into practice. They have operated in a more organised way providing residents with a number of house meetings every week and requiring them to be in twice weekly individual psychotherapy outside the house.

Although the PA continued to work to a large extent with people having experienced psychotic breakdowns, florid psychosis could sometimes not be contained in the houses. This was due to the lack of live-in staff and structured day activities which characterises many other therapeutic community settings. Unlike settings where mental suffering is dealt with by professionals, the philosophy of the PA houses is tied in with the idea that mental suffering is best dealt with by living in an ordinary setting with people who have an understanding of it through their own personal experience (Cooper 1989). Therefore, the limits of what will be tolerated in the house at any particular time are up for negotiation (Barnes and Berke 2002).

One of the main reasons that florid psychosis cannot always be accommodated in the PA houses, however, is to do with a shift in the political climate. The anti-psychiatry movement as inspired by R.D. Laing and others (Laing 1960; Laing and Esterson 1964) was part of the revolutionary movement in the 1960s. There was then a climate among intellectual circles ripe for the critique and deconstruction of the predominant psychiatric system along with the deconstruction of other mainstream sociopolitical structures (Goffman 1961). Some of these criticisms were partly taken on board and have since been reflected in the flourishing of the various therapeutic community settings within and outside hospitals (Ingleby 1981). Recent mental health regulation (Mental Health Act 1983) meant that when somebody's mental suffering seems to put into question their safety or that of others, they are strongly encouraged to spend some time in a hospital setting, ideally with an understanding of therapeutic community work (Janssen 1994).

The two long-term PA houses developed throughout the 1980s and 1990s in the post-1960s' political climate in relation to mental health, where various other therapeutic community settings were being established. More recently though, the mental health political climate has once again shifted in favour of short-term interventions and a goal-oriented, evidence-based practice. The setting up of a new PA community fell within this latter change of orientation in the philosophy around mental health. Within this context, it was an opportunity to rethink what the PA philosophy behind the therapeutic community households was and whether the original ideas were still valid or whether they had to be reviewed. Moreover, the difficulty of setting up such a community in a political climate opposed to this kind of project put into question whether the PA therapeutic households were still viable in the present culture.

The setting up of a new community has brought up questions such as: who are the people who would benefit most from living in a PA household? What are the implications and the risks of asking people often experiencing acute mental distress to live together in a meaningful way, without live-in staff? What are the limits of the PA invitation for residents to make themselves at home and what do these limits mean in terms of people feeling free to act out their distress? Is it possible for such a household to survive in a culture that seeks to fix mental distress through medication or quick therapies? How much space is there for the concept of a community in the present political climate of regulation? What is it that the PA houses can offer that is unique and of value?

The new PA community has so far survived and expanded against all odds. The residents who still live there and who were involved with its beginnings are very aware of the house's difficult history and its implications for the kind of support they received. Setting up a new community has proved a creative experience in terms of having to rethink the PA philosophy and practice regarding the place of its community households in the wider world. This chapter aims to identify the parameters of the debate about community living and the PA's contribution to it in the present culture.

The recent history of the houses within the PA

Running community households was one of the central aims of the Philadelphia Association's foundation. The PA was founded by R.D. Laing and others as a charity aiming to relieve mental distress primarily through the running of its community households. The first such community Laing opened was Kingsley Hall (Barnes and Berke 2002). Later on, the PA also became a philosophy and psychotherapy training organisation as well as a forum for philosophical and political debate around the notion of mental illness. However, the charity status of the organisation is still nowadays primarily linked with its work around the relief of mental suffering through community living.

In the 1980s, following Laing's distancing from the organisation and his subsequent sudden death, much activity around acquiring and opening new community households had quietened down. Equally, the predominant culture in the PA houses has changed dramatically over the recent years. The atmosphere has shifted from the houses being asylum places for people experiencing breakdowns or wanting to regress, to the atmosphere of longer stay community households that are based on the family household, 'home' model. Such a shift was not organised and planned but rather a natural progression in the history of the PA houses.

Since 1983 the PA settled down to running only two communities. These PA houses had been open for over the last 20 years and were to a large extent run by the same therapists who had come to identify and be identified with the houses. One of these houses belonged to the PA, while the other belonged to a housing association.

The most recent acquisition of the PA was its house in Islington, which was bought through fundraising and was the third PA house to open, this occurring in January 1996. The house became a symbol of the new PA and therefore, a divisive factor within the organisation. It soon became clear, that the organisation had evolved in a way that had made the running of a new community household rather uncomfortable and possibly a conflict-ridden issue for members.

The PA was now much more engaged with running a training in psychotherapy. The running of the houses as family households meant that fewer PA members were involved in the work of the houses and were interested in the link between the relief of mental suffering and community living. As a result of the new position of the organisation and of a number of its members, the new PA house never quite flourished in the way that the other two had.

It was centrally involved in and badly affected by the split of some members from the organisation in 1997. Once again, the split focused on the kind of therapeutic work that the PA was happy to endorse and what part psychoanalytic theory as well as the regulation of psychotherapy by an outside body could have in the PA's public profile. The PA members who were running the house at the time, seemed to operate increasingly separately from the rest of the organisation, excluding other members from a potential conversation about how the PA houses should be run and how they were part of the PA's philosophy and public profile. They eventually left to form with others another organisation more focused on the practice of psychoanalysis from a critical perspective.

The running of the house proved difficult after the split. As the original therapists opening the house had left the organisation, it was run by a new team of three therapists for a number of years. However, in 2002 one of the therapists resigned and some time after that, the other two resigned together as the low numbers of residents in the house meant that the external funding was being withdrawn. The two remaining residents had to be rehoused.

An opportunity presented itself to reopen this house under Supporting People funding in 2003. This coincided with a time when the way that the houses had been run separately from the organisation was being challenged. An attempt was made to re-integrate community living into the organisation by having debates around the philosophy underpinning the work of the houses and involving psychotherapy students in their running. My colleague, as a more established member of the PA, and I as a new, recently qualified member, reopened this community in March 2003. It began its new life with only two female residents, a very fragile initial setup, but the only option we had at the time other than deciding to close it down. It was a relief therefore, that they were soon joined by a third, male, resident.

At this point, partly because of circumstances, but also as a model that made sense, all three PA houses were each run by two therapists, one female and one male. Such a setup tied in with the idea of the parental couple as opposed to a community inspired by a charismatic leader.

The beginnings of the new PA community household were far from smooth as it was to be expected. Soon after it reopened the house lost its Supporting People funding primarily because it provided therapeutic support, even though it received a very positive feedback from the so-called service users. The viability of the project came to be questioned and there was considerable force within the organisation for closing it down, soon after it reopened. It was an unfortunate outcome of its difficult history that it came to be labelled as the bad or the weak PA house.

What came as a surprise during this turbulent time was that a second PA house, which was very well established and had full occupancy for most of its recent history also lost its Supporting People funding. As the building did not belong to the PA, there was no other option than to close it down.

The question was therefore raised of whether it was inevitable that all PA houses would have to close down, and the PA would have to reorient itself in terms of its charitable aims or whether the two remaining houses owned by the PA would have to survive through independent means.[2] This is still an open debate within the organisation. It ties in with less public funding and fewer resources being available for independent community projects. It seems that at the moment, the public authorities' 'goal-oriented approach' has led to the dismissal of difference and multiplicity of resources that independent charity work has provided for the public for many years.

Having to come up against funding difficulties and the very painful closing down of one PA household that had provided services to the community for a long time, was also an opportunity to re-evaluate what the PA community households can offer and to reappreciate the uniqueness of the service provided. It is these issues that have to be constantly revisited and be thought about in the current work of running the PA's newest community household.

Who would benefit from living in a PA community household?

The question of who would be most likely to be helped by living in a PA community household is tied up with the PA's philosophy and what the organisation stands for. The PA has traditionally questioned the idea of mental suffering as a form of illness during which the patient needs to be treated by experts who know what is wrong with him/her. This questioning is enhanced by some rigorous understanding of phenomenology and some continental philosophy (Gordon and Mayo 2004) which deconstructs the place of knowledge and scientific expertise in our understanding of the human condition (Heaton 2000: 34–42; Merleau-Ponty 1962).

The possibility of somebody benefiting from living in a PA house is not so much dependent on the severity of somebody's mental health history and on the diagnoses they have been given, but on the nature of what the person sees as the way forward. If somebody comes to a PA house wanting to be treated for their illness rather than to be given space to unravel their history and make sense of it on their own terms, then a PA house is not likely to be the best place for them. In a phenomenological sense, what a PA house offers is the possibility of lived time and experience, of 'coming into being' with others (Dasein) as opposed to a mechanical existence in terms of an imposed outside structure on one's time (Heidegger 1985: 135–223). What is also on offer in the house is the possibility to connect with one's history and to be able to see how it contributes to one's present situation as well as to the kind of relationships the person forms with others. As Gadamer argues, such an understanding is not about one's objective knowledge of the past, but about the embodiment of the past in the present moment (Gadamer 1975).

In practice, however, the understanding of what the PA houses stand for and what they can offer can be confusing for all concerned. This was probably one of the most crucial things that the reopening of a new PA community household has taught me. The fact that somebody's diagnosis and history of hospitalisation are not the deciding factor for whether they would make a good candidate does not mean that anybody can benefit from living in such a house. There are certainly some factors in somebody's history that are strong indications for their unsuitability such as a history of violence and current or recent alcohol or drug addiction. Such factors of exclusion are not based on the PA's therapists' expertise, but rather on common sense. As mentioned earlier, the PA houses operate with a minimum of imposed structure on the residents' week. In the case of the newest house, residents are required to attend three house meetings a week of 1½ hours each and twice-weekly individual psychotherapy. People who struggle with addictions or who have difficulty respecting others' boundaries might feel they have very little with which to get by in such an environment.

The real difficulty of assessing whether somebody will make good use of a PA house, however, is deciding on the more subtle ways in which living with others in a relatively unstructured environment might not help somebody thrive. When people are distressed, they often tend to either withdraw and minimise interaction with others or demand to have somebody else with them all the time, as being on their own can feel agonising. In fact, it is either of these factors that most people we interview describe as their most difficult behaviour. As mentioned earlier, one of the major cultural shifts in the PA houses' history has been the shift from relatively open communities that were often the forum of meetings of the organisation and inherently connected with the goings-on within it, to community households similar to a family home. The implications of such a shift for the everyday living in the community is that there is less scope for people having company most of the time if they need it or for withdrawing without endangering themselves while living in a PA household.

In this sense, the function of the PA households nowadays is based even more than in the past on the ability of the residents to exercise their own judgement over their situation. Residents need to constantly assess whether living with others in an ordinary way, where they have the opportunity to both address things and get space, but where neither of these comes as an immediate response to their distress when it is acute, is something that they can bear. The therapists' role in the process of considering a candidate for the houses is to assess whether connecting with one's history through examining their present relationship with others is something that the candidate is interested in doing at this particular moment in their life. For the therapists to assume that a potential resident is likely to manage to stay with their distress and not seek or need some other kind of intervention such as hospitalisation would be to believe that the therapists have some objective knowledge/expertise over the course of another person's suffering.

Therefore, the process of setting up a new community household has meant that new residents had to face up to the difficulty of bearing their suffering and the implications of doing so. Some of them decided they needed to alleviate their distress by going into hospital or leaving the house altogether. The consequent feelings of frustration, pain, failure, disappointment and/or endurance were what the whole of the community including the therapists and residents in less acute distress also had to bear.

Living in a PA house: what is on offer?

I would like to attempt to answer this question by briefly exploring a terrible incident that marked the beginnings of the newest PA community. In its early days, after its last reopening the house had three residents. The meetings seemed rather long. Residents had plenty of space to explore their histories, but took considerably less space to explore the difficulties of living with each other. We often acknowledged but rarely elaborated on the fact that the house felt rather fragile, unsure of its ability to survive aggression.

One of the residents (I will call him Alex), the third person who came to live in the house, and the only male resident for a while, was particularly fragile. He used the meetings to explore his past and to unravel the vast amounts of suffering he had had to endure as a child. It was clear to people who had developed a closer relationship with him that there was very little life force in his history.[3] There was a real question about what kind of reparative experience[4] he could have in the house.

The house developed and, about 6 months after its opening, it looked like new residents would be moving in. This opened up the possibility of more conflict and aggression within the house. It was clear that such a change did not agree with Alex. He quickly withdrew into his room, socialised much less and attended fewer meetings and therapy sessions. A lot of the ideas he expressed in the few meetings he did attend were about people following him and the house not being able to protect him from intruders. However, the predominant desire he expressed was to withdraw from the world, which could take the form of living in the countryside. He had indeed done this in the past, but had found that he could not really withdraw from people completely. He was left to do so in the house to an extent, but was frequently interrupted by other residents and the therapists expressing concern and residents offering to help or engage him by preparing a meal for him etc. Despite this, he withdrew further and further and with Christmas approaching there was real concern expressed by residents about his well-being, especially how he and the house would cope during the forthcoming break from house meetings.

He did not want to go into hospital. He had made that very clear. While we were discussing with the house residents what could be done to help him, it emerged that he was actually not in his room as we had thought and had not been there since the night before. His things were packed as though he was about to go. Later on that day, after reporting him missing to the police, we were told that he had been found dead in an area of London connected with his history. He had jumped from the top of a building.

It is difficult to describe the impact that his suicide had on everybody in the house who had been involved with him. There was, of course, anger and frustration that this had to be the outcome of his stay in the house. But the main feeling shared by everybody involved with him was that of deep sadness that his life had been so damaged that he could feel no hope for a reparative experience (Winnicott 1965). Residents said that he left a number of thank you notes within the house.

The night after he died, I had a dream of a grave in an open green space and the word peaceful written on it. It felt as though that dream were a communication from him or rather a manifestation of my experience of him. During the summer of the year he died, Alex had become very distressed and tormented by memories of abuse. During the summer holiday, he had called me a number of times and described his suffering. At the time, it had felt as though he was asking me to carry his suffering in a way that was not possible for another human being to do. He had then expressed a wish for peace, peace that seemed to me at the time to only belong to the pre-birth, pre-world, possibly womb environment. The dream of the grave seemed in a very sad way to be the fulfilment of his wish.

Alex had kept minimal contact with his family. We had no idea which, if any, relatives existed, let alone where they were. His funeral was undertaken by the PA and a close friend of his, who told us that he was always afraid he would hear the news of his death. The other residents were centrally involved in holding a reception in the house after his funeral for people he had lived with when he was young and his friends. The experience was undoubtedly disturbing and upsetting for them, as well as the whole of the house and the PA. It has marked the history of the house for many years since.

Had we been able to, we would, of course, have wanted to prevent his suicide from taking place. When we interview would-be residents, we do ask them whether they are likely to harm themselves while living in the house. The irony, of course, is that, often, people who express suicidal thoughts do so as a way of expressing anger, frustration and distress and are less likely to act on their thoughts. It is easier to focus on what could have been done or can be done in the future than to stay with the reality of the enormous suffering that people we work with often bring with them. It is precisely the reality of some people's tremendous emotional suffering that the PA's work takes on board.

The PA houses have traditionally been sanctuaries for people whose lives have fallen into pieces and who wanted a breathing space. More recently, there has been more of an emphasis on therapeutic work and what can be achieved through living in a PA house. What is often the case, however, and Alex's story is an extreme example of it, is that what people want to achieve out of being in a PA house, does not coincide with the therapists' idea of healing and health. Being given the opportunity, to have the space to think about how they want their lives to evolve is what residents find invaluable in a PA house.

In place of a conclusion: opportunities and limitations

Most people who come to a PA house believe that there is scope in their lives for reparation. However, in order to have a reparative experience, they engage in a painful process of looking at what has gone wrong so far. Having the space to reflect about one's life is particularly difficult when somebody feels they have had limited choices and control over the damage they have suffered.

Part of the process of feeling better and moving on is about recovering the ability to live in the present and realising that one can have more control over one's life as an adult. People who come to our houses often reach this conclusion, through their experience of living with others who attempt to understand and respect them. Being able to move on also involves coming to terms with one's losses. It is often a process that as well as enabling people to feel alive, makes them face up to their limitations.

We live in a culture that seeks concrete evidence of progress and achievement. Evidence often entails a fixed notion of what a well person is supposed to be like. The PA houses invite people to think about their own lives and histories and about how they want their lives to be as opposed to how they are expected to be. Their ideas about their lives are being tested in an environment where they attempt to live with others in a meaningful way.

Notes

1 The word 'therapeutic' is used in this chapter in its broader sense of facilitating healing rather than to indicate the application of a particular kind of therapy.
2 The two remaining PA houses are both PA properties. The fact that there is minimal therapeutic structure in the houses means, therefore, that they can be viable financially through the rent that the residents pay and that can be covered by housing benefit. However, relying on housing benefit as the only means of financing the houses makes their existence rather fragile, as full house occupancy is necessary for them to be financially viable.
3 I am referring to life force in the sense of the origins of creativity as Winnicott describes it in his book *Human Nature*. According to Winnicott, the infant discovers the breast, i.e. perceives the existence of continuous, sensitive to his needs, care as something he generates himself. According to Winnicott, this is the

basis of human creativity/aliveness cf. D.W. Winnicott, *Human Nature*, London: Free Association Books, 1988, pp. 100–115.

4 The term reparation is used in Kleinian theory to describe the infant's aggressive impulses towards the breast and its progressive realisation of the mother's ability to survive his aggression. Winnicott accepts the Kleinian basis of the term, but uses it primarily in relation to the mother's ability to tune into her baby and provide a sense of continuity (Winnicott 1965). In this chapter, I am using the words reparation, reparative experience to indicate the possibility of a facilitating, stable and sensitive environment in the Winnicottian sense.

Bibliography

Barnes, M. and Berke, J. (2002). *Two Accounts of a Journey Through Madness*. New York: Other Press.

Cooper, R. (1989). Dwelling and the 'therapeutic community', in *Thresholds between Philosophy and Psychoanalysis: Papers from the Philadelphia Association*. London: Free Association Books.

Gadamer, H.G. (1975). *Truth and Method*. New York: Seabury Press.

Goffman, I. (1961). *Asylums*. London: Penguin.

Gordon, P. and Mayo, R. (2004). *Between Psychotherapy and Philosophy*. London and Philadelphia: Whurr Publishers.

Heaton, J.M. (2000). *Wittgenstein and Psychoanalysis*. Duxford: Icon Books.

Heidegger, M. (1985). *History and the Concept of Time*. Bloomington: Indiana University Press.

Ingleby, D. (1981). Understanding 'mental illness', in *Critical Psychiatry: The politics of mental health*. London and New York: Penguin.

Janssen, P. (1994). *Psychoanalytic Therapy in the Hospital Setting*. London and New York: Routledge.

Laing, R.D. (1960). *The Divided Self*. London and New York: Penguin.

Laing, R.D. and Esterson A. (1964). *Sanity, Madness and the Family*. London and New York: Penguin.

Merleau-Ponty, M. (1962). *Phenomenology of Perception*. London and New York: Routledge.

Winnicott, D.W. (1965). *The Maturational Processes and the Facilitating Environment*. London and New York: Karnac.

Chapter 7

Psychosis and the community of the question: training therapists in therapeutic community

Alistair Black

ἀκοῦσαι οὐκ ἐπιστάμενοι οὐδ εἰπεῖν

Not knowing how to listen neither can they speak
(Heraclitus: Fragment XVII, cf. Kahn 1979)[1]

What might be called the four τόποι (*topoi*), the situating elements of a topography of practice on which the healing potential of the therapeutic community rests, have been articulated in terms of 'dialogue', 'dwelling', 'care', and 'community' (Tucker 2000).[2] Each of these *topoi* contributes structurally to the fundamental and enigmatic key, the attunement or mood, which has also been named the 'atmosphere', as that within which the life and breath of any therapeutic engagement takes its course. Placing each of these four structural terms in inverted commas, similarly so placing the word 'atmosphere' itself, indicates that they do not so much provide an answer to the question of what supports and constitutes the therapeutic essence of the therapeutic community, as much as each serves rather as the title of a question or an appeal to a possible questioning. The inverted commas indicate that each of these terms demands thought, calls for thinking or ought to be experienced as thought provoking inasmuch as each serves as a sign for an essential aspect of human existence, which means that they articulate existential structures, or dimensions of world, of the human being's being-in-the-world (Heidegger 1927, 1996).[3] As such they are not so much 'principles' if principle means the grounding and guiding representation on which a firm knowledge can be built, the moment of highest certainty, as if the meaning of the terms mentioned is already decided with clarity and distinctness and they are not brought forward again here with the intention or suggestion of replacing the already articulated essential qualities of the therapeutic community, but as elements open to questioning, not points of theoretical certainty from which practice takes its orientation, but signs that point to paths into the unknown (Haigh 1999; Rapoport 1960).[4] It is around these 'questionable' elements, inseparable in practice, each of which implies and includes the others, that training for therapists or therapeutic practitioners within a therapeutic community might be organised, as a sensitivity to each phenomenal dimension, if it is indeed to be training in a way of questioning. However what constitutes the kind of 'atmosphere' in which such questioning could possibly take place and how does questioning itself allow and preserve this atmosphere? (Clark 1999; Cox 1998; Haigh 1999).[5]

Questioning community

The basic articulation of the essence of the therapeutic community, of that which is essential and distinguishes this kind of community from others, is that it is a community of questioning, a culture of enquiry (Main 1989)[6] or open communication, and this is already implicit in the idea of a 'living–learning' experience (Jones 1968). There can be no learning without adequate and appropriate questioning. Questioning is the interpretative unfolding of understanding in the disclosing of meaning. It is not necessarily a theoretical kind of questioning, it is not necessarily an inquisition or the more or less violent forcing of a causal explanation where this kind of knowing might indeed be inappropriate to the kind of beings apprehended, as such it is not always simply a representational (objectifying) thinking which provides grounds. Questioning is not necessarily only a path toward the procuring of such an objectifying knowledge that is held over against a knowing subject, by that subject, from which the subjectivity of the subject in question is an element to be minimised if not totally eliminated. Such an intellectual or theoretical questioning leaves the questioner as such unquestioned. Rather, there is need, in therapy, of the kind of questioning that places the questioner, along with the whole, in question and that, through the unfolding of the questioning, brings about a transformation of the questioner. Such interpretative or hermeneutic questioning is rather the release into meaning, whereby things become more meaningful the more they can be taken up into questioning and held within it. Questioning as a path into further questioning does not seek answers, at least not primarily, but rather seeks to develop and unfold the question itself, through which human existence becomes ever more questionable. Here again it should be emphasised that this is not a merely intellectual or theoretical questioning of the essence, in its traditional metaphysical interpretation as idea defining the whatness of something, it is not purely an academic questioning of the essence of dialogue, of dwelling, of care, of community, which would seek to arrive at an adequate conceptual definition of each of these terms, giving a theoretical answer. Rather essence is here understood as the way and manner in which something presences, comes to presence and maintains itself in presencing. The clinical practice itself, the everyday practice of therapeutic community circles around within these elements of the 'atmosphere', not merely theoretically (although clear and well-articulated theory should and must always inform and guide practice if practice is, in turn, meaningfully to inform our interpretations) but through the encounter with the existential question, the question which brings the meaning and limits of human existence, here and now, into question. Thus the answer to the questions of dialogue and dwelling, care and community is not an objectifying knowledge but rather a transformation of the questioner with respect to these phenomena.

Instead of questioning we could also say thinking, and with respect to thinking, listening. To question, to think, is to allow to become thoughtful, to give oneself over to thought, to allow thought to enter by deciding against thoughtlessness. Thoughtfulness begins with listening, with learning to listen (Wilberg 2004).[7] Thinking here is in no way to be understood as opposed or external to feeling or attunement. Each of the named components of the 'atmosphere' of the therapeutic community demands thought in its own way, that is, to be continuously given thought, explicitly maintained in thinking and developed in thoughtfulness. Each of the elements cannot be thought without the others: without thought 'dialogue' becomes empty chatter, impoverished communication repeating worn formulas and reduced to public relatedness as the transfer of information; without thought 'dwelling' becomes merely living in a particular place, that place having no particular meaning as a dwelling place; without thought 'care' becomes indifferent passing one another by and irresponsibility with respect to the other; without thought 'community' becomes individualised minimal interaction without an obligating bond or shared destiny, without the act that inaugurates and maintains community as such. So the 'atmosphere' – could we even dare say spirit? – that is the distinguishing feature of the therapeutic milieu is further characterised, in essence, by thoughtfulness. It is an 'atmosphere', as that which envelops and permeates whatever happens and each situation that unfolds, of thought, in which the possibility of reflection is preserved and sheltered. Does not what has been said so far present a somewhat idealised picture of the therapeutic community as a spiritual world imbued with thoughtfulness, a community without illness, without the many elements that militate against thought and propel into thoughtlessness, without indeed the need for therapy? Yet to the essence understood existentially and phenomenologically, the in-essence or counter-essence also belongs and, with the absence of thought, even comes to dominate. The essential is always accompanied by the inessential and the latter overshadows the former as the always possible, as that which the essence brings with it. The inessential presences as the deficit or privation of the essential, when that which is essential slips out of remembrance. When we enquire concerning the essence of something, we are seeking the truth of its being. Yet semblance always accompanies being and masks our access to its truth. That phenomena can presence in semblance, distorted or come to be forgotten and covered up is the reason that there is need of phenomenology. Precisely because, first and for the most part, phenomena do not present themselves in their truth, there is need of a philosophical discipline that attempts to return to the things themselves and to preserve their truth in the word. Only in and through explicit reflection on the belonging together of the essential and the inessential is the difference preserved. Thought dwells on the inessential as such (not, that is, inessentially) in order to allow the essence to remain in presence. In the factically existing community thought battles with thoughtlessness, the in-essence of thought; with the *un*thought in its many guises, thoughtlessness being possible only for a being capable of thought. Indeed, without the explicit call to reflection, the preservation and opening of the space of and for thought, any community decays into thoughtlessness, into empty repetition of formulas, into the performance of meaningless rituals which only serve the perpetuation of institutions and practices devoid of compassionate therapeutic action (Main 1990).

Questioning psychosis

In whichever way we attempt to think about the essence of psychosis and how it is to be understood and interpreted, whether pathologised as mental illness, whether as a state or series of psychic–emotional states, an ongoing or developing structuration of experience or a way of being, an existential bearing or stance, the interpretation will need to take account of the disturbances in meaning and language, on the one hand, and the disintegration and fragmentation of the awareness of self or identity, on the other.

Phenomena that are usually categorised as psychotic include: hallucinations whether auditory or more specifically verbal (hearing voices), visual or tactile; the conviction that one is being watched, observed, spied on, usually by some supposedly malevolent being or higher power; the feeling of being persecuted, punished or tested by this power or powers; the enigmatic experience (Laurent 2004) of an overabundance of meaningful connections that bear directly on the person (certainty); the belief that thoughts are being controlled from without, ideas being inserted, broadcast or transmitted to a receptivity that cannot be filtered or switched off; a conviction that one is special, chosen or selected to undergo this suffering for a reason the meaning of which further eludes the sufferer; and following on from this the grandiosity associated with this special mission.

To the question of psychosis also belongs that of the trigger, of what releases a psychosis from a supposedly prodromal state, the premonitory phenomena of pre-psychotic experience and how this, in turn, relates to the pre-psychotic structuration of experience, however this is conceived. Then there is the question of the course, the growth or development of a psychosis (psychotic breadth, width, and depth), a process which is by no means uniform or standardised with respect to the historical unfolding of the psychotic formation, but perhaps in relation to which we can make some broad temporal conceptual divisions. As just mentioned, prior to a psychotic breakdown proper there is the preliminary structuring and the prodromic states in which the pre-psychotic person finds themselves, characterised by a withdrawal or loss of a sense of the coherence of shared meaning, emotional instability, increased inner speed or the flight of ideas, accompanied by premonitions of destruction, of disaster and catastrophe (prominent for example in dreams), giving rise to the fear of collapse and the attempted avoidance through various strategies of this inevitability.

On this state of precarious instability and vulnerability the trigger acts, so to speak, to remove the keystone and the edifice collapses. This constitutes the acute phase of psychotic destruction. Out of the enigmatic experience arise anxious strategies to re-establish meaning following the shift in the centre and collapse of the fragile pre-psychotic world. The boundaries and provenance of the self, of I and other, self and world are caught up in the maelstrom. There is then the desperate tendency to construct delusional formations in an attempt to rebuild a semblance of a meaningful world and hallucinatory experiences everywhere confirm these delusions. Trust in other human beings cannot survive such a collapse and resistance to developing trusting relations with those attempting to help or with those who were formerly trusted, emphasises the acutely psychotic form of existence and its oscillation between grandiose omnipotence and abject loneliness.

Later in the psychotic process even the delusional structures, established as a means of reconnection and attempt at recovery, themselves may become the object of doubt and their formations begin to be dismantled, islands of relative sanity may then emerge with greater frequency and be sustained for longer periods. The euphoria of grandiosity or the dysphoria of persecution and powerlessness can give way to depressive moods. There is then the possibility of questioning, of establishing a distance from the gravitational centre of the psychotic core, a distance necessary for any therapeutic engagement, the possibility of trusting another human being again and of sharing social and common meanings may develop, community in some sense again become possible in its most basic form.

There then follows the possibility of reconstruction. In this phase there is the increased capacity to separate out self and other, the boundaries of an I emerge from fusion states, yet shadows of psychotic disturbance may continue to cast themselves over the newly emerging stability. Feelings of shame, of guilt, and of relief may predominate, yet also those of loss, of disillusionment and of dispossession, similar to the experience of anyone who is confronted with the rigours and responsibilities of the day on awakening from a particularly absorbing dream. Yet the after-effect in the life history of the reconstructing person of the psychotic collapse can maintain itself through a traumatising form of repetition. Trauma always involves the difficulty of the return from an extreme experience, which shatters the sufferer on the limits of meaning, to the everyday world of consensual and conventional reality. When someone is suffering from trauma, they literally cannot find the words with which to make sense of their experience, the meaning remains disintegrating and disintegrated with respect to the continual sense-making activity of their existence, they cannot forget. Without this integration, the wound remains open or the scarring problematic and inhibiting. Psychosis is a massive intrusion into the emotional existence of a human being which can bring about permanent damage. Such damage is the equivalent of scarring or scarification. Colloquially we say that a person has been emotionally scarred by an experience. Psychotic scarification may take a lifetime to come to terms with. The scar can remain painful, shameful and disfiguring. Yet within this cycle, from pre-psychotic to reconstructive there are many traps and catches, many holes and ditches. What has been presented here as a psychotic logic is rarely linear but as might be expected, rather baroque. Like the game of snakes and ladders an unlucky throw can lead to setbacks and circulations. It is possible that a single episode may be successfully reconstructed and reintegrated, such an episode may even lead to creative responses and transformations in a person's existential stance. Yet the gravitational force of a psychotic formation may equally take hold and recurring relapses capture a person's existence. The longer a life is embroiled in the cycle of psychosis, the more difficult is any therapeutic effort and the more meagre the outcome. Such is the importance of early psychotherapeutic input.

The disintegration of the person and loss of the responsibility of selfhood, the many problems that cluster around the continuity and boundaries of the I, the withdrawal from involvement in relationship with others, even to the point of the non-recognition of their otherness, the apparent collapse of world and the intensity of the emotional field that the psychotic person communicates, the overwhelming anxiety, anger and fear or hopelessness that may be engendered, all these factors add up to make therapeutic work difficult, demanding both emotionally and personally and potentially hazardous for the emotional well-being and integrity of the therapist or therapeutic team. When it is a question of a team working with a group of psychotically disturbed persons, the difficulties, the demands and the dangers for those attempting to engage in therapeutic work are magnified. Thus one of the most important factors in training therapists undertaking such work which involves emotional engagement, the use of the self or working with relational depth should attempt to impart the capacity and resources necessary for this work both at the level of understanding and emotionality. Psychosis conceived of as a painful disturbance of a person's structured being-in-the-world and as such a dis-ease more than any other calls for thought about what it means to be a human being, of what properly constitutes our humanity, our selfhood and access to meaning. Psychosis in the modern world, as in the pre-modern where madness was on occasion recognised as a call for reflection on the limits of human existence, leads us to question our own sanity and the meaning of sanity in general, of the meaning of our shared and consensual reality and of the limits of our conventional reason. Fragmentation and alienation seem to be the basic characteristic of psychotic experience, both with respect to the experience of self and in relation to others, leading to corruption in both meaning and identity (Hinshelwood 2004).[8] Thus working therapeutically with psychotic experience perhaps demands that we are all somewhat drawn, most reluctantly in all probability into 'metaphysics' in the sense of a provocation to question the meaning of being and the essence of human existence, to reflect on the phenomena that arise in relation to such experiences and move beyond the everyday understanding of such phenomena and the everyday kind of responses and inasmuch as such questioning beyond our own everyday experience of the ordinary and the usual leads us to question our selves, necessarily places ourselves, and the existence of the human being in general, into question along with the whole (Heidegger 1998).[9] This is not, of course, to suggest that therapists need to study academic philosophy before they practise or engage in their clinical work, but we might remember here that Hippocrates himself recommended that before learning the art of medicine his students should have a proper grounding in philosophy (Gadamer 1996).[10] Lacan also makes a similar point precisely in his seminar on the psychoses where he begins to speak about the phenomenon of psychosis. He here finds it necessary to remind his listeners that he is not engaged in the metaphysics of the Freudian discovery (in which presumably he felt he might be so understood) yet his trainees would 'lose nothing in inquiring into the metaphysics of the human condition' (Lacan 1993) and presumably he suggests this because he thinks that such questioning would help in the clinical work with the psychoses (Boss 1963; Gale 2000; Heidegger 2001; Ylla 1990).[11] Rather the practice of therapy with those suffering psychotic experiences or states necessarily impinges on the therapists' own understanding of themselves and their world, on their own meaning, purpose and identity. Hence with respect to all the phenomena that could be included under the rubric of countertransference, such ability to question self and world should not be minimised. Therapists will need to be trained to recognise and wield their own desire in ways which are therapeutically beneficial in their encounter with psychosis, a sensitivity to the manner in which their desire figures or disfigures the shared world in such an encounter and the way in which they are figuring in the psychotically structured world (Searles 1965).[12]

If the training of therapists for therapeutic community practice orients itself around the themes or elements of dialogue, dwelling, care, and community, then this can only mean that it is in these that the therapeutic interventions they are trained to offer are expected to bring about qualitative change. It is within these elements of the therapeutic community that interventions can help guide towards the facilitating atmosphere or alternatively allow the slip into forgetfulness. Reflective practice that is the cornerstone of such work means disclosing and preserving in thoughtfulness, or mindfulness, each of the elements, each in its own way. Yet it is precisely in these elements or dimensions of existential structure that the dis-ease of psychosis factically brings an impoverishment, a deterioration, a fracturing. If each are essential dimensions of the worldality of the world (*Weltlichkeit der Welt* cf. SZ 63; BT 59) in psychosis each suffers a privation, a withdrawal and a diminishing. In psychosis many aspects of the factical shared world collapse, all the more readily does the existential opening of world, the nothing of world shine forth, that the human world is primarily constituted by lack. Rather than bear this nothing, the psychotic process seeks to rebuild a meaningful world for itself out of the symbolic elements cast away as the flotsam and jetsam of the wreckage of world. This attempted rebuilding of world structures the enigmatic experience of the developing psychosis within elements that externally can be labelled delusional, according to the formula stating that which has been precluded from the symbolic dimension, returns in the real. The developed delusional system offers a complete world which as Freud long ago realised should be considered as an attempt at recovery rather than the primary illness (Freud 1958).[13]

Four *topoi*

Dialogue means through language, in speaking with one another (Tucker 1998).[14] Through dialogue or conversation we disclose the world and bring ourselves into a relation to the beings that surround us in their presence and absence. Human beings are distinguished by being within language, which is to say that they find themselves always within a language and understand themselves and their world through this language. Yet, for the most part, speaking with one another is not concerned to disclose but rather to close off and conceal, to cover up and to maintain a particular level of disclosedness with which we are all comfortable and familiar. Heidegger names this kind of everyday speaking with one another *Gerede*, which might be translated as chatter or 'empty talk' (SZ 167ff; BT 157ff.).[15] Chatter articulates in discourse the predominant understanding and interpretations, it is basically an uncreative way with language, a speaking without thinking about the words and language we are speaking. Human beings are initially and within certain limits constantly entrusted to the interpretedness which has already been expressed which offers the possibilities of the average understanding and the attunement belonging to it (the tranquilisation of indifference). In communication with others, interpretations are handed down with the intention of bringing the hearer to participate in the disclosed being towards what is being talked about. Being with one another in dialogue takes place but only with an approximate and superficial under-standing, communication becomes 'gossiping and passing the word along' (SZ 168; BT 158).[16] Discourse then takes the form of everyday chatter. In this average understanding, everything is understood and chatter is the possibility of understanding everything. As such a mode of discourse chatter, rather than opening up the world, has the tendency to close up, cover over and hide the relationship to beings. This is not necessarily a conscious desire to deceive. Yet chatter 'holds any new questioning and discussion at a distance because it presumes it has [already] understood' (SZ 169; BT 158). We get to know many things initially in this way and can never completely escape this everyday way of being interpreted into which we have grown initially and within which we find ourselves at home. This public way of being interpreted even delimits 'the possibilities of being attuned' (SZ 170; BT 159). Chatter configures the average everyday way of human existence and tranquilises through establishing the limits and possi-bilities of familiarity, homeliness, the ordinary and the usual. The tranquil-ised indifference of average everydayness is certainly not indifferent with respect to beings with which it is preoccupied and within which it loses itself. Rather this indifference is a concealed relation to extreme possibilities of its own being, to its finite existence, disclosed as such. Therapeutic dialogue, however, seeks to allow the subject to experience themselves and their truth as free as possible from disguises and dissimulations. Therapeutic dialogue builds the therapeutic relationship. Yet involved in this engagement in dialogue the therapist questions themselves in relation to the work of the dialogue, inasmuch as they always attempt to move the therapeutic rela-tionship deeper into this work. In psychosis, the possibility of true dialogue seems to have all but broken down. It is often unclear in the speech of the psychotic subject who is being addressed, who is speaking and what exactly is being spoken about. Yet through the perseverance of the therapist in providing a containing and holding openness to dialogue, understanding can be developed and meanings articulated. Most important in this endeav-our is the ability of the therapist to listen and to hold this listening in a questioning stance. In the therapeutic community, the dialogue is the ongoing attempt to disclose the truth of the community, its members and their relationships. The therapeutic work is conducted through the invita-tion to each member to join in this ongoing dialogue, which develops as a shared language. Such dialogue is not everyday chatter but is imbued with a seriousness that allows each member of the community to be heard and establish for themselves a voice that meets with a thoughtful response. The questioning therapist always asks themselves whether dialogue is truly taking place here in a therapeutic sense.

Dwelling means to stay, to remain, to find oneself at home, to find a place to be. Dwelling seems to have connotations of shelter of hearth and home, of familiarity, comfort, safety. In addition to this it means the relation with place and rootedness. We speak about putting down roots and mean something like allowing our sense of dwelling to mature and grow. Yet can this at home be reduced to a place become familiar? Is dwelling merely lasting and lingering or persisting somewhere? Yet dwelling as finding oneself 'at home' denotes intimacy and belonging and also the relationship with a boundary, an outside. Home as the place of dwelling also includes this relation to the threshold, whether this is constituted by the doorway, the boundary stone or the ocean's edge. Dwelling is not merely given in the familiar, the unquestioning acceptance of that which has been passed on. Rather, dwelling is a struggle, an exile and a return, a homecoming. Returning home one appreciates home as if for the first time. Human beings must always set out to learn to dwell, but before this they need to recognise that they are, indeed, homeless. To dwell is then to cultivate home through an appreciation of the other, the strange or the foreign. Human beings do indeed dwell on the earth but mostly in forgetfulness of the quest for home. In psychosis, this homelessness and absence of home seem intensified. Psychotic experience seems eminently lost and without moorings, adrift in a language without shared meaning. Even the question of home seems barred, psychotic homelessness is not recognised as such by the sufferer, often such exile is accepted and preferred to other even less appealing possibilities. The therapeutic community is a place in which the question of dwelling and it privation are kept open. We often speak in the therapeutic community movement of the need to build a therapeutic culture. In contradiction to the idea that building precedes dwelling Heidegger will say: 'Only if we are capable of dwelling, only then can we build' (Heidegger 1971: 160). But how then do we become capable of dwelling in the modern technical machine age in which the absence of the possibility of dwelling seems to announce itself? When it seems that homelessness and desolation cover the earth, when 'gods no longer step out of things'? One way is by asking this question about building and dwelling, by attempting to think about what is thoughtworthy in their relationship. As for Heidegger thinking itself is a kind of building that belongs to dwelling. Both building and thinking as a kind of building are necessary for dwelling and help dwelling so long as they listen to one another. Heidegger concludes his essay 'Building dwelling thinking' by asking about our dwelling in the modern world, he indicates that the real plight of dwelling does not lie in lack of houses but that mortals 'ever search anew for the essence of dwelling, that they *must ever learn to dwell*' (Heidegger 1971: 161). And this learning involves thinking what it means to dwell and giving thought to this homelessness (Cooper 1989; Tucker 2000).[17]

Care means here caring for or concern, which in an existential sense denotes that we are always in relation to other human beings and find ourselves only in and through relating to others. Heidegger calls this care or concern for other human beings, as essentially relational, *Fürsorge* (SZ 121;

BT 114). Our world is always a shared world in which we encounter other human beings and they encounter us. Even the hermit can choose isolation from other human beings because, essentially, existence is shared, being with others (SZ 117ff; BT 110ff). Such a choice is an active recognition of this shared being together in the world and an attempt to minimise its impact. Yet factical isolation is not the only or the most obvious way in which we might find ourselves alone in the shared world. Precisely in our everyday world, in the hustle and bustle of the marketplace, we enter into a privative mode of being with one another, of passing one another by, of not mattering to one another or avoiding one another. Here our concern for the other is minimised and concern becomes negative, coming to be characterised by 'distance and reserve' and 'mistrust' (SZ 122; BT 115; Boss 1963). Yet there are many factical occasions for positive concern, of being responsible to and for the other. In terms of actively helping other human beings when they are in need, positive concern has two essential forms. Concern can 'leap in' (*einspringen*) for the other, take their responsibility away, relieve the burden and fix their difficulty for them. Boss names this kind of care or concern *intervening*, in which 'the other person can become dependent and dominated, even though such domination may be silent and remain hidden to the one who is dominated' (Boss 1963: 73). Here Boss echoes Heidegger who observes that in such concern 'the other is thus displaced, he steps back so that afterwards when the matter has been attended to, he can take it over as something finished and available or disburden himself of it completely' (SZ 122; BT 114). This positive mode of concern, Heidegger continues, 'is to a large extent, determinative for being with one another' (SZ 122; BT 114) inasmuch as everyday being with one another is first and foremost taking care of useful things and other human beings come to figure in our world according to their usefulness to us in our everyday projects taking care of useful beings. An example of this kind of positive concern from medical practice would be exemplified by the surgeon. The surgeon exercises positive concern for the patient by performing the operation for which they take ultimate and sole responsibility, emphasised by the fact that the patient is usually anaesthetised during the operation and with the aim of returning to the patient the use of his body. The patient gives up his responsibility to the surgeon. Concern in the second positive sense does not so much take away a person's responsibility from them as attempt to hand it back to them to the extent that they can bear it. Boss contrasts this kind of concern, which he calls *anticipating*, with intervening, in this concern the therapist 'does not take over for the patient but tries to hand back to him what has been cared for . . . it helps the other person to become transparent to himself and free for his existence' (Boss 1963: 73). This kind of concern is not so much that which steps in as that which 'leaps ahead' (*vorausspringt*) in order to hold open possibilities and opportunities for the human being to grasp for themselves. This concern

Heidegger observes 'essentially pertains to owned care (*eigentliche Sorge*); that is, the existence of the other, and not to a what which it takes care of, helps the other to become transparent to himself in his care and free for it' (SZ 122; BT 115). So Heidegger contrasts two forms of positive concern for others one which he names *einspringend-beherrschenden*, domineering leaping in, and the other *vorspringend-befreienden*, freeing leaping ahead (SZ 122; BT 115). The latter mode of positive concern is precisely the domain of the analyst or psychotherapist. In psychosis, the ability and possibility of taking responsibility for oneself seems to be greatly diminished and concern for others often also seems reduced to negative forms. Therapeutic community practitioners learn to be attuned to the differing modes and polarities of concern and yet keep open for themselves the question, while trying to minimise their lapse into negative concern, of the kind of positive concern they bring into their work with such psychotic experience.

Community means that which is shared beyond all differences, a shared world. Community is at once the most elusive and the most important element of the healing atmosphere of the therapeutic milieu the most ineffable, the inexorable, as it touches most directly on questions of spirit (Gale and Sanchez 2005). It is this element that is singled out in the sense that it names the specific mode of therapy, the therapeutic community, yet this indicates that there can be community that is untherapeutic and, in fact community, is itself mostly experienced in a deficient mode of its being. Yet as such community suggests that there is something intrinsically healing in the experience of genuine community and this something has connotations of belonging, of sharing, of mutual understanding and participation. Community has its epiphany only through a commitment that strives after an ideal beyond itself. Such togetherness is seldom and fragile. Just living in the same place and doing the same kind of things does not give rise to community, an assumed external shared identity based on interest is the empty shell of community. Community is inaugurated and preserved in the act of communion, a gathering identification, a mutual bond and obligation. Community as such must be freely entered into, affirmed and valued by its members. Yet community as that which is most easily lost and forgotten is that which needs to remain always in question, community must be a questing and questioning community, questioning itself and its limits. A community that is not a community of the question is not a mutual quest for its potential healing power, but merely a convenience. Thus the decay of community is the most dangerous and the most insidious. Psychosis is perhaps a sign of the end of community, it is the extreme expulsion from communal existence, seemingly bringing the impossibility of commitment and communication. Community in itself implies a shared or a common language. The work of community attempts to approach the possibility of μετοχή, a sharing or communion, a joining in meaning and purpose, a μετέχω, a participation in one another's being such that it constitutes a μέτοχον, a spiritual community of the practice of health, well-being, growth and mutual striving. Psychosis brings the collapse of the possibility of a fully shared world of everyday consensus and commonality. Thus therapeutic community practice is constellated around the question of community, all else circles around this point as around its polar star. This pole gathers around itself the rules and boundaries of the community and it is this that makes its questioning necessarily a politics. The question of community always leads back to that of the therapeutic process of the community as a whole and the work of community itself as therapeutic process.

The four *topoi* of therapeutic community here outlined as questionable in the sense of remaining in question, each contributes in its own way to the elusive atmosphere in which the healing potential of this modality of 'treatment' can grow. Each of these *topoi* is in its questioning enactment a *hodos*, a pathway, to travel these pathways and to follow after them constitutes the *methodos*, the method. The key to unlocking this potential lies in the provision, the centrality and the preservation of reflective practice, not merely as an adjunct to the clinical work, but as fully integrated and interwoven within the work itself. Reflective practice is the heartbeat of a culture of enquiry or a community of questioning. Yet reflective practice is that which is so easily forsaken through the endless pressures and concerns of the day, allowing thoughtlessness to prevail. The ability to productively utilise the appropriate space for reflective practice, itself needs to be learnt and this constitutes an essential element of reflective practice itself. Working with psychosis within a therapeutic community inevitably has a dramatic impact emotionally on therapeutic practitioners and the ability to reflect openly and honestly on this impact is the key to effective therapeutic engagement. Perhaps it is now more than ever that therapeutic community practitioners require an education in reflective practice, what it consists in and how to pursue it and indeed why it is necessary? Is it not time that thoughtful practitioners devoted themselves to this question?

Notes

1 Kahn (p. 34) places Fragment XVII directly after the fragment in which ψυχή appears for the first time in extant literature directly related to language and hence defining human being. Heraclitus first introduced psyche as a thoughtful word in relation to *Logos*, being human intrinsically connected to speaking and participating in language.

2 The present contribution is indebted to this collection and situates itself with respect to the opening up of the questions that it articulates. Tucker introduces what she refers to as the 'four fundamental themes' in order to show how these underlie the work of therapeutic community practice (p. 19ff). As will become evident the four *topoi* entered here are not the only way to explore the 'placing' of therapeutic community practice, yet such a topography allows access with a comprehensive view to certain phenomenal structures.

3 Subsequent references appear as SZ followed by page number and BT followed by page number in text. Cf. SZ p. 52ff. BT p. 49ff.

4 Rapoport suggested permissiveness, communalism, reality confrontation and democratisation, while Haigh expanded on these principles giving attachment, containment, communication, involvement and agency, these being correlated with their actualisation in therapeutic community practice and culture to give belonging, safety, openness, living–learning, and empowerment.

5 Clark (p. 33) quotes the World Health Organization Report (1953) *Expert Committee on Mental Health: 3rd Report* Geneva, in which the 'most important single factor', the foundation of a therapeutic milieu, is claimed to be 'an intangible element' only to be 'described as its atmosphere'. This atmosphere is developed by: the preservation of the patient's individuality; the assumption of trustworthiness; the positive reinforcement of 'good behaviour'; the assumption of retention of a capacity for responsibility; and the need for meaningful occupation. Cox articulates: respect for persons; therapeutic ability belonging to both staff and clients; an emotionally containing environment linked to clear leadership; an understanding of group dynamics; a living–learning experience; and a culture of enquiry.

6 Main first articulated the idea of the 'culture of enquiry' into the unconscious dynamics of the community claiming that the hallmark of a therapeutic community is 'not a particular form of social structure but a culture of enquiry' (p. 141).

7 Wilberg muses 'The way we come to ourselves "through the word" (*dia-logos*) depends on the way we ourselves come to words, i.e.: the way we listen to ourselves before we speak. To think before we speak is to listen before we speak, for thinking itself is the process of translating what our listening awareness brings to light' (p. 93).

8 Hinshelwood describes the 'subjective features that occur with regularity in the experience of psychotic people' as: 'turning away from the real world; a self-absorption that makes one's imaginings real; the cognitive loosening of links between thoughts; the loss of abstraction and symbolisation; and missing the sense of a consistent self' (p. 49). While acknowledging the importance of Hinshelwood's formulations, and indeed of the book as a whole for the reflections being attempted here, each of these formulas seems to me to be susceptible of further questions that would need to be constellated around the possible meanings of 'reality' and the 'real', the essence of 'world', the being of the 'imaginary' and 'thought', the relation of the human being to language and language to being itself and, last but not least, the constitution of human selfhood. And this constellation in turn articulated with respect to a whole economy of human health and illness, within which an existential phenomenology of psychosis would claim a privileged position. This would not be to oppose an existential phenomenological ontology to psychoanalytic interpretation and tradition but rather to engender a conversation between these movements of modern thought that has hardly yet begun, for the benefit of therapeutic discourse and practice. This conversation, it seems to me, is increasingly urgent with respect to adequately formulating the philosophical and theoretical grounds of a therapeutics that reaches beyond the tendency to individualise, reify and medicalise, such a therapeutics as should perhaps characterise any group analytics and therapeutic community practice.

9 Here, in introducing the question of metaphysics, Heidegger first invokes Hegel's words in which philosophy or metaphysics is described from the vantage of 'sound common sense' to appear as 'the inverted world' or the everyday world

turned upside down. Heidegger continues 'every metaphysical question always encompasses the whole range of metaphysical problems . . . [and] . . . every metaphysical question can be asked only in such a way that the questioner as such is also there within the question, that is, is placed in question' (p. 82). Such questioning of being is prior to scientific investigation of beings and opens the conceptual space, as a region of the being of beings, in which a particular science can then unfold.

10 Commenting generally on the pre-eminence of philosophy in relation to the Greek's view of medicine Gadamer states: 'Plato's suggestion that the physician, like the true rhetorician, must take the whole of nature into view remains valid. Just as the latter must draw on true insight to find the right word which will influence those who listen, so too the physician must look beyond the immediate object of his knowledge and skill if he is to be a true physician' (p. 42).

11 It is perhaps apposite to echo here some remarks by John Gale who recalls here that the therapeutic community movement, in its attempts to think about itself as such, that is, in its engagement with psychoanalytic theory and group analysis was first led to question the appropriateness and provenance of this tradition with respects to its foundations, in a manner which inevitably invoked a conversation with philosophy at its limits. Unfortunately, this engaging conversation seems, however, to have more recently petered out. Gale, in turn, echoes Ylla who claimed that Heidegger's existential ontology 'offers the most genuine philosophical bases for therapeutic communities' (p. 10) 'Philosophic sources underlying diverse aspects which characterise therapeutic communities of psychodynamic orientation' (ibid.). Why and how this might be cannot be explored further here. Yet it might also be noted Heidegger's active role in the attempted conversation between his thought and psychotherapeutic theory and practice through his association with the Swiss psychiatrist, psychoanalyst and Daseinsanalyst, Medard Boss. Boss even states in his book *Psychoanalysis and Daseinsanalysis* that the 'view of man' arising from the *Daseinsanalytik* of Heidegger's thinking 'enables us to see that every human existence consists of a primordial being-with (*Mitsein*) . . . it provides us for the first time sound fundamentals for all the sociological sciences in general and for a social psychiatry and social psychoanalysis in particular' (p. 56). He continues with a statement that could be the leitmotif of therapeutic community thinking that 'no psychopathological symptom will ever be fully and adequately understood unless it is conceived of as a disturbance in the texture of the social relationships of which a given human existence fundamentally consists, and that all psychiatric diagnoses are basically only sociological statements' (p. 56). Also of importance with respect to this question is the collection edited by K. Hoeller, *Heidegger and Psychology* originally published as volume 16 nos. 1, 2 and 3, (1978–79) of the *Review of Existential Psychology and Psychiatry*, Seattle, later reissued as a book in a special edition in 1988; Boss, M. *Existential Foundations of Medicine and Psychology* (trans. S. Conway and A. Cleaves), 1979, London: Jason Aronson. Interestingly, Benedetti (one of the founders of the International Society for the Psychological Treatment of Schizophrenia and the other Psychoses) was for a while under Boss's supervision as Benedetti's training analyst.

12 Searles discusses the importance of therapists engaging in reflective practice with respect to recognising the prevalence of projection and introjection in working with psychotic clients.

13 Freud formulates it thus: 'He builds it up [his world] of his delusions. *The delusional formation, which we take to be the pathological product, is in reality an attempt at recovery, a process of reconstruction*' (p. 71).

14 Tucker here elaborates on the importance of dialogue, from the perspective of its educative function. She highlights the importance of integrating theory, experiential self-learning and supervised practice in the training of therapeutic community therapists. She emphasises the role of the therapist as educator with respect to the client. My emphasis here is perhaps the inverse, the client as the educator of the therapist, insofar as the therapist is able to listen and bear with the clients psychotic disturbance holding in questioning with the client rather than modelling.

15 Stambaugh translates *Gerede* by idle talk. Yet chatter is very rarely idle, rather its concern is with busyness itself.

16 It should be stated that no negative or moralistic judgement is intended through these terms.

17 See Cooper 1989 for an attempt to think about the kind of dwelling made possible within the therapeutic community with the help of Heidegger's thought concerning dwelling For a more philosophically engaged introduction to Heidegger's thought about dwelling see J. Young, What is dwelling? The homelessness of modernity and the worlding of the world, *Heidegger, Authenticity, and Modernity: Essays in Honor of Hubert L. Dreyfus, Volume 1*. (eds) M. Wrathall and J. Malpas, 2000, London: MIT press.

Bibliography

Boss, M. (1963). *Psychoanalysis and Daseinsanalysis* (trans. L. Lefebre). London: Basic Books.

Clark, D. (1999). Social psychiatry: the therapeutic community approach, in P. Campling and R. Haigh (eds) *Therapeutic Communities: Past, present and future*. London: Jessica Kingsley.

Cooper, R. (1989). Dwelling and the 'therapeutic community', in R. Cooper, J. Friedman, S. Gans, J. Heaton, C. Oakley, H. Oakley et al. (eds) *Thresholds between Philosophy and Psychoanalysis: Papers from the Philadelphia Association*. London: Free Association Books.

Cox, J. (1998). Reflection on contemporary psychiatry: where is the therapy? *Therapeutic Communities* 19(1): 3–10.

Freud, S. (1958). Psycho-analytic notes on an autobiographical account of a case of paranoia (dementia paranoides), in *The Standard Edition of the Compete Psychological Works of Sigmund Freud* Vol. XII (trans. and ed. J. Strachey). London: Hogarth Press.

Gadamer, H.-G. (1996). *The Enigma of Health: The art of healing in a scientific age* (trans. J. Gaiger and N. Walker). Stanford, CA: Stanford University Press.

Gale, J. (2000). The dwelling place of meaning, in S. Tucker (ed.) *A Therapeutic Community Approach to Care in the Community: Dialogue and dwelling*. London: Jessica Kingsley.

Gale, J. and Sanchez, B. (2005). Reflections on the treatment of psychosis in therapeutic communities. *Therapeutic Communities* 26(4): 433–447.

Haigh, R. (1999). The quintessence of a therapeutic environment: five universal qualities, in P. Campling and R. Haigh (eds) *Therapeutic Communities: Past, Present and Future*. London: Jessica Kingsley.

Heidegger, M. (1927). *Sein und Zeit*. Tübingen: Max Niemeyer.

Heidegger, M. (1971). Building dwelling thinking, in *Poetry, Language, Thought* (trans. A. Hofstadter). New York: Harper & Row.

Heidegger, M. (1996). *Being and Time* (trans. J. Stambaugh). New York: State University of New York Press.

Heidegger, M. (1998). What is metaphysics?, in W. McNeill (ed.) (trans. F. Krell) *Pathmarks*. Cambridge: Cambridge University Press.

Heidegger, M. (2001). *Zollikon Seminars: Protocols, conversations, letters* (trans. F. Mayer and R. Askay). Evanston, IL: Northwestern University Press.

Hinshelwood, R.D. (2004). *Suffering Insanity: Psychoanalytic essays on psychosis.* Hove and New York: Brunner-Routledge.

Jones, M. (1968). *Social Psychiatry in Practice.* Harmondsworth: Penguin.

Kahn, C.H. (1979). *The Art and Thought of Heraclitus: An edition of the fragments with translation and commentary.* Cambridge: Cambridge University Press.

Lacan, J. (1993). *The Psychoses: The seminar of Jacques Lacan Book III 1955–1956* (trans. R. Grigg). London: Routledge.

Laurent, E. (2004). Three enigmas: meaning, signification, jouissance. *Psychoanalytic Notebooks* 12: 27–40.

Main, T.F. (1989). *The Ailment and Other Psychoanalytic Essays.* London: Free Association.

Main, T.F. (1990). Knowledge, learning and freedom from thought. *Psychoanalytic Psychotherapy* 5: 59–78.

Rapoport, R.N. (1960). *Community as Doctor.* London: Tavistock.

Searles, H.F. (1965). The schizophrenic's vulnerability to the therapist's unconscious processes, in *Collected Papers on Schizophrenia and Related Subjects.* London: Maresfield Library.

Tucker, S. (1998). Dialogue: training for active citizenship. *Therapeutic Communities* 19(1): 41–53.

Tucker, S. (ed.) (2000). *A Therapeutic Community Approach to Care in the Community: Dialogue and dwelling.* London: Jessica Kingsley.

Wilberg, P. (2004). *The Therapist as Listener: Martin Heidegger and the missing dimension of counselling and psychotherapy training.* Sussex: New Gnosis Publications.

Ylla, L. (1990). Philosophic sources underlying diverse aspects which characterise therapeutic communities of psychodynamic orientation. *International Journal of Therapeutic Communities* 11(1): 7–11.

Part 2

Treatment settings and clinical models

The dimensions of meaning and the intertwining of these dimensions, the terms, the tone, the volume of the voice, the gestures, the silences, the repetitions, the discourse of the speaker show that he is situated in his words and that through them he is situated in the events that he recounts.

Henri Maldiney 1961

Chapter 8

The therapeutic community approach in forensic settings

Sarah Davenport

A recent systematic review of papers on therapeutic environments and schizophrenia (Smith 2000) concluded that the optimum environment for inpatients with psychosis should be 'highly supportive, with an emphasis on relationships and orientated towards individual needs. There should be little expression of anger and aggression, a relaxed, non-restrictive regime of care and opportunities for user involvement' (Smith 2000: 37).

The review went on to argue that 'a therapeutic community model, modified to provide high levels of emotional support and individual care, may help' (Smith 2000: 46). This provides an informed view that a therapeutic community-style approach may be beneficial to people with psychosis who need inpatient care. However, there are particular problems in applying this approach to people with psychosis in a forensic setting.

Tension between therapeutic community principles and secure forensic settings

The provision of a therapeutic community in a secure forensic setting generates a fundamental tension between the provision of that therapeutic community approach and the constraints imposed by the structure and organisation of the secure forensic setting. In the latter, the management and reduction of risk is the primary task, whereas in the former, personal growth and social learning are the primary objectives.

The therapeutic community approach demands freedom and equality (democracy) for all participants while a secure forensic setting demands order and obedience to certain guidelines and protocols.

The therapeutic community expects that its residents should be safely *psychologically* contained while the secure forensic setting demands that its residents are safely *physically* confined, to reduce the risks to the general public in the community outside the hospital.

A therapeutic community assumes that it can create its own rules for the safety of its resident community; a secure forensic setting is subject to statutory rules associated with the Mental Health Act and Home Office, to reduce the risks with the resident community.

A secure forensic setting needs safe physical boundaries to prevent absconding, safe procedures to exclude contraband items such as weapons and illicit substances and sufficient skilled staff to engage patients, manage aggression and promote recovery and insight into offending behaviour.

Most if not all patients are detained and some will also be under the supervision of the Home Office. All these restrictions reduce individual choice and individual freedoms, which, in turn, are the basic rights expected within a therapeutic community.

Moreover, opportunities to make personal choices and to be exposed to the social consequences constitute the social learning environment of the therapeutic community. Many personal choices are limited within a forensic setting, including the fundamental choice over whether a person wishes to be there or not. Many are sent from court to receive treatment for their psychosis.

People with psychosis and offending behaviour may not share the same aspirations for treatment as those that work in the setting; they may have limited rights under the Mental Health Act 1983 to refuse treatment.

Assuming, as Jay Smith (2000) does in her review, that the therapeutic community model may be of some help to inpatients with psychosis in a secure setting, the challenge is to deliver care based on conflicting principles, while ensuring that the therapeutic milieu is calm, clearly boundaried and consistent.

There are two different styles of therapeutic community usually employed, the democratic (non-hierarchical) type and the concept (hierarchical) type. While these two models appear to be incompatible, there are commonalities, which lend themselves therapeutically to an intrinsically challenging environment such as a secure forensic setting.

Two basic types of therapeutic community

Democratic therapeutic community (TC)

This model of therapeutic communities originated with Maxwell Jones (Kennard 1998) and was developed as a group-work method to treat people suffering with a range of psychiatric difficulties, although not primarily, psychosis; it uses social learning principles (Jones 1952, 1968).

Rapoport (1960) described the following four principles of democratic therapeutic community treatment:

- *Permissiveness*. Residents can freely express their thoughts and emotions without any negative repercussions (in the sense of punishment or censure).

- *Democracy*. All residents and staff members have equal chance and opportunities to participate in the organisation of the therapeutic community.
- *Communalism* Face-to-face communication and free interaction to create feelings of sharing and belonging.
- *Reality testing*. Residents can be, and should be, continually confronted with their own image (and the consequent impact of that) as perceived by other clients and staff members.

Concept or hierarchical therapeutic community

This type of therapeutic community evolved from a self-help movement for people who abuse substances, where the crucial concept is 'community as method' or 'the purposive use of the peer community to facilitate social and psychological change in individuals' (De Leon 1997: 5).

It comprises the following elements:

- *Community*. Living together in a group and showing responsible concern and belonging is the main agent for therapeutic change and social learning.
- *Hierarchy*. Daily activities take place in a structured setting where people act as if they have no problems and where older residents act as role models.
- *Confrontation*. Negative behaviour, which interferes with the community concepts, values and philosophy, is confronted and the residents are urged to stop the negative behaviour,
- *Self-help*. The resident is the protagonist of his own treatment process. Other group members can only act as facilitators.

There are some commonalities between these two approaches, and recent literature emphasises a gradual tendency towards integration of the two models (Broekaert et al. 2000). Both types are essentially democratic, but address different objectives through treatment; the concept therapeutic community is designed primarily for behaviour change, which is highly relevant to outcome for psychotic offenders. Treatment of illness and modification of offending behaviour is sought.

The democratic therapeutic community promotes social maturation and personality change which is highly relevant to recovery, adoption of non-offending more adaptive social roles and the type of social learning which may improve resistance to relapse for people with psychosis. Essentially both types of therapeutic community aim to achieve social learning with all participants.

The therapeutic community approach in prison settings

Therapeutic communities have been delivered to specific client groups within the British Prison Service, since HM Prison Grendon Underwood was opened in 1962. Grendon followed the democratic (or non-hierarchical) model for a group of personality-disordered men, with a high prevalence of sexual offending. More recently three concept (or hierarchical) therapeutic communities have been opened within the prison system for the specific treatment of drug- and alcohol-dependent prisoners.

Although there is little formal evidence of effectiveness, the fall in reconviction rates following exposure to therapeutic communities as part of a rehabilitation programme has led to renewed commitment to the delivery of therapeutic communities models in prison.

The therapeutic community approach is used in secure units treating people with personality disorders and offending behaviour. The dangerous severe personality disorder units in high secure settings are examples, but are outside the scope of this chapter.

The therapeutic community in a forensic setting

There is as yet no evidence of effectiveness of a therapeutic community approach used in a secure forensic setting for people suffering from psychosis. However, some therapeutic community principles are becoming incorporated into the overall treatment approach in some forensic units. It may be that the tide of change associated with user involvement, the recovery movement and the explicit partnership working proposed in the national service framework for mental health are impacting on service delivery in positive manner. These user-centred initiatives are synergistic with a therapeutic community approach; all focus on respect for the individual patient's views, on empowerment to participate in their own care and to make personal choices about their route to recovery.

Modifications of a therapeutic community approach in a secure forensic setting

The user and recovery movements have influenced inpatient service delivery at all levels of security through the National Service Framework. Service users can be more meaningfully involved at many levels of activity, ranging from their own individual care planning, participation in patient care team meetings, through to service management, development and monitoring. This is probably best developed in rehabilitation services. However, most services now have user forums, which aim to deal democratically with services users views and concerns about the service they receive. These forums vary in their remit, content and effectiveness and the way in which they influence the service management structures.

Most inpatient wards have regular community groups to discuss ward-specific issues; again these vary in content and usefulness in producing user-centred change.

Many mental health units are now involving service user representatives in strategic development, service planning and service monitoring at a level beyond mere tokenism. The degree to which service users receive support and training to participate meaningfully in these activities also varies. The degree to which service management acts on representatives' views is not consistent, but at best, real representation is respected. It can be a powerful force for change, towards a more democratic process and a more recovery-oriented service.

Such groups do provide opportunities for a more democratic exchange of views between service users and staff; they also give a real opportunity to influence the manner in which care is delivered. These groups can increase a service user's sense of belonging within a service and afford opportunities to experience alternative social roles to that of the patient. Participation in such groups may also help to regain a sense of personal responsibility, not only individually but also for those they represent.

These diverse types of group meeting can be used to promote some of the principles of the therapeutic community, e.g. the ward community group can be safely facilitated to promote permissiveness, communalism and reality testing. Used well it can promote a sense of living together in a group and promote responsible concern for others and a safe forum in which negative behaviour such as violence can be challenged.

The manner in which therapeutic community principles can be incorporated into a secure forensic setting is illustrated by the brief case history that follows. The service user on whom this account is based gave her consent for her story to be used here, much as she has contributed to workshops and training events to promote user empowerment and involvement.

Mrs A's story

Mrs A made a remarkable recovery journey from prison, through high security, then to a women-only medium secure service and out to her home in the community. She had a conviction for armed robbery and a diagnosis of schizoaffective disorder. She has recovered to the point where she is living the life she has chosen in her community tenancy; she is in paid employment and lives with her teenage son, for whom she was able to recover parental responsibility.

She received most of her psychiatric care in a medium secure forensic service, on a ward where many of the other women had a psychotic disorder. By her own account, her recovery was most enhanced by the opportunity to participate within a range of user-focused groups as the democratically elected representative of the secure service users. She began by tackling issues to do with food and catering, progressed to setting up a consultation about service user participation in care programme approach reviews and subsequently influenced the provision of advocacy services to the unit. She then trained as an advocate and worked in a voluntary capacity with a local advocacy service before her discharge. Having a job and a social role was central to the recovery of her self-esteem and empowered her to work within the community of the secure service and then outside of it, within 'real life'. She is now a paid employee of the same advocacy service.

While in the secure hospital, she represented herself and her co-residents in management committees, met with service commissioners and described her experiences to a visiting judge, who wanted an update on the service to which he was sending some convicted offenders.

She helped to develop a sense of community on the ward on which she lived for 2 years. She began by proposing a more democratic and communal approach to Sunday lunch; this promoted responsible concerns for each other among the resident group and approximated to 'communalism', one of the four cardinal principles of a therapeutic community (Rapoport 1960). All the women on the ward had a say in the menu planning and food preparation. The meal acted as a focus for discussion of the coming week and often provided items for the weekly ward community meeting. This was facilitated by a member of nursing staff and developed into a forum where the women's concerns could usually be expressed without too much anxiety over potentially negative repercussions. The ward community meeting also served as forum in which some unacceptable behaviour could be challenged and peer feedback given about its impact on other residents. In this manner, it functioned to serve the principles of permissiveness, democracy and reality testing (Rapoport 1960), although the degree of challenge to those more fragile residents often had to be contained or modified by staff.

Mrs A was in the forefront of developing new philosophies to underpin care and treatment. She acted as a powerful role model for the other women. She maintains her role as mentor to some of the other women who remain in the service. She continues to assist the Trust on womens' service development. She became a leader, able to negotiate with other leaders of the service in a responsible and reciprocal manner. She was ever vigilant about the uses and abuses of power within the secure service and able to reflect on them with staff in a manner that promoted a better understanding of the therapeutic community democracy principle.

She acknowledged the importance of the correct medication, appropriate psychological interventions and support to re-establish her family relationships and her family role. She even acknowledged the role of the Home

Office, which was persuaded to grant leave from the hospital for her to train as a national MINDLINK representative. All the team working with her had their own roles in making the system more responsive to her individual needs. Mrs A became the living embodiment of self-help and modelling, working in concert with a more democratically informed and self-reflexive forensic service.

The interventions that made the most difference to her remarkable recovery journey were those opportunities for social learning described above. These are consistent with the core principles of the therapeutic community. Her story lends credibility and weight to the importance of incorporating therapeutic community principles into practice within a forensic setting. As described by Maxwell Jones (1982) respect for the patients' integrity, the unique roles of residents as well as staff and a distinct type of leadership with provisions to check the abuse of power are crucial elements in this approach and, to some extent, were those that promoted Mrs A's recovery. It may be that the necessary focus to add value to a forensic service, should be the application of therapeutic community principles to the existing structures of the unit, e.g. ward meetings and management meetings with proper service user representation. Some dedicated research is needed in this area.

Bibliography

Broekaert, E., Vanderplasschen, W., Temmerman, I., Ottenberg, D.J. and Kaplan C. (2000). Retrospective study of similarities and relations between American drug-free and European therapeutic communities for children and adults. *Journal of Psychoactive Drugs* 32: 407–417.

De Leon, G. (1997). Therapeutic communities: is there an essential model?, in G. De Leon (ed.) *Community as Method: Therapeutic Communities for special populations and special settings*. Westport, CT: Greenwood Publishing Group.

Jones, M. (1952). *Social Psychiatry: A study of therapeutic communities*. London: Tavistock.

Jones, M. (1968). *Beyond the Therapeutic Community: Social learning and social psychiatry*. New Haven, CT: Yale University Press.

Jones, M. (1982). *The Process of Change*. London: Routledge.

Kennard, D. (1998). *An Introduction to Therapeutic Communities*. London: Jessica Kingsley.

Rapoport, R.N. (1960). *Community as Doctor: New perspectives on a therapeutic community*. London: Tavistock.

Smith, J. (2000). The healing elements of an environment for those with chronic psychosis. *Therapeutic Communities* 21: 37–46.

Chapter 9

The treatment of substance use and mental health problems in Bulgaria

Peter Vassilev, Teodora Groshkova and Vassil Jenkov

Background

A variety of contemporary meanings of co-morbidity exist and they are rarely explicitly stated (Starcevic 2005). For the purposes of this chapter, the term is used in its meaning as a diagnostic and clinically significant co-occurrence of two mental health disorders.

Co-morbidity between schizophrenia and substance use disorders (SUDs) is seen at particularly high rates, both compared with the normal population and with patients suffering from other psychiatric disorders. Studies have suggested that up to 60% of patients with schizophrenia have a history of abusing illegal drugs. Cannabis and psychomotor stimulant drugs are abused at particularly high rates by patients with schizophrenia.

Legal drugs are also used at higher rates than in the general population. Between 70% and 90% of patients with schizophrenia have a history of nicotine dependence and approximately 35% have had alcohol abuse problems (Regier et al. 1990). The high rate of co-morbid substance misuse with schizophrenia is not immediately understandable and is, superficially, somewhat paradoxical. Schizophrenia has long been postulated to be associated with hyperactivity within the mesolimbic dopamine (DA) pathway, originating in the ventral tegmental area (VTA) and innervating the nucleus accumbens (NAcc). The DA hypothesis of schizophrenia suggests that the positive symptoms of the disorder result from this DA hyperactivity. Drug taking is also linked to hyperactivity within the mesolimbic DA system. Drugs of abuse cause increases in DA levels within this system and this is thought to underlie their addictive nature (Di Chiara 2002; Robinson and Berridge 1993, 2003). Thus, drug taking by patients with schizophrenia may actually worsen some of their symptoms and make antipsychotic medication regimes more difficult to implement (Duncan et al. 1999; Margolese et al. 2004). So, why would a patient with schizophrenia take a drug that actually exacerbates some of the symptoms of their disorder? There are at least two possible explanations for co-morbid schizophrenia and addiction that must be considered. The first is the self-medication hypothesis, which suggests that drug abuse is a consequence of schizophrenia. Given the evidence for the worsening of some symptoms in drug-taking schizophrenics, this may seem to be an unlikely explanation. However, although this may be the case for some of the positive symptoms of the disorder, there is some evidence for other symptoms being relieved by drug taking. The alternative approach is that there is some common underlying neuropathology that makes an individual susceptible to both schizophrenia and substance misuse.

Patients with schizophrenia and with co-morbid SUD are more likely to have experienced significant trauma during childhood, often on more than one occasion – e.g. death of a parent, abuse, domestic violence – than those without (Scheller-Gilkey et al. 2002), although the cause–effect relationship between these factors is not clear. However, it is clearly possible that SUD may be more common in patients with schizophrenia than in the general population because drugs are being used to help the individual cope with the effects of traumatic and stressful experiences. It is also possible to apply the self-medication hypothesis of substance use to the problem of co-morbid schizophrenia in a more directed manner, linking drug use with specific symptoms. The relatively high rates of alcohol and cannabis use may be due to the effects of these drugs on the positive symptoms of the psychotic disorder, maybe reducing the incidence and/or severity of psychotic episodes or enabling the patient to cope better with such episodes through their anxiolytic properties. However, evidence for these suggestions is limited (Krystal et al. 1999). There is greater evidence to support the suggestion that patients with schizophrenia may use drugs, specifically psychomotor stimulant drugs such as amphetamine and cocaine, in order to ameliorate negative symptoms that they may be experiencing. So-called negative symptoms include motor inactivity, apathy, loss of initiative and social withdrawal. It is thought that such symptoms may result from hypoactivity within frontal cortical regions (O'Donnell and Grace 1998). Drug use is particularly associated with increased levels of dopamine (DA) within the mesocorticolimbic system of the brain, which includes the frontal cortex. It has been reported that patients with schizophrenia smoke less when on medication that is effective in reducing negative symptoms (Lyon 1999). This is also supported by the finding that negative symptoms are less severe in patients with schizophrenia who have drug abuse problems than in those who do not (Green et al. 2004), although the positive symptoms that they experience are worse. Nicotine is by far the most commonly used drug amongst patients with schizophrenia. This preference for nicotine over other drugs of abuse may simply be due to its availability and social acceptability.

However, it is also possible that high rates of smoking are due to nicotine's effects on some of the subtle attention and cognitive deficits from which patients with schizophrenia suffer. It is well established that patients with schizophrenia exhibit deficits in sensory gating, e.g. the ability to pay attention selectively to relevant stimuli, while ignoring irrelevant ones

(Ludewig et al. 2003; Weiner 2003). There is also evidence for the presence of deficits in verbal memory function and on reaction time task performance (Smith et al. 2002). These types of cognitive deficit are ameliorated by nicotine (Larrison-Faucher et al. 2004; Smith et al. 2002) and may, in turn, reduce the severity of the positive symptoms that are thought to be particularly related to the incidence of sensory-gating deficits (Weiner 2003).

An unresolved question has been the role that drugs of abuse have in triggering psychosis in individuals with no previous psychiatric history. The theory that stimulants can cause psychosis through the increase of dopamine concentration in the extra-cellular site does not explain the way in which patients continue to have psychosis when they do not use stimulants. A study by Sekine et al. (2003) reports an association between loss of dopamine transporters and positive symptoms in methylamphetamine abusers with histories of methylamphetamine-induced psychosis. Since dopamine transporters are the main mechanism for removing extra-cellular dopamine concentration, their loss in methylamphetamine abusers could result in high levels of extra-cellular dopamine even when methylamphetamine is no longer present. Other possible explanations are related to mechanisms such as postsynaptic changes, over-adaptation of undamaged dopamine terminals, or improper rewiring of recovering dopamine terminals. In contrast, Volkow (2001) showed an association between dopamine transporter losses in methylamphetamine abusers and psychomotor impairment compatible with decreased brain dopamine activity. Another interesting question is why some methylamphetamine abusers develop psychosis and others do not.

Is cannabis etiologically important in the development of psychosis or do individuals use cannabis to relieve the distress associated with prodromal symptoms? In an historical cohort study of 50,087 Swedish conscripts, Zammit et al. (2002) reported that the use of cannabis during adolescence increases the risk of developing schizophrenia with a dose-dependent relationship. This was also independent of the effects of other drugs or social personality traits. The authors concluded that cannabis increases the risk of schizophrenia by 30%. Similarly, Arseneault et al. (2004) in a recent review on the association between cannabis and psychosis found that cannabis use in adolescence leads to a two- to threefold increase in relative risk for schizophrenia or schizophreniform disorder in adulthood; earlier uptake of cannabis use showed a propensity for greater risk of psychotic outcomes. However, the authors point out that cannabis does not provide a causative factor for the development of psychosis but forms part of a causal relationship. It is important to bear in mind that the knowledge of the possible mechanisms may be limited by the animal models of psychiatric conditions that are presently available. Animal models of both addiction and depression or schizophrenia are a long way from allowing examination of all aspects contributing to the development of such conditions. Relatively few studies have been done investigating the neuropsychology of co-morbidity and it is clear that more research needs to focus on this in order that we may progress in the understanding of co-morbidity. However, there is an important degree of concurrence between the results of animal and those human studies that have been done, which emphasises the importance of animal studies in this context.

Treatment implications

In recent years new approaches to the treatment of the dually disordered client have been developed (Stohler and Rössler 2005). Among those, the application of therapeutic community (TC) model and cognitive-behavioural integrated treatment (C-BIT) will be emphasised, among others, as evidence-based approaches to the treatment of dually diagnosed clients.

Therapeutic community (TCs)

Therapeutic communities have evolved a potent model for modifying drug abuse behaviour and reducing psychological symptoms (Jainchill 1994). The traditional therapeutic community is distinguished from other major drug treatment modalities in several ways, including coordinating a comprehensive range of interventions and services in a single treatment setting, e.g. vocational counselling, work therapy, recreation, group and individual therapy and educational, medical, family, legal and social services. An important feature of the therapeutic community model is that the primary approach to treatment is community-as-method (De Leon 2000), that is the primary therapist and teacher in the therapeutic community is the community itself, consisting of peers and staff members who serve as role models, with staff members also serving as authorities and guides in the recovery process. Residents live together in a drug-free environment, organised and structured, in order to promote changes in attitudes, perceptions and behaviours associated with drug use and make possible a drug-free life in the outside society. In addition to the importance of the community as a primary agent of change, a second fundamental therapeutic community principle is self-help. Self-help implies that residents are the main contributors to the change process. Mutual self-help means that individuals also assume partial responsibility for the recovery of their peers, an important aspect of an individual's own treatment. The community as a whole is seen as providing a crucial therapeutic milieu that occurs 24 hours a day, 7 days a week and serves as a context for continued learning in which individual changes in conduct, attitudes and emotions are monitored and mutually reinforced in the daily regimen (Galanter and Kleber 2004).

The therapeutic community has been recognised as a promising residential model from the substance abuse field for those with substance use and serious mental disorders (e.g. Carroll and McGinley 1998; De Leon 1999; French et al. 1999). The principles and methods of the therapeutic community are being applied to the circumstances of the client, making three key alterations: increased flexibility, more individualised treatment and reduced intensity. The last point refers especially to the conversion of the traditional encounter group to a conflict resolution group, which is highly structured, guided, of very low emotional intensity, geared toward achieving self-understanding and behaviour change. The central feature of therapeutic community treatment is retained: a culture is established in which clients learn through mutual self-help and affiliation with the peer community to foster change in themselves and others.

Cognitive-behavioural integrated treatment approach

The cognitive-behavioural integrated treatment (C-BIT) approach to substance misusing clients with mental health problems is based on the premises of the cognitive therapy model (Beck 1976; Salkovskis 1996), which has been established as an effective treatment of emotional disorders (Clark and Steer 1996). Cognitive therapy has been successfully applied to the treatment of substance abuse, suggesting that an important difference between individuals who use substances in a problematic way and those who do not is the beliefs held about the substances (Beck et al. 1993). Within the cognitive model of substance abuse (Beck et al. 1993; Liese and Franz 1996), cognitions at different levels, core beliefs, dysfunctional assumptions, automatic thoughts and substance-related beliefs, are pivotal in the development and maintenance of addictive behaviour.

Cognitive therapy has also been successfully extended to the treatment of severe mental health problems, particularly psychosis (Fowler et al. 1995). The cognitive model put forward by Tarrier and Calam (2002) emphasises a stress–vulnerability link. According to this model, life stressors, such as family conflict, increase the risk of destabilisation and activation of individual's underlying vulnerability characteristics. The experience of psychosis and the associated experiences are said to be mediated by beliefs. According to the C-BIT of substance abuse in clients with severe mental health problems, developed by Graham, Copello and Birchwood (2003), positive substance-related beliefs are key factors in maintaining patterns of addictive behaviour and poor mental health. Thus, C-BIT aims collaboratively to identify, challenge and undermine unrealistic beliefs about drugs that maintain problematic use and replace them with more adaptive beliefs that will lead to and strengthen behavioural change. It also seeks to facilitate an understanding of the relationship between problem substance use and mental health problems. Finally, it teaches specific skills for controlling and self-managing substance use and the early warning signs of relapse to mental health problems and for developing social support for an alternative lifestyle. An important advantage of a C-BIT intervention is that the psychological, emotional and behavioural issues implicated in the factors leading to substance misuse and mental illness, can be described or formulated and then used to inform interventions (Persons 1989).

Epidemiology of SUDs and co-morbid mental health problems in Bulgaria

The period 1990–2000 saw epidemic spread of substance misuse in Bulgaria. Epidemiological investigations carried out over the last 5 years among adolescents in Sofia and other parts of the country showed that one in four pupils had smoked herbal cannabis. According to expert estimations made by the Ministry of Health the number of people dependent on heroin is around 30,000. The figures for cocaine and cannabis were 5000–10,000 and 80,000–110,000 respectively. Regular amphetamine users were said to be between 10,000 and 15,000. The misuse of heroin in Bulgaria became a real and significant public health issue. The rate of intravenous users infected with hepatitis C has dramatically increased reaching 70% in 2001. The epidemic spread of drug misuse has led to increased demands on the national health system. The number of drug misusing clients in residential/ inpatient treatment has increased more than six times for the period 1990–1999. During 2003 the psychiatric clinics in Sofia treated 1600 heroin-dependent individuals and 1200 clients with alcohol dependency.

Prior to 1990 the common terms used in psychiatry to describe the parallel presence of substance abuse problems and psychiatric problems were secondary alcoholic abuse and symptomatic alcohol abuse. These terms explained symptoms of substance abuse and alcohol dependency occurring in the context of an existing psychiatric problem.

The authors refer to the term 'secondary alcoholism' (ibid., *passim*) to describe alcohol dependency that is directly related to a particular phase of a main psychiatric disorder, e.g. drinking to relieve an anxious or depressive state. In these cases, alcohol use and misuse may mask the underlying psychiatric symptoms and they may not be recognised. Portnov and Petnitskaya (1971) pointed out that unmotivated alcohol misuse is a sign of an endogenous process. In these cases clients often try to normalise their mental state through use of alcohol by self-medicating themselves. An investigation among clients with borderline personality disorder in Bulgaria showed that alcohol dependence is more common among women with this disorder (Onchev 1994).

Treatment of substance dependent individuals with mental health problems in the therapeutic community Phoenix

Clients referred to therapeutic community Phoenix (TC Phoenix) come with a range of different mental health problems, mostly heroin dependence and psychosis. Between two and four cases of clients experiencing psychotic symptoms in addition to their heroin dependence are being referred to TC

Phoenix every year. Others have depression, an anxiety or an eating disorder in addition to heroin dependence. During 2006 two residents with co-occurring depression, one with social phobia and one with bulimia nervosa, have undergone the programme at Phoenix.

Theoretical framework

The TC Phoenix programme has a solid grounding in the existing professional literature that describes the therapeutic community theory and treatment model. Programme activities are logically linked to the theoretical foundation of addictive behaviours change in people with mental health problems. The treatment fully integrates therapeutic community procedures, e.g. clinical groups, community meetings, vocational and educational activities and community and management activities and C-BIT e.g. cognitive case formulation, relapse prevention and specific skills teaching procedures.

Historical background and overall structure of TC Phoenix

TC Phoenix was established in June 2001 by Peter Vassilev, MD, and his team. In 2002 therapeutic community Phoenix became a member of the Association of Therapeutic Communities (ATC) and was involved in the Royal College of Psychiatrists research project Community of Communities, A Quality Network of Therapeutic Communities. In 2003 TC Phoenix became a full member of the European Federation of Therapeutic Communities (EFTC). A link and close collaboration was set up with the Ley Community, Oxford, in 2003. It allowed for exchange of residents and training internships of clinical staff. So far eight people from therapeutic community Phoenix, six staff members and three residents, have undergone practical training at the Ley Community. In September 2003 Anthony Slater, President of EFTC, made a work visit to therapeutic community Phoenix. The same year collaborative links were established with therapeutic community Phoenix Haga, Norway, KETHEA, Greece, and Trempoline, Belgium. This provided opportunities for improved ongoing staff training and integration of the experience of European colleagues. For example, in 2003, two people, one staff member and one resident, from Phoenix, Bulgaria, went through the 1-month rehabilitation training at Phoenix, Haga.

Programme stages

Therapeutic community Phoenix programme is structured in three stages that reflect increased levels of personal and group responsibility. The orientation phase or initial entrance period lasts 2 to 4 weeks and involves bio-psycho-social assessments, introduction to the therapeutic community philosophy and routine, engagement and building motivation for personal change. Primary treatment is a 6-month period of living and working in the therapeutic community, with increasing levels of personal and social responsibility and privileges. The main therapeutic work is towards members' gaining understanding and awareness of their dysfunctional habits, challenging their personal limits and developing skills for relapse prevention. There is also an emphasis on developing and demonstrating leadership skills. The primary treatment stage residents are expected to provide appropriate self-disclosure in groups and present educational seminars to the community. The re-entry stage involves community re-entry over a 1–3-month period, with daily work or education and development of a local social support network; clients live in a safe and sober home environment that continues the therapeutic community philosophy. The resocialisation stage lasts 6 months. The aim is to prepare individuals for a worthwhile life by means of professional skills training, assistance in job searching, family therapy, individual and group counselling and club activities.

Staff selection and qualifications

TC Phoenix staff are qualified and committed to the programme. A supportive environment for staff and encouraging continued professional development, including skills acquisition, values clarification and competency attainment is ensured. A key feature that is present in the list of essential components of treatment at therapeutic community Phoenix is enhanced staffing that incorporates professional mental health specialists and psychiatric consultation. The staff team consists of one psychiatrist, seven psychologists (with either BSc or MSc in clinical psychology), two social workers, a psychiatric nurse and four ex-residents working as volunteers. Two of the staff members are licensed cognitive-behavioural therapists: All staff members have undergone specialised training in the therapeutic community model. The therapeutic community is staffed at all times including evenings and weekends. While the responsibility of running the community is placed on residents, the therapeutic community is ultimately reliant on residents' internalisation of learned concepts and the desire to change, they are a group of individuals who have long histories of poor decision-making and poor impulse control. To effect the cognitive and behavioural changes necessary in many aspects of their lives a broad plan of staff cover is necessary.

Therapeutic approach and interventions at TC Phoenix

Community as method

The therapeutic approach consists of the group and its rules, the culture and expectations. The educational process is a built-up system aimed at stimulating positive behaviour and giving negative responses to the unacceptable behaviour of the residents. It provides a goal and meaning for moving up in the hierarchy in the programme. Each move toward a higher position brings more opportunities for learning. The approach at Phoenix to problem substance use among those with mental health problems is structured but flexible. This refers to the level of expectations for participation in programmed activities as well as to the length of core programme treatment phases. For example, some clients may need to spend as much as 2 months in the orientation phase (that is engagement and building motivation to change), whereas other clients may have already thought about changing their drug use or have made changes themselves.

All activities and interpersonal and social interactions are considered important opportunities to facilitate a resident's individual change. Treatment methods include clinical groups, e.g. encounter group, group for personal growth, relapse prevention group, goal group and groups for persons with similar issues, to address significant life problems and specific issues, community meetings, daily house and general meetings and seminars, to review the goals, procedures and functioning of the therapeutic community, vocational and educational activities to provide work, communication and interpersonal skills training, community and clinical management activities, systems of positive and negative reinforcements for behaviour shaping, learning experience, house ban and daily house runs to maintain the physical and psychological safety of the environment and ensure that resident life is orderly and productive.

One important aspect of the programme is individual treatment plans including residents' main problem areas, treatment goals and an outline as to how problems will be resolved within the therapeutic milieu. At programme entry each resident is allocated a referent – a staff member who is completely engaged with the individual treatment plan of the resident. Treatment planning begins with assessment, covering the following areas: current functioning, patterns of substance use, effects of use, reasons for use and beliefs about substance use, relationship between substance use and mental health and motivation to change and goals. Once an assessment has been carried out the information is used to guide the development of the treatment plan and the case formulation. The client and their referent work together on developing the treatment plan, following it while the resident remains in the programme as well as preparing them for entering the programme for resocialisation. The referent also serves as a main source of support for the resident when it comes to developing the cognitive formulation as well as coping with difficulties in the therapeutic process.

Cognitive-behavioural therapy techniques

Identifying thoughts and beliefs. Three techniques are being applied for identifying problematic thoughts and beliefs: identifying hot thoughts through Socratic questioning, thought diaries, and drug diaries.

Identifying hot thoughts

The key question asked to elicit these key cognitions is: 'What went through your mind just before you last used?' Was it what typically goes through your mind before using? In order to identify positive substance related beliefs, residents will also be asked what they liked about the substance, how they felt the substance was helping them and what they believed the benefits of using the substance were.

Thought diaries

Thought diaries are helpful in providing a functional analysis of the factors that trigger and maintain problematic patterns of thoughts, behaviours and moods. Residents are recording situational and contextual antecedents – where they were and what were they doing when the problematic feelings/behaviours occurred, mood – the feeling they had in this situation and automatic thoughts – the thoughts that went through their mind just before they felt that way (Greenberg and Padesky 1995).

Drug and alcohol diaries

Drug and alcohol diaries are based on the same principle as thought diaries, but the focus here is on providing a functional analysis of substance-using behaviour. Residents are recording the situational and contextual ante-cedents – day, time, where they were and what was happening, thoughts and feelings in the particular situation, behaviour – how much substance they used and money spent and consequences – how they thought and felt after having used. Application of this technique in the therapeutic community is retrospective. However, it allows residents to become aware of the factors that have maintained addictive behaviour, particularly the role of positive substance-related beliefs.

Modifying and re-evaluating thoughts and beliefs: identifying cognitive distortions

One strategy to help residents re-evaluate and modify their beliefs is by identifying any errors in their logical reasoning of why they are using the substances. The distortions in the beliefs/reasons clients give for using/against change allow them to give themselves permission that it is ok to continue using. Reviewing the evidence they use to support those beliefs, clients may find that they are not 100% truthful all of the time.

The Three-Question Technique

Another technique for assisting residents to re-evaluate and modify the positive reasons for use is the Three-Question Technique, where through a series of questions they are encouraged to consider an alternative perspective that reflects, in a balanced way, the evidence (Padesky 1993). The three questions typically used to guide the discussion are the following:

- What is the evidence for that belief?
- Are there times when that is not the case?
- If there are times when that is not the case, what are the implications?

Behavioural experiments

Behavioural experiments give residents the practical opportunity to test out and re-evaluate their beliefs in real-life situations (Greenberg and Padesky 1995). They also allow residents to discover what will happen in these situations, which is often not the same as what they think will happen. Initially behavioural experiments are designed to be carried out in situations in the community life. At later programme stages residents have the opportunity to test out specific beliefs outside.

Case formulation

As part of their treatment residents at TC Phoenix develop and present an individual formulation – a description of their problem within the CBT framework. The cognitive formulation integrates information about residents' early development, schemas, stimulus situations, emotions and maladaptive behaviours. This link between the cognitive and developmental profiles is based on the cognitive-developmental model of substance abuse (Beck et al. 1993). The main purpose of the cognitive case conceptualisation is raising awareness about an individual's dysfunctional mechanism. A final point in the process of development of the conceptualisation at Phoenix is an established procedure: each resident presents in front of the whole community their hypotheses about the following: what factors maintain the current problems, how these problems developed and what relationship exists between the various problems, particularly drug use and mental health problems.

Several other features are present in the list of essential components of treatment at TC Phoenix, including psychoeducational classes, e.g. mental disorders and substance abuse, relapse prevention and specific skills teaching based on Marlatt and Gordon's (1985) model. Some of these components, such as assertiveness training, teach coping methods for specific types of situations: managing negative emotions, interpersonal conflicts. Others, like leisure education, assist the residents in developing more global strategies to manage stress and develop a balanced lifestyle.

Medication

The use of proper medication is an essential programme element, helping clients to stabilise and control their symptoms, thereby increasing their receptivity to programme elements. The staff's role is first to provide the prescribing physician with an accurate description of the client's behaviour and symptoms, which ensures that proper medication is chosen, and then to assist the client in adhering to the medication regimen. Staff and the peer community help and support individual efforts to follow prescription instructions.

Conclusion

The existence of mental health problems in substance misusing clients is a common phenomenon, although research in Bulgaria has found somewhat lower prevalence rates. Co-morbid mental health problems complicate the treatment picture of SUDs. Nevertheless, on the basis of our clinical experience, we suggest that application of an integrated approach of a therapeutic community model and cognitive-behavioural techniques is a promising treatment for clients presenting with co-morbidity. Assessing and understanding clients' problems provides a therapeutic window for modifying idiosyncratic dysfunctional beliefs they hold of drug use, their mental health problems, of themselves, the world and the future.

Bibliography

Alderson, H.L. and Matthews, K. (2006). The neurobiological and neuropsychological perspectives in comorbidity. *ECCAS Monograph* 4: 61–75.

Arseneault, L., Cannon, M., Witton, J. and Murray, R.M. (2004). Casual association between cannabis and psychosis: examination of the evidence. *British Journal of Psychiatry* 184: 110–117.

Beck, A. (1976). *Cognitive Therapy and the Emotional Disorders.* New York: International Universities Press.

Beck, A.T., Wright, F.W., Newman, C.F. and Liese, B. (1993). *Cognitive Therapy of Substance Abuse.* New York: Guilford Press.

Carroll, J.F. and McGinley, J.J. (1998). Managing MICA clients in a modified therapeutic community with enhanced staffing. *Journal of Substance Abuse Treatment* 15: 565–577.

Clark, D.A. and Steer, R.A. (1996). Empirical status of the cognitive model of anxiety and depression, in P.M. Salkovskis (ed.) *Frontiers of Cognitive Therapy.* New York: Guilford Press.

De Leon, G. (1999). Modified therapeutic community for homeless mentally ill chemical abusers: emerging subtypes. *American Journal of Drug and Alcohol Abuse.* Accessed on 21 January 2007 from http://www.findarticles.com/p/articles/mi_m0978/is_3_25/ai_55816079

De Leon, G. (2000). *The Therapeutic Community: Theory, model, and method.* New York: Springer.

Di Chiara, G. (2002). Nucleus accumbens shell and core dopamine: differential role in behavior and addiction. *Behavioural Brain Research* 137(1–2): 75–114.

Di Furia, L., Pizza, M., Gordon, C. and Schifano, F. (2006). The psychological/psychiatric perspectives of comorbidity. *ECCAS Monograph* 4: 77–93.

Duncan, G.E., Sheitman, B.B. and Lieberman, J.A. (1999). An integrated view of pathophysiological models of schizophrenia. *Brain Research Reviews* 29(2–3): 250–264.

Fowler, D., Garety, P. and Kuipers, E. (1995). *Cognitive Behaviour Therapy for Psychosis: Theory and practice.* The Wiley Series in Clinical Psychology. Chichester: John Wiley & Sons.

French, M.T., McCollister, K.E., Sacks, S., McKendrick, K. and De Leon, G. (1999). Modified therapeutic community for mentally ill chemical abusers: outcomes and costs. *Evaluation of Health Professions* 22: 60–85.

Galanter, M. and Kleber, H.D. (eds) (2004). *Textbook of Substance Abuse Treatment* (3rd edn). Washington DC: American Psychiatric Publishing.

Graham, H.L., Copello, A. and Birchwood, M.J. (2003). *Cognitive-Behavioural Integrated Treatment (C-BIT): A treatment manual for substance misuse in people with severe mental health problems.* New York: John Wiley & Sons.

Green, A.I., Tohen, M.F., Hamer, R.M., Strakowski, S.M., Leiberman, J.A., Glick, I. et al. (2004). First episode schizophrenia-related psychosis and substance use disorders: acute response to olanzapine and haloperidol. *Schizophrenia Research* 66(2–3): 125–135.

Greenberg, D. and Padesky, C.A. (1995). *Clinician's Guide to Mind over Mood.* New York: Guilford Press.

Jainchill, N. (1994). Co-morbidity and therapeutic community treatment. *NIDA Research Monographs* 144: 209–223.

Krystal, J.H., D'Souza, D.C., Madonick, S. and Petrakis, I.L. (1999). Toward a rational pharmacotherapy of comorbid substance abuse in schizophrenic patients. *Schizophrenia Research* March 1(35, Supplement): S35–49.

Larrison-Faucher, A.L., Matorin, A.A. and Sereno, A.B. (2004). Nicotine reduces antisaccade errors in task impaired schizophrenic subjects. *Progress in Neuropsychopharmacology Biological Psychiatry* 28: 505–516.

Liese, B.S. and Franz, R.A. (1996). Treating substance use disorders with cognitive therapy: lessons learned and implications for the future, in P.M. Salkovskis (ed.) *Frontiers of Cognitive Therapy.* New York: Guilford Press.

Ludewig, K., Geyer, M.A. and Vollenweider, F.X. (2003). Deficits in prepulse inhibition and habituation in never-medicated, first-episode schizophrenia. *Biological Psychiatry* 54: 121–128.

Lyon, E.R. (1999). A review of the effects of nicotine on schizophrenia and antipsychotic medications. *Psychiatric Services* 50(10): 1346–1350.

Margolese, H.C., Malchy, L., Negrete, J.C., Tempier, R. and Gill, K. (2004). Drug and alcohol use among patients with schizophrenia and related psychoses: levels and consequences. *Schizophrenia Research* 67(2–3): 157–166.

Marlatt, G.A. and Gordon, J.R. (1985). *Relapse Prevention: Maintenance strategies in the treatment of addictive behaviours.* New York: Guilford Press.

O'Donnell, P. and Grace, A.A. (1998). Dysfunctions in multiple interrelated systems as the neurobiological bases of schizophrenic symptom clusters. *Schizophrenia Bulletin* 24(2): 267–283.

Onchev, G.N. (1994). Clinical psychological research of personality disorder of borderline type. Doctoral thesis, Medical University Department of Psychiatry. Sofia: Central Medical Library.

Padesky, C. (1993). *Socratic Questioning: Changing minds or guided discovery?* London: European Congress of Behavioural and Cognitive Therapies.

Persons, J.B. (1989). *Cognitive Therapy in Practice: A case formulation approach.* New York: W.W. Norton & Co.

Portnov, A.A. and Pyatnitskaya, I.N. (1971). Clinical issues on alcoholism in an inpatient department in Leningrad, in A.N. Petrov (ed.) *Alcohol Clinic* [in Russian]. Moscow: Medicina.

Regier, D.A., Farmer, M.E., Rae, D.S., Locke, B.Z., Keith, S.J., Judd, L.L. et al. (1990). Comorbidity of mental disorders with alcohol and other drug abuse: results from the Epidemiological Catchment Area (ECA) study. *Journal of the American Medical Association* 264(19): 2511–2518.

Robinson, T.E. and Berridge, K.C. (2003). Addiction. *Annual Review of Psychology* 54: 25–53.

Robinson, T.E and Berridge, K.C. (1993). The neural basis of drug craving: an incentive-sensitization theory of addiction. *Brain Research Reviews* 18(3): 247–291.

Salkovskis, P.M. (1996). *Frontiers of Cognitive Therapy. The state of the art and beyond.* New York. Guilford Press.

Scheller-Gilkey, G., Thomas, S.M., Woolwine, B.J. and Miller, A.H. (2002). Increased early life stress and depressive symptoms in patients with comorbid substance abuse and schizophrenia. *Schizophrenia Bulletin* 28: 223–231.

Sekine, Y., Minabe, Y., Ouchi, Y., Takei, N., Iyo, M. and Nakamura, K. (2003). Association of dopamine transporter loss in the orbitofrontal and dorsolateral prefrontal cortices with methamphetamine-related psychiatric symptoms. *American Journal of Pathology* 160: 1699–1701.

Smith, R.C., Singh, A., Infante, M., Khandat, A. and Kloos, A. (2002). Effects of cigarette smoking and nicotine nasal spray on psychiatric symptoms and cognition in schizophrenia. *Neuropsychopharmacology* 27(3): 479–497.

Starcevic, V. (2005). Psychiatric comorbidity: Concepts, controversies and alternatives. *Australasian Psychiatry* 13(4): 375–378.

Stohler, R. and Rössler, W. (eds) (2005). Dual diagnosis. The evolving conceptual framework. *Bibliotheca Psychiatrica* 172: 137–156.

Substance Abuse and Mental Health Services Administration, U.S. Department of Health and Human Services (2002). *Evidence-Based practices for Co-Occurring Disorders – The Evolution of Treatment for Co-Occurring Disorders.* Washington, DC: SAMHSA.

Tarrier, N. and Calam, R. (2002). New developments in cognitive-behavioural case formulation. Epidemiological, systemic, and social context: an integrative approach. *Behavioural and Cognitive Psychotherapy* 30: 311–328.

Volkow, N.D. (2001). Drug abuse and mental illness: progress in understanding comorbidity. *American Journal of Psychiatry* 158(8): 1181–1183.

Weiner, I. (2003). The two-headed latent inhibition model of schizophrenia: modeling positive and negative symptoms and their treatment. *Psychopharmacology* 169: 257–297.

Zammit, S., Allebeck, P., Andreasson, S., Lundberg, I. and Lewis, G. (2002). Self-reported cannabis use as a risk factor for schizophrenia: further analysis of the 1969 Swedish conscript cohort. *British Medical Journal* 325: 1199–1201.

Chapter 10

Medication as a tool in therapeutic and rehabilitative programmes in communities for people suffering from schizophrenic disorders

José Mannu and Federica Soscia

Introduction

Psycho-pharmacotherapy as the one and only approach to psychiatric treatment is traditionally considered to be an intervention which is both authoritarian and reductionist. It is considered as authoritarian because it implies a decision taken by the doctor that is poorly negotiable by the patient, conferring him low empowerment, hence, characterised by strong asymmetry; it is reductionist because it considers the person from an exclusively biological standpoint.

Our aim is not to settle the endorsement versus refusal issue of medication use, but to understand whether and which way a community paradigm may modify an intervention (pharmacological) that, besides being a healing tool, has always been the vector of the doctor's power.

To this goal, we will examine how medication prescribing relates with other treatment options in rehabilitative community programmes and whether it constitutes an alternative or one out of many options. We will attempt at identifying possible elements supporting the interdependence between a biological and a community paradigm. As happens with trading, each one of the two parties will have to give up something. The issue is whether a compromise can be accepted by both parties or whether there is a dichotomy, a fracture that cannot heal.

The community paradigm

The community programme addressing rehabilitation deals with what we could define as the preverbal domain:

> Most often the patients we work with appear as if their psychic space is filled with memories of actions and interaction about which they can talk, but which are disconnected from their emotional quality and which seem unavailable for reflexive thought.
>
> (Vansina-Cobbaert 2005: 55)

To tackle this domain implies to enter a context that has not been thoroughly analysed, but that is extremely important during the rehabilitation process. All too often rehabilitation focuses on the visible aspects of rehabilitative practice as, for instance, personal care, communicative skills and occupational placement programmes. In contrast, much less attention is focused on acts taking place before visible results are obtained. Rehabilitation, in other words, does not identify itself with placement in the work environment, but with the programme that precedes this placement and makes it possible. Rehabilitation can be defined as a care process with a definite and testable objective.

The treatment process is the basis of rehabilitation, not its objective. Considering self-care, it is not an element of rehabilitative work, it is only its effect. Rehabilitation is a process whose objective is self-care. Furthermore, the process leading to verbalisation of one's own emotional world or, in other words, to its mentalisation, is a process that is part of the rehabilitative work.

Rehabilitation, in the treatment of psychoses, is therefore an early intervention that must precede psychotherapeutic interventions that require mentalisation and relational abilities, which may constitute objectives rather than starting points. Instead, all too often patients are placed in the community as a last chance, after a long history of treatment failures. Sometimes we assist with the situation of psychotic patients who have been referred to our community after a long period of psychotherapeutic work, in one instance as long as 13 years. Hence, one problem of community rehabilitation is its inappropriate use; although it is not indicated as such, community placement is in many cases connected with the *failure* of previous treatment plans. In our opinion, an appropriate community placement should not be based on time considerations, but rather on contextual and individual ones, e.g. on the careful evaluation of the patient's needs and resources.

The rehabilitative process

It is commonly believed that the objectives of rehabilitation coincide with normal requirements for social life, e.g. personal care, hobbies and personal interests, social skills, getting a job. However, these are only the surface elements of a work that is much more complex and elaborate, being the rehabilitation process in the community but one aspect of the complexity of the entire programme.

If we accept that any therapeutic intervention technique is not applied in a vacuum, but rather in an environment on which it acts and whose influences it absorbs, in the case of a therapeutic community the environment is an integral part of the technique itself. Environmental community therapy is the framework wherein it is possible to structure a reflexive system.

Defining this integral part of the technique is a difficult task, but a large part of it may be identified with the relation:

> Perhaps 'active interpersonal environment' would be more correct, as the milieu can also be non-therapeutic, depending on who is at the centre and what is going on . . . Generally the milieu deals with the practicalities of day-to-day living together. In other words it mediates external reality.
>
> (Berke et al. 2002: 88)

The community environment stimulates the various forms of relations in everyday life. The community environment is not a non-specific variable, but rather an element that must contribute to the therapeutic process through the following:

- The environment must enable the patient to collect experiences that minimised his or her distortion of reality.
- It must promote reality-based and meaningful communication with others.
- It must facilitate cooperation with others, leading to a sense of security and satisfaction.
- It must contribute to the reduction of anxiety and to the enhancement of feelings of well-being.
- It must promote the patient's self-respect.
- It must increase the awareness of the patient as to the possible causes and various manifestations of his or her disorder.
- It must support a mobilisation of the patient's initiative to realise his or her potential creativity and productivity.

(Perris 1989: 107)

Admitting that the environment may be therapeutic, we should try to establish how its therapeutic potential should impact on a condition that represents the sum of interactions between constitutional factors and factors linked to the individual's life context.

Currently, there is an attempt to identify possible endophenotypes of schizophrenia (Keri and Janka 2004; Snitz et al. 2006; Stefanis et al. 2007) that would be present in the patient's genetic material and confer vulnerability to the construction, in the presence of particular life events which may be envisaged as catalysts, of the psychotic process. Cognitive deficits have been proposed to herald this vulnerability (Saperstein et al. 2006).

The deficit hypothesis is important because it prompts us to consider the severity expressed not so much by the florid symptoms of psychosis, the positive symptoms, such as delusions and hallucinations, but by the defects or negative symptoms, such as anhedonia, alogia, lack of motivation, blunted affect etc., and also disorganised ones, such as impaired thinking and relational skills, which place the person in a disadvantaged condition. Rehabilitative and psycho-educational interventions, such as social skills training, cognitive remediation or reduction of expressed emotion, have been conceived with the specific aim to reduce the deficit and disadvantage, to counteract the effects of vulnerability. We believe that community work with people affected by schizophrenic psychosis must precede and make possible such interventions.

Our hypothesis is that community work impinges on social disability and this represents a priority issue because it has to do with the possibility to develop attachment relationships, an essential element for a person's cognitive and emotional development. In a recent naturalistic study carried out in Italian communities hosting mainly psychotic patients (Soscia et al. 2005), we observed that most of the improvement obtained during 1 year of community work was related to improved cognitive abilities, despite no specific cognitive rehabilitation technique aimed at improving such abilities being employed, but instead the rehabilitative work focused on the various pre-symbolic and symbolic relational levels.

In this context, the medication enters in the developing therapist–patient relationship at the pre-symbolic and symbolic level.

Medication

The administration and subsequent action of medication has both a symbolic and a biological value. Concerning the former, medication given in a community context has to give up its role of a necessary prescription and become a contract for an agreed objective. This underlies the compliance versus adherence issue. If compliance is the patient's reliability in following therapeutic prescriptions (Hulka et al. 1976), it re-proposes a doctor–patient relationship characterised by the latter's dependence on the former, but this is what community work is set to counter. Contrariwise, treatment adherence is the patient's informed and conscious adhesion to a treatment programme after having weighed the pros and cons of the programme. The taking of medication should be viewed in this context; it is only a means to reach an optimal state so that other interventions could work better.

Rex Haigh (1999), speaking of the concept of authority in community routines, underlines that 'authority must always remain negotiable – authority is something that exists *between* people rather *in* individuals or policies' (Haigh 1999: 255). Hence, medication cannot function without negotiability and the doctor's authority must take into account this community culture of empowerment. In psycho-education associated with medication, the objective is to obtain better adherence to an overall programme, comprising both rehabilitative work and pharmacotherapy.

The patient in the community brings his own inner world and the modalities of its construction and reconstruction; these modalities are plotted against the construction and reconstruction of the community programme's rules, roles, relations and interactions. The objective of obtaining adherence assumes a meaning inasmuch it is framed within a global reconstruction of the patient's inner world and of relational mechanisms. It is in this perspective that we intend the action of a medication not so much as the treatment, but rather as a means of caring.

Medication from a rehabilitative perspective

The prescription of medication in a community context has to become part of a psychotherapeutic and rehabilitative project; within this project, the medication is the tool that will enable the patient to gain access to all other forms of therapeutic interventions.

Recently we have been witnessing a change in the definition of the target of psychopharmacological therapy and, hence, of its biological value in the treatment of psychosis. This appears to be the consequence of the interplay of many factors, such as enhanced insight into the mode of action and the effects of traditional anti-psychotics, acknowledgement of the potential of a new generation anti-psychotics, increased knowledge of the biological bases of schizophrenia and, finally, a change of paradigm in the way we conceive the relations between medication and rehabilitation in schizophrenia. With the introduction of the first anti-psychotics, the main role recognised for medication in the context of an integrated treatment was that of rendering the patient a reduction in positive psychotic symptoms, which was considered an absolute necessity for psychosocial treatments to be introduced (Keith and Matthews 1984).

The interventions during the crisis and, then, during the course of the illness were considered factors preventing the expression of residual effects inasmuch they favoured treatment continuity outside the hospital, as well as access to rehabilitative interventions. The objective to control positive symptoms and stabilise the patient at all costs, the underestimation of the importance of other symptomatological dimensions and iatrogenicity in the determination of the course of the illness and in the treatment and rehabilitation process itself, all derive from prognostic and ideological errors. Therapeutic pessimism related to the belief that schizophrenia will inevitably progress toward deficit (dementia praecox) prompted crisis interventions. These interventions were taken from short term, rather than a long-term maintenance treatment perspective and led psychiatrists to consider the neuroleptic drug-induced depressive and negative symptoms as an inevitable expression of the illness or, worse, of the healing process. Many a physician mistook extra-pyramidal symptoms as an index of therapeutic effects between 1960s and 1980s. Furthermore, the claim, on the one hand, to treat a biological deficit pharmacologically and, on the other, to rehabilitate the ensuing biological or iatrogenic deficit, was based on a core belief that drug treatment and psychotherapy were two dissociated and independent interventions.

Longitudinal studies on the evaluation of treatment outcome in schizophrenia, the advent of atypical anti-psychotics and the expanded possibility to study their cellular, ultra structural and genomic effects, gradually led to a radical re-examination of these concepts.

A correlation has been shown between the negative dimension and cognitive impairment in schizophrenia (Tamminga et al. 1998). Also, it is the severity of negative symptoms and cognitive impairment more than that of positive symptoms that predicts lack of efficacy of treatment (Schuepbach et al. 2002, 2004) and specifically of rehabilitative techniques and lower quality of life in the long term (Yeung and Chan 2006). Furthermore, the role of side-effects in interfering with functional recovery and in protracting the clinical course of the illness has been recently acknowledged (Voruganti et al. 2000). These effects comprise extrapyramidal movement disorder, hyperprolactinaemia, dystonia, dysphoria, akathisia, tardive dyskinesia and neuroleptic malignant syndrome; the first five are common during neuroleptic intake. The interference with recovery may occur along numerous paths:

- Subjective suffering and stigmatisation connected with the presence of extra-pyramidal symptoms are responsible for reduced compliance with drug treatment and are associated with increased mortality, cognitive dysfunction and movement disorders (Cortese et al. 2004).
- Neuroleptics can worsen some cognitive functions, such as attention, short- and long-term semantic memory, abstraction capacity and semantic organisation, information processing and problem-solving abilities (King and Henry 2002) and cause a negative syndrome that is the expression of deficit. Yet these very cognitive abilities are the main target of rehabilitative interventions.

These side-effects are the expression of neurotoxicity, blockade of neuronal depolarisation, neuronal apoptosis, excessive excitation of some neuronal pathways, namely in the striatum (Gil-Ad et al. 2001). These weaken an already biologically vulnerable organism, reduce the resources that therapeutic–rehabilitative processes are attempting to implement and enhance the social withdrawal most often seen in schizophrenic syndromes.

From the perspective of a rehabilitative process that aims at reducing social disability and at favouring improved quality of life for the patient in the long term, medication must have some characteristics, i.e., efficacy, the ability to counteract autism, but most of all, safety and tolerability, so to ensure patient adherence to the therapeutic programme.

Cognitive dimension and neuroplasticity: a meeting point between medication and rehabilitative intervention

How can medication carry out an anti-autistic action and favour the rehabilitative process?

From a clinician's viewpoint

An ideal anti-psychotic drug should be able to relieve a variety of psychotic and mood symptoms; it should also have an improved cognition profile and insight-enhancing properties to allow the patient to participate actively in treatments and increase his quality of life.

In fact, low level of insight (Rittmannsberger et al. 2004), the presence of cognitive alterations (Malla et al. 2002) and social instability constitute clinical correlates of lack of adherence to treatment (Elbogen et al. 2005), whereas depression (Elbogen et al. 2005) and negative symptoms (Rettenbacher et al. 2004) tend to yield better compliance. The last result should not be taken to mean that it is useful to leave depression and negative symptoms as they are to obtain better adherence; it only means that people with such symptoms before beginning treatment show better compliance, a fact that can be exploited when planning a community intervention.

New-generation anti-psychotics are more tolerable and safe with respect to classical neuroleptics and ensure better adherence to treatment thanks to their reduced tendency to elicit extra-pyramidal side-effects (and consequent neurotoxicity) and increased efficacy on negative (Remington and Kapur 2000)[2] and mood-related symptoms of schizophrenia (Awad and Voruganti 2004). Not only are new-generation anti-psychotics, considered as a class, better than classical neuroleptics for cognition (Keefe et al. 1999), but they also directly and independently improve performance in various neuropsychological tasks (in particular attention, memory and executive functions), with much reduced tendency to extra-pyramidal side-effects (Clemente and Bersani 2004).

Cognitive deficits seem to be present in some patients with schizophrenia, as shown by neuropsychological tests. Cognitive deficits represent a distinct construct compared to other psychopathological dimensions; it affects planning, as well as patient ability to initiate and regulate goal-directed behaviour (Stip 2006). The impact of cognitive impairment on social functioning and on long-term outcome of patients with schizophrenia has been extensively documented (Green 1996; Milev et al. 2005). Neuropsychological measures such as memory, abstraction or problem solving prove to be of crucial importance in social abilities and their alteration is without any doubt responsible for the important functional disability connected with schizophrenia.

Atypical anti-psychotics, therefore, would intervene directly by reducing biological vulnerability factors and contributing, together with environmental protective factors (therapeutic context of the community 'environment'), to construct the rehabilitative process and improvement of quality of life, according to the Skantze et al. (1992) model, based on inter-correlations between the dimensions vulnerability, stress, adaptation and quality of life.

From a biological standpoint

The long-term anti-autistic and rehabilitative action of drugs is linked to the induction of neuroplasticity processes, which are able to reduce the negative effects of altered neurodevelopment and neurotoxicity. Such an action could be important in reversing chronic syndromes resulting from neurotoxicity, i.e. EPS, tardive dyskinesia, secondary autism etc.

According to the neurodevelopmental hypothesis of psychoses,[1] a delay in neuronal migration during the second and third trimesters of pregnancy would lead to neuronal miswiring in the prefrontal cerebral cortex and in the limbic system, with resulting altered neuronal plasticity (Feinberg 1983; Keshavan et al. 1994). Neuronal plasticity enables neurones to reorganise relationships both between and inside brain areas, leading to lasting cognitive and behavioural changes. This process initially underlies a change in neurotransmission-dependent synaptic efficacy, while changes in the long term require the expression of genes and protein synthesis, which lead to changes in neural connectivity. Although the neuroplasticity potential is higher during early developmental stages, it is still a prominent phenomenon in the mature adult brain. In fact, neuroplasticity changes are involved in memory and learning, in recovery after brain damage, in behavioural disorders and in the therapeutic effects of medication and rehabilitative interventions.

Recent animal studies found that atypical anti-psychotics, unlike neuroleptics which induce neuroplasticity only in the limbic system and the striatum (Doraiswamy et al. 1995), are able to increase neuroplasticity in specific cortical areas (Konradi and Heckers 2001) and this increase parallels the improvement in cognitive performance (Gemperle et al. 2003a, 2003b; Le Pen and Moreau 2002). The neuroplastic effects of anti-psychotic drugs may be additive to those induced by the community milieu; in fact, it has been shown that protected social environments increase hippocampal neurogenesis and neuronal plasticity in the rat (Lu et al. 2003); further, novel environments counter the effects of stress on hippocampal neuroplasticity (Yang et al. 2006). The community environment is likely to provide such a protective, stress-reducing environment, which might potentiate the biological effect of anti-psychotic medication.

Anti-psychotic medication within the context of a community therapeutic and rehabilitative programme constitutes a tool that should be rendered available to the patient; but we should never cease to explore the meaning of the medication for the individual patient, as well as what side-effects are considered acceptable by him, in order to guarantee access to the various forms of treatment, intervening in the short term to regulate the crisis but favouring, in the long term, an anti-autistic action. Neuroplasticity constitutes the meeting point as well as the result of the integration of interventions at various levels, whether pharmacological or otherwise, as the common aim is to reduce the patient's social disability, to increase his sense of self-efficacy/empowerment and to improve his quality of life. In this perspective, the drug may more properly become a rehabilitative tool.

Notes

1 For a review see S. Marenco and D.R. Weinberger, The neurodevelopmental hypothesis of schizophrenia: following a trail of evidence from cradle to grave *Developmental Psychopathology*, 2000, 12(3): 501–527.
2 See comment in *Psychopharmacology*, 2000, 148(1): 20–21 and 22–23.

Bibliography

Awad, A.G. and Voruganti, L.N.P. (2004). New antipsychotics, compliance, quality of life and subjective tolerability: are patients better off? *Canadian Journal of Psychiatry* 49(5): 297–302.

Berke J.H., Fagan M., Mak-Pearce G. and Pierides-Müller, S. (2002). *Beyond Madness: Psychosocial interventions in psychosis*. London: Jessica Kingsley.

Clemente, R. and Bersani, G. (2004). Cognitive deficits in schizophrenia and profile of response to different atypical antipsychotics *Italian Journal of Psychopathology* 10: 1.

Cortese, L., Jog, M., McAuley, T.J., Kotteda, V. and Costa, G. (2004). Assessing and monitoring antipsychotic-induced movement disorders in hospitalized patients: a cautionary study. *Canadian Journal of Psychiatry* 49(1): 31–36.

Doraiswamy, P.M., Tupler, L.A. and Krishnan, K.R. (1995). Neuroleptic treatment and caudate plasticity. *Lancet* 345(8951): 734–735.

Elbogen, E.B., Swanson, J.W., Swartz, M.S. and Van Dorn, R. (2005). Medication non-adherence and substance abuse in psychotic disorders: impact of depressive symptoms and social stability. *Journal of Nervous and Mental Disease* 193(10): 673–679.

Feinberg, I. (1983). Schizophrenia: caused by a fault in programmed synaptic elimination during adolescence? *Journal of Psychiatric Research* 17(4): 319–334.

Gemperle, A.Y., Enz, A., Pozza, M.F., Lüthi, A. and Olpe, H.R. (2003b). Effects of clozapine, haloperidol and iloperidone on neurotransmission and synaptic plasticity in prefrontal cortex and their accumulation in brain tissue: an *in vitro* study. *Neuroscience* 117(3): 681–695.

Gemperle, A.Y., McAllister, K.H. and Olpe, H.R. (2003a). Differential effects of iloperidone, clozapine, and haloperidol on working memory of rats in the delayed non-matching-to-position paradigm. *Psychopharmacology* (*Berlin*) 169 (3–4): 354–364.

Gil-Ad, I., Shtaif, B., Shiloh, R. and Weizman, A. (2001). Evaluation of the neurotoxic activity of typical and atypical neuroleptics: relevance to iatrogenic extrapyramidal symptoms. *Cellular and Molecular Neurobiology* 21(6): 705–716.

Green, M.F. (1996). What are the functional consequences of neurocognitive deficits in schizophrenia? *American Journal of Psychiatry* 153: 321–330.

Haigh, R. (1999) The quintessence of a therapeutic environment, in P. Campling and R. Haigh (eds) *Therapeutic Communities: Past, present and future*. London: Jessica Kingsley.

Hulka, B.S., Cassel, J.C., Kupper, L.L. and Burdette, J.A. (1976). Communication, compliance, and concordance between physicians and patients with prescribed medications. *American Journal of Public Health* 66(9): 847–853.

Keefe, R.S., Silva, S.G., Perkins, D.O. and Lieberman, J.A. (1999). The effects of atypical antipsychotic drugs on neurocognitive impairment in schizophrenia: a review and meta-analysis. *Schizophrenia Bulletin* 25(2): 201–222.

Keith, S.J. and Matthews, S.M. (1984). Schizophrenia: a review of psychosocial treatment strategies, in J.B.W. Williams and R.L. Spitzer (eds) *Psychotherapy Research: Where are we and where should we go?* New York: Guilford Press.

Keri, S. and Janka, Z. (2004). Critical evaluation of cognitive dysfunctions as endophenotypes of schizophrenia. *Acta Psychiatrica Scandinavica* 110(2): 83–91.

Keshavan, M.S., Anderson, S. and Pettegrew, J.W. (1994). Is schizophrenia due to excessive synaptic pruning in the prefrontal cortex? The Feinberg hypothesis revisited. *Journal of Psychiatric Research* 28(3): 239–265.

King, D.J. and Henry, G. (2002). The effect of neuroleptics on cognitive and psychomotor function: a preliminary study in healthy volunteers. *British Journal of Psychiatry* 160: 647–653.

Konradi, C. and Heckers, S. (2001). Antipsychotic drugs and neuroplasticity: insights into the treatment and neurobiology of schizophrenia. *Biological Psychiatry* 50(10): 729–742.

Le Pen, G. and Moreau, J.L. (2002). Disruption of prepulse inhibition of startle reflex in a neurodevelopmental model of schizophrenia: reversal by clozapine, olanzapine and risperidone but not by haloperidol. *Neuropsychopharmacology* 27(1): 1–11.

Lu, L., Bao, G., Chen, H., Xia, P., Fan, X., Zhang, J. et al. (2003). Modification of hippocampal neurogenesis and neuroplasticity by social environments. *Experimental Neurology* 183(2): 600–609.

Malla, A.K., Norman, R.N., Manchanda, R. and Townsend, L. (2002). Symptoms, cognition, treatment adherence and functional outcome in first-episode psychosis. *Psychological Medicine* 32(6): 1109–1119.

Milev, P., Ho, B.C., Arndt, S. and Andreassen, N.C. (2005). Predictive values of neurocognition and negative symptoms on functional outcome in schizophrenia: a longitudinal first-episode study with 7-year follow-up. *American Journal of Psychiatry* 162(3): 495–506.

Perris, C. (1989). *Cognitive Therapy with Schizophrenic Patients*. New York: Guilford Press.

Rapoport, R.N. (1960). *Community as Doctor. New perspectives on a therapeutic community*. London: Tavistock.

Remington, G. and Kapur, S. (2000). Atypical antipsychotics: are some more atypical than others? *Psychopharmacology* (*Berlin*) 148(1): 3–15.

Rettenbacher, M.A., Hofer, A., Eder, U., Hummer, M., Kemmler, G. and Weiss, E.M. (2004). Compliance in schizophrenia: psychopathology, side-effects, and patients' attitudes toward the illness and medication. *Journal of Clinical Psychiatry* 65(9): 1211–1218.

Rittmannsberger, H., Pachihnger, T., Keppelmuller, P. and Wancata, J. (2004). Medication adherence among psychotic patients before admission to inpatient treatment. *Psychiatric Services* 55(2): 174–179.

Saperstein, A.M., Fuller, R.L., Avila, M.T., Adami, H., McMahon, R.P., Thaker, G.K. et al. (2006). Spatial working memory as a cognitive endophenotype of schizophrenia: assessing risk for pathophysiological dysfunction. *Schizophrenia Bulletin* 32(3): 498–506.

Schuepbach, D., Hill, S.K., Sanders, R.D., Hell, D., Keshavan, M.S. and Sweeney, J.A. (2004). Early treatment-induced improvement of negative symptoms predicts cognitive functioning in treatment-naive first episode schizophrenia: a 2-year followup. *Schizophrenia Bulletin* 30(4): 837–848.

Schuepbach, D., Keshavan, M.S., Kmiec, J.A. and Sweeney, J.A. (2002). Negative symptom resolution and improvements in specific cognitive deficits after acute treatment in first-episode schizophrenia. *Schizophrenia Research* 53(3): 249–261.

Skantze, K., Malm, U., Dencker, S.J., May, P.R. and Corrigan, P. (1992). Comparison of quality of life with standard of living in schizophrenic out-patients. *British Journal of Psychiatry* 161(12): 797–801.

Snitz, B.E., Macdonald, A.W. III and Carter, C.S. (2006). Cognitive deficits in unaffected first-degree relatives of schizophrenia patients: a meta-analytic review of putative endophenotypes. *Schizophrenia Bulletin* 32(1): 179–194.

Soscia, F., Ruberto, A., Girardi, P., Torricelli, D.F., Mannu, J., Recchi, G. et al. (2005). Approccio evidence-based alla valutazione del trattamento comunitario: Outcome di pazienti psichiatrici nelle comunità terapeutico-riabilitative del Lazio. *Psichiatria e Psicoterapia* 24: 273–290.

Stefanis, N.C., Trikalinos, T.A., Avramopoulos, D., Smyrnis, N., Evdokimidis, I., Ntzani, E.E. et al. (2007). Impact of schizophrenia candidate genes on schizotypy and cognitive endophenotypes at the population level. *Biological Psychiatry* 22 (Supplement 1): S19–20.

Stip, E. (2006). Cognition, schizophrenia and the effect of antipsychotics. *Encéphale* 32(3 Pt 1): 341–350.

Tamminga, C.A, Buchanan, R.W. and Gold, J.M. (1998). The role of negative symptoms and cognitive dysfunction in schizophrenia outcome. *International Clinical Psychopharmacology* 13 (Supplement 3): S21–26.

Vansina-Cobbaert, M.J. (2005). A therapeutic community: a space for multiple transitional change, in G. Amado and L. Vansina (eds) *The Transitional Approach in Action*. London: Karnac.

Voruganti, L., Cortese,L., Oyewumi, L., Cernovsky, Z., Zirul, S. and Awad, A. (2000). Comparative evaluation of conventional and novel antipsychotic drugs with reference to their subjective tolerability, side-effect profile and impact on quality of life. *Schizophrenia Research* 43(2–3): 135–145.

Yang, C.H., Huang, C.C. and Hsu, K.S. (2006). Novelty exploration elicits a reversal of acute stress-induced modulation of hippocampal synaptic plasticity in the rat. *Journal of Physiology* 577(Pt 2): 601–615.

Yeung, F.K. and Chan, S.H. (2006). Clinical characteristics and objective living conditions in relation to quality of life among community-based individuals of schizophrenia in Hong Kong. *Quality of Life Research* 15(9): 1459–1469.

Chapter 11

Consent, accountability and the future of therapeutic communities in the light of accompanied self-rehabilitation: the chemical asylum and the right to be socially sanctioned

Alberto Fergusson in collaboration with Alba Realpe

Introduction and background

The principles and the phases of accompanied self-rehabilitation and the understanding of psychosis as a process of psychological destruction and decomposition (PDD) have been described since 1997 (Fergusson 1997, 2000, 2001; Diaz et al. 2004). Working since 1976 with people diagnosed with schizophrenia, I was able to describe and develop the approach that he initially called accompanied auto-analysis and later accompanied self-rehabilitation (AS).[1] Recognising failures was a key to adopting a humble scientific attitude. This together with a profound awareness of the extent to which we ignore how both the mind and the brain work and how little we know about psychosis and schizophrenia led to this new approach. In fact, available scientific knowledge is not sufficient, in our opinion, to justify many of the diagnoses that we make, the treatments we recommend or the prognosis that we establish (Breggin 1994; Harding and Zahnizer 1994; Szasz 1999). It is, in fact, time to honour Emil Kraepelin who in 1901 wrote, with considerable intuition: 'It is true, that in the strictest terms, we cannot speak of the mind as becoming diseased' (Szasz 1999).

The only way forward seems to be to hand over the responsibility and the leadership of the rehabilitation process to the accompanied person. They have to assume, as far as possible, full responsibility for themselves and for their rehabilitation process. This was the origin of the two key words, self-rehabilitation (initially auto-analysis) and accompanied. Since the beginning in accompanied self-rehabilitation, we have insisted that people with disabilities should be the leaders of their own rehabilitation process. Among other things, this enables them to become experts in their illnesses and in themselves and to redesign their everyday life according to such expertise. This is very clear when we look at the mentally ill, especially people diagnosed with schizophrenia. After several observations, we have concluded that consent and accountability are the main tools through which people are really able to become leaders of their rehabilitation processes.

We have observed that if consent and accountability are present, leadership on the part of the patient will be natural and up to certain point inevitable. In the philosophical statement of accompanied self-rehabilitation, as it was initially presented at St Elizabeth's Hospital in Washington, DC, in April 2001, one can see that both concepts are essential to the whole approach:

> So-called mentally ill people have been subject to too many forced treatments: forced into psychiatric hospitals, forced out of hospitals, forced out of their families, forced into their families, forced out of their communities, forced into their communities, forced into psychiatric medication, forced out of medication, forced into certain lifestyles, forced out of other lifestyles and so on.
>
> Parallel to that the tendency has been not to hold them accountable for their acts. The approach that we call Accompanied Self-rehabilitation tries to change both trends. We propose that so-called mentally ill people should be forced the least possible and that they should be held accountable for their acts as much as possible. Many things can be said to support this approach, but it is enough if we remember that forcing oneself or being forced by others to feel and act in certain ways, is frequently in the first place one of the most important causes of so-called mental illness or what we prefer to call mental injury and destruction.
>
> (Fergusson 2001: 1)

The first part of the statement has to do with consent and the second part with accountability. In fact, the best way to make sure that someone is not being forced is to guarantee that real consent took place and that he/she had real choices. Although the word consent is frequently used and although we often have lengthy documents elaborated by lawyers that are usually signed by all the parties involved, unfortunately, real consent is seldom present in everyday practice within the mental health professions. It is part of human nature to demand that consent should be allowed for, and when consent is honoured, people tend to feel accountable for their actions. Nevertheless, it is also true that within that same human nature, there are forces, which possibly originate during the long years of infantile dependency, that tend to avoid consent and let others consent for you. In such cases, people also tend to avoid accountability for their actions.

Recently we have added a new phase to those originally described for accompanied self-rehabilitation (Fergusson 1997). We go through this phase together with the person who is entering the process and with anybody else that might be actively involved for whatever reason. During this phase we try to build an agreement that will secure, as far as possible, that consent and accountability will be central to the process at all times. We discuss and explain why it is that the rehabilitation process can only happen if such agreement is honoured, throughout the process as far as possible. Currently this is a prerequisite to begin the process of accompanied self-rehabilitation as such and usually it takes several months before we can enter the next phase. We have come to recognise that one of our greatest mistakes in the past was precisely that the evaluation and the preparation phase was extremely short and somewhat superficial. In fact, this is not an uncommon mistake in mental health activities. We are talking of a period during which both the accompanied and the accompanying person take enough time to decide if they can work together. This is, of course, a bilateral evaluation process and not an old style unilateral evaluation in which the expert, the therapist, used to evaluate if he/she would accept the patient. In our approach it is crucial that the accompanied person does a thorough evaluation of his/her therapist or therapists and we try to create conditions where he/she has a real choice. One of the most complicated problems in institutions (and most therapeutic communities are institutions) is that they tend to require therapists and patients to work together to suit the needs of the institution rather than those of the patient and the therapist. Nevertheless, we still use the classic therapeutic community and will continue to do so in the future, for all those people that have special difficulties in achieving a reasonable level of consent and accountability.

It could be argued that if consent and accountability were firmly established no further therapy would be needed. In a certain sense, that is true. In this process we find the same thing that strategists have discovered with respect to war, that you first have to win the war in your own mind before you go to the battlefield. That is exactly the case with any rehabilitation process. If, right from the beginning, you manage to obtain those attitudes – after all consent and accountability are, in the long run, mainly attitudes – you can guarantee that you are on the right track. As the right to fail and try again, in any part of the process, is essential to the accompanied self-rehabilitation approach, everybody can try again and again until they familiarise themselves with the importance of consent and accountability. However, the most important point we wish to make with regard to consent is intimately related to scientific knowledge. Power in medicine and in any health profession is closely related to the control of diagnosis, treatment and prognosis. As this is done in the name of science, the consequences are serious. We then face a very complicated practical and ethical problem. In fact the prognosis of mental illness usually becomes a self-fulfilling prophecy. It is interesting to notice how we suddenly change what we think and say depending on whether we are with other professionals or with patients. In scientific and academic settings we are perfectly comfortable to admit that science ignores much with regard to the way the mind and the brain work. Whereas when we are in front of patients we suddenly seem illuminated, as if by magic, and we tell them exactly what is wrong with them (diagnosis), what they should do with it (treatment) and what is going to happen to them (prognosis). We speak with an amazing sense of certainty. It is here, that the most complicated issues related to consent emerge. Accompanying and accompanied persons tend to assume, usually in good faith, that their diagnosis, treatments, prognosis and consent processes are scientifically based. As a result they are misled. During the new preparatory phase we currently take all the time that is necessary to show, based precisely on all the available scientific data, that it is currently very difficult to justify the diagnosis, treatment plans and prognosis of a mental illness. In order to obtain a valid consent, the person must have enough clarity with regard to the current state of scientific knowledge in matters related to the mind, the brain and human behaviour. It is also true that only a therapist or caregiver who has the same clarity is in a position to ask for consent in the right way.

Case example

JB was diagnosed, according to *DSM-IV-TR Fourth Edition* with disorganized schizophrenia. He was told that he had a chemical disease that was currently incurable and that he had to be on medication for life. He was told that there was serious scientific evidence with regard to the organic and genetic causes of the disease. He was advised that psychotherapy was sometimes useful and that he should learn about the external and internal events that triggered his crisis. Emphasis was made in the fact that if he kept taking his medication and if he was serious with his psychiatric monthly appointments, he could most probably lead a reasonably healthy life.

JB came to our programme to obtain a second opinion. We agreed in principle with the DSM-IV diagnosis. He joined our study groups where he began to learn the basics of AS and to study different theories about schizophrenia, ranging from biological psychiatry to anti-psychiatry, including the systemic, cognitive and psychoanalytic points of view among others. After that he realised that he had several choices and that he had to become the leader of his own rehabilitation process. He realised all that science ignores about the mind and so called mental illness. He found the International Classifications of Functioning (WHO 2001) especially useful for his rehabilitation process. He was then ready to face choice, consent and accountability.

Once consent for any treatment or rehabilitation process is obtained, within this context, accountability begins to happen naturally. People tend to feel accountable for their actions if they follow on from real consent. The best excuse to avoid accountability is to feel that you have been somehow forced. That is why we say that consent and accountability are part of the same psychological process. One of the consequences of deploying the process of accountability is that a peculiar right that we have called the 'right to be socially sanctioned' (Fergusson 2007) begins to emerge, especially in those diagnosed with schizophrenia. In fact, one of the most complicated and serious forms of discrimination against them, is not to sanction them socially, while at the same time declaring them legally unfit, although this last issue varies significantly from country to country. We have observed that there is a tendency of any society to deprive the mentally ill of their right to be socially sanctioned. This type of discrimination is paradoxically presented as a privilege. A typical example of what we have just seen occurs when, on the one hand people diagnosed with schizophrenia are denied jobs just because of their diagnosis, but, on the other hand, society tends to forgive them if they steal something because they are known to be suffering from so-called schizophrenia. This is another example of the tendency, on the one hand, to discriminate against such persons in many ways, while on the other not holding them accountable for their actions. In our opinion, both tendencies should be reversed. Obviously some extreme cases and situations should be considered un-indictable and should not be sanctioned socially (Szasz 2005). We frequently tend to apply to the majority what is applicable only to a minority. Most people diagnosed with schizophrenia, especially after they recover their capacity for consent and accountability, should also recover, as soon as possible, the right to be treated both legally and socially as any other citizen with all their rights and duties.

Consent and accountability and the future of therapeutic communities

We are currently facing great changes in the way we understand therapeutic communities. For example Al-Khudhairy (2000) discussed the different meanings of community besides the simple geographical designation. She said that: 'People today have many technological ways of keeping in contact, and these may provide a sustaining way of keeping one's membership of a community in between actually meeting with people.' And later: 'In a dispersed community, people can engage in a commitment-to-struggle together in different ways' (Al-Khudhairy 2000: 177). Some therapeutic communities in Europe, which in the past applied psychoanalytic principles and enjoyed some success, disappeared after a few years. Others became institutionalised. This was the case in the UK at Mill Hill with Maxwell Jones, at Fulbourn Hospital, Villa 21 and Kinsley Hall. The same was the case with Paul-Claude Racamier's community in Besançon France and Basaglia in Italy (Kennard 1983; Pedriali 1997).

In our case, we have been working in a therapeutic community for more than 25 years, using the general principles of accompanied self-rehabilitation together with most of the classical principles of therapeutic communities

(Rapoport 1960). As we have mentioned, consent and accountability have been paramount in the process. We have gradually come to realise that new forms of therapeutic communities have developed worldwide with great success. It could be the case that some of them should not be called therapeutic communities any longer. Nevertheless, some of them do owe their very existence to traditional therapeutic communities. Those of us who have worked within the therapeutic communities paradigm must join forces to conceive new ways to understand and accompany all those that will continue to be diagnosed as mentally ill, especially those with schizophrenia. In doing so we need to preserve the key elements that come from the therapeutic community tradition while developing new modalities of treatment more suited to the present time. Yet no matter what these new developments are we will continue to need to use traditional therapeutic communities for some people for certain periods of time, possibly in some cases even for life. We must never forget that traditional therapeutic communities were especially effective in uncovering many of the abuses of the old asylum. They greatly helped to diminish coercion, stigmatisation and discrimination in general. They showed the road to recovery, but frequently failed to achieve it, in our view mainly because they were never able to avoid some of the basic problems of institutionalisation. At least that is our experience of therapeutic communities. In one way or another it is time to move further. Hinshelwood (2004) seems to agree with this when he writes:

> I shall suggest that the distress of the inmates and their carers affects the institution itself. The institution as an entity is consumed by the same psychotic processes – but on a different scale. That is to say the organization itself subverts meanings, and treats personal identity as a highly impersonal thing.
>
> (Hinshelwood 2004: 108)

No matter how hard we try to develop healthy institutions, they will always be in a complicated struggle to create a culture in which freedom and creativity thrive. It would not make sense to deny that, as well as their enormous achievements, therapeutic communities in the past have failed, in many ways, to achieve their own goals. Furthermore, they have complicated side-effects. In our opinion, and as far as we know, consent and accountability could never really develop within traditional therapeutic communities. Currently, in our group, we only use the more traditional therapeutic community model for a minority while always trying to preserve the main links that the person has with society. Frequently, people benefit from the challenge of new and real living environments and it is important to avoid the artificiality that we sometimes observe in the relationships that develop in therapeutic communities. We must, therefore, prepare ourselves for new developments, including what we call the new virtual therapeutic community (VTC) and the multi-accompanying person (MAP) approach. The internet, with all its possibilities, has generated a great revolution in favour of those diagnosed with a mental illness. Just as an example, in AS where it is crucial for the accompanied person to become an expert in his/ her illness, the internet enables the patient to become much more informed, despite the undeniable risks it may have due to the quality of such information. One of the most important features of the internet is its ability to bring together large numbers of people from diverse backgrounds. Some may argue that most internet-based relationships are pathological. But this is just the latest in a string of moralistic and discriminatory arguments that have no evidence to support them. People have the right and we would add that those diagnosed with schizophrenia have the obligation towards themselves to relate to others with creativity, without moralistic restrictions (Fergusson 1998, 2000). One of the main goals of accompanied self-rehabilitation is to redesign everyday life with creativity especially with regard to relations with other human beings and this has become much easier thanks to the internet. Contrariwise, the practice of accompanied self-rehabilitation and of other forms of psychotherapy has changed as a result of the internet. All of these are also examples of what we now call the multi-accompanying person (MAP) approach. In this approach the accompanied person chooses his accompanying persons or therapists. It does not have to be just one and the choice rests with the accompanied person. Of course, the consent of the accompanying person is also needed.

According to our view, new developments coming from therapeutic communities should be based on recognising that the leadership of the whole process must be in the hands of the so-called mentally ill person and that as far as possible institutions should not be allowed to develop. According to accompanied self-rehabilitation, becoming an expert in oneself and redesigning everyday life according to that expertise, will continue to be central to the process, together with new ways to facilitate consent and accountability. We have described the rights of the accompanied person and the importance of consent and accountability with regard to them. But what about accompanying persons, such as therapists or caregivers?

Strange as it may seem, in practice it is frequently the case that the accompanying persons do not really consent to work with the patient. This is either because they are employed and have to take on cases that are assigned to them by a manager or by a computerised referral system or because the financial constraints of private practice mean they end up accepting most of the people who come to them.

We are beginning a new transitional era involving complex but fascinating challenges. It has been interesting to realise that our effort to create a therapeutic community where people do not live together has been tried elsewhere. In fact, whatever we do, contact with other accompanied and accompanying persons will always be crucial. When we emphasise the importance of the patient becoming the leader of the treatment process, this by no way means to underplay the importance of interactions with other people.

In any new developments we must be careful to avoid the complicated side-effect of the developments in psychopharmacology, which we refer to as the establishment of a chemical asylum (Fergusson 1988). Although people with a mental illness are no longer placed in asylums and remain living in society, they are sophisticatedly coerced by the chemical asylum created by their medication. This is because psychiatric medication is frequently given without real consent. As far as it is reasonable and humanly possible, the accompanied person should decide on their medications, as in all other aspects of the treatment process. We must on the other hand recognise that most of the non-pharmacological approaches to handle psychosis were developed in therapeutic communities. Recently, we made a very simple observation. In a typical modern city building chosen at random, we found that more than 80% of the people were taking some sort of psychiatric medication but only 5% of those reported really having given their consent to take their medication. The main failures that had occurred in the consent process had to do with the lack of real education and information with regard to the medications side-effects and the lack of different choices and alternatives offered to handle their mental suffering, whatever it happened to be.

Conclusion

There is enough evidence to show that therapeutic communities are responsible for some of the most important developments in understanding and taking care of people diagnosed with so-called mental illnesses. It is also true that using the general principles of AS, it is possible to understand why therapeutic communities have not been able to meet some of their own goals. Only if and when the leadership of the rehabilitation process is assumed by the accompanied person and when consent and accountability become paramount to that process will it become really possible to achieve greater treatment efficacy and avoid the institutional side-effects that therapeutic communities have been struggling with for decades. That leadership on the part of the accompanied person should be the essence of new developments in the rehabilitation process, both in therapeutic communities and in other settings.

Note

1 We have serious doubts with regard to words and concepts such as but not limited to therapist, patient, treatment, rehabilitation process, mental illness, mental

health, schizophrenia, madness, psychosis and so on. The reader must always assume a slight pause, as it were, before those words wherever they appear in this chapter.

Bibliography

Breggin, P. (1994). *Toxic Psychiatry*. New York: St. Martin's Griffin.

Diaz, S., Fergusson, A. and Strauss, J. (2004). Innovative care for the homeless mentally ill in Bogotá, Colombia, in J. Jenkins and J. Barrett (eds) *Schizophrenia, Culture and Subjectivity: The edge of experience*. Washington, DC: Cambridge University Press.

Fergusson, A. (1988). *The Chemical Asylum*. Paper presented at the meeting of medical staff executive committee, Fungrata, Bogotá.

Fergusson, A. (1997). *The Technique of Accompanied Auto-analysis and the Theory of Psychosis as Psychological Destruction and Decomposition*. Paper presented at the 12th ISPS conference, London.

Fergusson, A. (1998). La normalidad a la luz de la locura, in A. Perez (ed.) *Monografías, Foros y Debates Clinicos*. Bogotá: Universidad de los Andes.

Fergusson, A. (2000). Accompanied autoanalysis: an emphatic approach. *Ethical Human Sciences and Services: An International Journal of Critical Inquiry* 2(1): 9–20.

Fergusson, A. (2001). *On Accompanied Self-rehabilitation*. A paper presented at the meeting of medical staff executive committee, St Elizabeth Hospital, Washington, DC.

Fergusson, A. (2007). *Social Sanctions in Mental Illness*. Paper presented at the meeting of medical staff executive committee, Fungrata, Bogotá.

Harding, H.M. and Zahnizer, J.M (1994). Empirical correction of seven myths about schizophrenia with implications for treatment. *Acta Psychiatrica Scandinavica* 90 (Supplement 384): 140–146.

Hinshelwood, R. (2004). *Suffering Insanity: Psychoanalytical essays on psychosis*. Hove: Brunner-Routledge.

Al-Khudhairy, N. (2000). The changing idea of community, in *A Therapeutic Community Approach to Care in the Community*. London: Jessica Kingsley.

Kennard, D. (1983). The rise and fall of moral treatment, in *Introduction to Therapeutic Communities*. London: Routledge.

Pedriali, E. (1997). Italian therapeutic communities: from historical analysis to hypotheses for change. *Therapeutic Communities* 18(1): 3–13.

Rapoport, R.N. (1960). *Community as Doctor*. London: Tavistock.

Szasz, T. (1999). Is mental illness a disease? *The Freeman* 49: 38–39. Accessed on 16 May 2007 at http://www.szasz.com/iol10.html

Szasz, T. (2005). Idiots, infants, and the insane: mental illness and legal incompetence. *The Freeman* 55: 26–27. Accessed on 16 May 2007 at http://www.szasz.com/freeman9.html

World Health Organization (WHO) (2001). *International Classification of Functioning, Disability and Health*. Accessed on 22 May 2007 at http://www.who.int/classifications/icf/site/intros/ICF-Eng-Intro.pdf

An exploration of the term autonomy: attitudes and philosophy for a modern concept in mental health

Raúl Gómez and Beatriz Sánchez España

The concept of autonomy, as it is used in relation to the chronic mentally ill, needs to be coherently defined if we want to achieve an authentic intervention that is therapeutic and rehabilitative. This is particularly relevant for therapeutic communities (TCs) that treat people with psychosis, as it touches on some fundamental principles. The key questions here concern the nature of autonomy and whether our interventions are oriented towards the promotion of the patient's autonomy or simply at getting them to adapt.

Defining autonomy

Autonomy as having one's own life under control

There are at least two different ways of understanding the concept of autonomy[1] in the context of patient functioning. First, autonomy can be understood as the patient's ability to carry out tasks without depending on social or health services. In other words being able to be independent without any need for support. Second, autonomy can be understood as having one's own life under control. Being able to direct one's own actions so as to be able to carry out the tasks one wants to do, whether one needs help to achieve these or not. The concept of autonomy as we develop it in this chapter follows the latter definition. It is a view that comes from the Enlightenment, specifically from Kant and one which has recently been revived by José Antonio Marina (1997). It is a concept we consider central to the therapeutic communities approach.

Psychosocial rehabilitation, a philosophy of intervention

Autonomy, according to Marina (1997), does not imply a lack of commitment but the choice to commit, the intelligence applied to direct one's own behaviour. Those disorders that produce an incapability of adapting or a suffering that does not seem to be based on any objective difficulty is considered a mental illness. There is always a loss of autonomy here. The patient is excessively vulnerable to a given situation and feels unable to change it. Whereas happiness consists of recovering an acceptable degree of autonomy, e.g. an extended capability of controlling one's own behaviour to come out safely at the other end. The majority of the pathological behaviours represent the wrong way to resolve a situation, like for example, delusions and compulsive behaviours. The aspiration of human intelligence, its claim to autonomy, is to find the right path and not just any path.

The old aspiration to be the owner of oneself, which was the ideal of a conscious life, has been preserved, in the modern era, in the different ways of understanding autonomy that have proliferated in the discourses of philosophy, literature and social sciences. Autonomy, understood in this sense as a faculty and a distinctive feature of individuals, is one of the central concepts of the Enlightenment. In the formulation of Mill (1997), one is free to look for happiness in one's own way. Here, autonomy is understood, not as a condition, but as a faculty that one has to exercise, because nobody is autonomous per se, but one makes oneself autonomous. Yet nobody can be autonomous in isolation and therefore creating a network of inter-subject relationships that respect the autonomy of each individual becomes the goal. Hence psychosocial rehabilitation can be described as a philosophy of intervention.

Therapeutic communities and their understanding of autonomy

In the UK, psychiatry began to be questioned in the 1970s particularly by those working in therapeutic communities. The questions they asked were about the nature of mental illness and the role of professionals. Psychiatrists and psychoanalysts, such as Cooper (1967), Laing (1967), Lacan (1988) and Basaglia (1968) published books that became historic in the anti-psychiatry movement (Kennard 1998). They questioned whether the role of professionals was to preserve the social peace by getting mentally ill people to behave in a way that was socially accepted or to help them become healthy individuals by promoting autonomy.

There are three fundamental attitudes we need to consider when reflecting on the relationship between professional and patient and they lie at the centre of the concept of autonomy and the principles of therapeutic communities. They are that the patient has agency, empowerment and democracy.

There are two attitudes that we need to avoid when relating to people with mental health problems. To treat them as infants and to act as parents by satisfying their demands (Tarí García and Dozza de Mendoza 1995: 32). We should avoid thinking that the patient does not fully understand what is going on around them and that they do not understand unless we use a form of regressive communication. There are times when we do not fully explain things to patients because we assume it might be unhelpful. What this attitude does is to contribute to the patient's dependence and chronicity. By the same token, attending to the constant demands of the patient does not mean necessarily that we are acting therapeutically. We should avoid giving into our patient's demands without careful consideration. Sometimes this might be anxiety provoking for us, however, by giving in to them we keep them in a dependent position.

In a therapeutic community, patients are given agency (Haigh 1999). Patients are treated as adults and are given as much responsibility as possible. This was one of the main interventions Bion made in the first therapeutic communities in the UK in 1943. Bion was given the challenge to change the training wing of a military hospital in Birmingham, in which soldiers were recovering from the traumas of war. The wing was chaotic and the patients were given the responsibility to solve it (Harrison 2000). In therapeutic communities patients are asked to participate actively in the running of the household and taking full responsibility for whatever social culture the community adopts. Whether this is a predominantly healthy and open culture in which everyone is progressing in their journey and contributing towards the journey of others or whether this is a predominantly unhealthy and closed culture, in which members of the community are isolated and maintain a disruptive environment, in both scenarios, patients are held just as responsible as staff for its maintenance or for taking the necessary steps to change it. In this way the power relationship between therapist and patient is reversed and this modification gives back the dignity and respect that a person suffering from psychosis deserves and this is intimately linked to the concept of autonomy. All residents in a therapeutic community have the opportunity to say what they think and to be listened to by other residents and staff, and they also have the opportunity to make decisions that are collective. 'Residents are trusted and encouraged to take responsibility and initiative' (Kennard 1998: 22). Thus there are both rights and responsibilities for patients in a therapeutic community and this is one of the core principles for re-integration in the wider society.

Raising the professional's expectations

Professionals in mental health services always need to remember that low expectations of what patients can achieve can establish a vicious circle in which reduced hopes diminish opportunities by reinforcing the assumption of low achievement. If a mental health professional has the idea that a mentally ill person cannot work, most probably he will transmit this attitudes to the patient who will accept it. Moreover, employers believe the experts and resist employing the mentally ill (Perkins 2005).

Challenging the idea of the professional as the expert: democratisation and dialogue

Autonomy enables patients to take control over their own lives. The relationship developed between professionals and patients, where the professional is seem as the expert, can be compared with how the teacher–student relationship develops when the leader is the one believed to have all the knowledge and the student a passive recipient of the knowledge to be delivered. This is what Buber (1965) classifies as the compulsory model of education in which the master uses directive approach and tells the student how things are and what to do. When this type of relationship takes place in the mental health field, it serves to hide the inability of the professional to acknowledge that as the patient develops the professional will not always have all the answers. This could be seen as a defence and if it is not effectively identified can become a barrier hindering the development of a therapeutic alliance. The patient with psychosis wants to be understood in each plea he makes to the professional. From here comes his constant question: Do you understand? But we should also know and accept that it may also cover the accusation 'You do not understand!' Accepting one's ignorance leads to respecting the tendency of patients to draw a veil over a psychotic episode, as if it were a tragic experience. The therapist should allow the patient to follow his own rhythm and deepen his discourse only when he is ready.

Flattening the hierarchy is one of the key principles of therapeutic communities. This is a condition of democratisation and allows for freedom and shared power. This sharing of power means that professionals take decisions on behalf of patients as little as possible. 'Each member of the community should share equality in the exercise of power in decision-making about community affairs – both therapeutic and administrative' (Kennard 1988: 163):

> The relation we enter into with clients is not one of carer to passive, essentially helpless people, stuck in their isolation, who require looking after. Rather it is one of tutor student who have the capacity to actively learn, participate and eventually take responsibility for their own lives, entering into relation with other people and the world around them.
>
> (Tucker 1998)

Conclusion

In a therapeutic community, autonomy is understood as the capability of the patient to lead his own actions to manage constructively different situations. The principles of democratisation, liberty, equality, social participation and responsibility underlie the notion of authority. It is a concept that situates the subject within an ethical dimension in that it refers to the possession of rights as well as responsibilities. This is central in the treatment provided by a therapeutic community, as patients are believed to have agency and are given the responsibility to take an active part in the life of the community.

Note

1 Autonomy comes from the Greek words *auto*, self, and *nomos*, custom or law and means, in general terms, the capability of taking decisions without the help of anybody else. It opposes to heteronomy, to being under the domination of an outside authority and is not about a condition, but about a faculty that is learnt.

Bibliography

Basaglia, F. (1968). *L' Istituzione negata*. Torino: Einaudi.

Buber, M. (1965). *I and Thou*. Edinburgh: T. & T. Clark.

Cooper, D. (1967). *Psychiatry and Anti-Psychiatry*. London: Tavistock.

Haigh, R. (1999). The quintessence of a therapeutic environment: five universal qualities, in P. Campling and R. Haigh (eds) *Therapeutic Communities: Past, present and future*. London: Jessica Kingsley.

Harrison, T. (2000). *Bion, Rickman, Foulkes and the Northfields Experiments*. London: Jessica Kingsley.

Kennard, D. (1988). The therapeutic community, in M. Aveline and W. Dryden (eds) *Group Therapy in Britain*. Milton Keynes: Open University Press.

Kennard, D. (1998). *An Introduction to Therapeutic Communities*. London: Jessica Kingsley.

Lacan, J. (1988). Book I: *Freud's Papers on Technique* (ed. J.-A. Miller). New York: W.W. Norton & Company.

Laing, R.D. (1967). *The Politics of Experience*. Harmondsworth: Penguin.

Marina, J.A. (1997). *El misterio de la voluntad perdida*. Barcelona: Anagrama.

Mill, J.S. (1997). *Sobre la Libertad* (trans. P. de Azcarate). Madrid: Alianza Editorial.

Perkins, R. (2005). Más allá de la independencia de los Servicios Sociales y de Salud Mental: apoyo, control y oportunidad, *La salud mental es cosa de todos*. Ministerio de Trabajo y Asuntos Sociales. Colección Documentos. Serie Encuentros 108–113.

Tarí García, A. and Dozza de Mendoza, L. (1995). Estrategias asistenciales para pacientes graves: un intento de conceptualización, *Revista Área* 3: 29–40.

Tucker, S. (1998). Dialogue: training for active citizenship, *Therapeutic Communities* 19(1): 41–53.

Chapter 13

Holding structures in a crisis centre: an applied psychoanalytical model

Tamar Schonfield and Kannan Navaratnem

The Arbours Crisis Centre is a small therapeutic community that applies psychoanalytic thinking to its therapeutic work with very disturbed individuals as well as to the conceptualisation of its own structures. In the first section of this chapter, we introduce the structures of the Arbours Centre in terms of its psychological function and meaning. In the second, we discuss the work with one individual.

The crisis centre (CC) was one of a number of communities which developed out of R.D. Laing's radical anti-psychiatric experiments of the 1950s and 1960s. These included Kingsley Hall, the Philadelphia Association, Soteria and others in Britain, France, Italy, Israel and the United States of America. They were also influenced by an earlier generation of social psychiatrists, such as Maxwell Jones and Tom Main, who had pioneered therapeutic communities in psychiatric hospitals.[1]

The centre has evolved over the years and has become more structured, from its radical early days, but it still combines psychodynamic thinking within a sociodynamic framework, working with the individual as part of a group, within the community milieu (Berke et al. 2002). The Arbours Crisis Centre's particular approach is based on the therapeutic community model, enriched by modern psychoanalytic thinking.

The structure

The underlining philosophy of the centre is that the endeavour to find meaning, by connecting seemingly disparate experiences and moving towards a sense of internal unity (Symington 1986) is curative and can help individuals regain a degree of autonomy and take responsibility for themselves. The individual with his or her particular personality and needs, is the focus of the centre's thinking. Our technique fits around them. This is true in relation both to our guests, as residents at the centre are referred to and to our Resident Therapists, who live and work with them. The structure of the Arbours Crisis Centre has evolved over the past 35 years in response both to intrinsic needs and to external demands. It provides a network, which holds together not only the guests' experiences but the centre's creativity as well. We would like to introduce the work and the structure of the CC through making sense of what they might mean.

In his paper 'On Psychotherapy', Freud (1904/1953) lists the criteria for suitability of patients for psychotherapy and says:

> Psychoses, states of confusion and deep-rooted depression are . . . not suitable for psycho-analysis; at least not for the method as it has been practised up to the present . . . I do not regard it by any means impossible that by suitable changes in the method we may succeed in overcoming this contra-indication – and so be able to initiate psycho-therapy of the psychoses.
>
> (Freud 1953: 264)

Over the century since this was written, many changes have been tried in and out of mental hospitals.[2] The thinking behind such changes was based on the understanding of the particular needs of borderline and psychotic patients, living with intense feelings and anxieties, which are truly unbearable. In order to benefit from psychoanalytic therapy and attempt to make sense of their experiences, these patients need structures that can help them bear that which is unbearable and process emotions with which they cannot live. Independent living is not an option for people trying to reach areas within themselves, which have been locked away for safety reasons. Analysts and therapists working with these patients also need support since they too find the anxieties and the projections too difficult to bear on their own.

Over the decades, a number of therapeutic communities have been established to support patients and therapists involved in this kind of work. In this respect, the crisis centre occupies an unusual and unique position as a modified therapeutic community. The structure of a therapeutic team which carries the primary responsibility of working with the individual, in individual therapy, is central to its community life (Berke 1995). What we hope will emerge in this chapter is that, through its 'psychoanalytically informed practice of living-together routines' (Hinshelwood 2002: 11), the centre often functions at its best when psychotic actions are met with therapeutic actions as well as reflective thought in the therapy conducted in the group and the milieu of the community.

The Arbours Crisis Centre is housed in a nine-bedroom Edwardian terraced house in north London, which is home to three resident therapists, who live there for up to three years. They invite into their community six houseguests for limited periods of up to 6 months at a time. The resident therapists and the guests, as patients are referred to at the crisis centre, form the house group. The choice of the phrase 'guests' denotes two meanings. One is the actual status of people who are invited to stay as houseguests.

They have their own set of keys and are expected to become gradually more involved in the practical chores. The other is the crisis centre's attempt to minimise the potential institutional atmosphere in the house.

This house group is supported by people who work at the crisis centre on a sessional basis. Some are nearly full-time workers, such as the administrative assistant, who coordinates crisis calls and office work and the centre and nurse managers, who coordinate administrative and nursing matters and others who spend only a limited time in the house.

Among those there is a small group of trainees on placement, who visit regularly over a period of 6 months, an art and a movement therapist and a group of experienced sessional therapists who are referred to as team leaders. The team leaders provide individual therapy for the guests as well as supervision and support for the resident therapists, the trainees and other people involved in the crisis centre.

People can refer themselves or be referred to the crisis centre by their health or social workers. A few are able to fund their stay on their own, but most need to apply for funding from health authorities and social services. As funding is becoming more difficult to come by, some authorities would only fund those people who they consider as having exhausted all their resources. The crisis centre is seen as the last resort for people who by their ways of dealing with their own anxiety produce intolerable levels of anxiety in their carers. Although occasionally people come to us in need of a short crisis intervention, these days many of our guests come after some hospital stays, diagnosed with severe mental illness and modes of coping with their troubled feelings which have become life threatening. We hope that our clinical presentation will illustrate the severity of the psychological difficulties and problems facing our guests and how we address them. Therapeutic intervention in the crisis centre takes place in terms of three interlinked holding structures, the individual, the group and the milieu.

The team: therapy for the individual

Individual therapy in the centre is carried out in a team setting. This is a variant of the usual setting for one-to-one individual psychotherapy (Berke 1995). The guest has three (or more) weekly team meetings with their team leaders, resident therapists and, at times, a trainee therapist as well. The team is a closed group defined by its membership, by time (three 50-minute sessions), and space (the room) and is held by a weekly supervision session not attended by the guest. One-to-one psychotherapy, per se, is not carried out in the crisis centre.

Groups

The house group changes on a predictable roll-in/rollout basis. It meets for three weekly formal group sessions and also has weekly art therapy and movement therapy with sessional therapists. Another weekly house meeting, the creative, as it is called, involves the trainees as well. This is a themed meeting, led in turn by members of the group who volunteer to run it and it is supported by a short debriefing meeting of the resident therapists and trainees and by their group's weekly supervision, facilitated at present by a team leader. The resident therapists, who are involved in all group therapy, are also supported by one supervision session with the director and another one with an external consultant psychotherapist. Each resident therapist has individual supervision with one of the team leaders as well as individual therapy or analysis independent of the crisis centre or the Arbour's umbrella.

The milieu

The milieu includes everyone involved in the crisis centre and all that happens in the house. Although a much looser structure, involving the everyday lives of many people, there is still a differentiation between the house group, involving the nine people who live in the community, and all the others who are usually absent in the evenings and during the weekends. The milieu is held by supervisory spaces such as the Wednesday clinical meeting, the trainees' and the resident therapists' supervision group and the fortnightly process group involving all staff members.

In describing each of these therapeutic structures, we have tried to define their boundaries and support systems or, in other words, that which holds the structures. In talking about holding we are referring to its therapeutic function in the way Winnicott describes it. Regarding analytic work with borderline patients, he argues that the clarity, reliability and stability of the analyst's attitude and of the therapeutic structure are essential (Winnicott 1963/1990). Borderline patients in his view need to be able to develop dependency and 'may take a long time to get there because of all the tests that have to be made by the patient who has become very wary because of previous experiences' (ibid.: 240). The analyst 'holds' the patient by indicating that he knows and understands the anxieties the patient experiences. 'What is not called for', he adds, 'is cleverness' (ibid.: 238).

At the crisis centre, the three resident therapists, in their function and through their presence, provide the lynchpin of the organisation. The fact that they share their lives with the guests and participate in all therapeutic structures provides continuity between the different areas of life and treatment. However, their ongoing relationships with the guests expose them to huge demands from the guests, in the form of testing and the expression of needs, only some of which can be met. They are also exposed to powerful projections of anxieties and emotions. It is not to be expected that they will be able to contain and maintain a therapeutic stance all the time. The centre is not only the resident therapists' workplace, but also their home and the major focus of their existence during their period of stay. Their relationships with the guests vary in terms of the quality of the space in which they are located. First there is the safely bound team space, where the resident therapist can feel protected by the team leader. The formal groups provide clear boundaries, but the resident therapists are in the frontline, with no team leader between them and the guests. In the more open-ended everyday life in the house, the resident therapists, like the guests, are exposed and vulnerable. The intensity of the experience can be overwhelming and institutionalisation is a risk of which we are constantly aware. It is for this reason that resident therapists can hold the post for no longer than 3 years.

In supervision, the resident therapists have the opportunity to internalise a paradigm of a well-defined thinking space, which can help them cope with their unbound relationships with the guests. They have the time and distance from the house to think about their experiences, to begin to unravel their own reactions and to think about what they are carrying for the guests.

The team leaders are able to provide support and supervision not only because of their experience and further education. They differ from the resident therapists in having only a limited involvement with the centre, so are less affected by the day-to-day anxieties and less subjected to the powerful projections. This allows them to regain and maintain their own reflective space and to support the house group through supervision and their availability on call.

In fact, like with radiating ripples in the water, the further one is from the centre, the weaker the experience of the anxiety borne there. In this way, the crisis centre is held by a few professionals and services who are not directly involved in its daily life and therefore are more able to bear the anxieties. These include a consultant psychiatrist, who sees the guests occasionally to oversee their medication but is kept informed by receiving the minutes of the Wednesday clinical meeting, a consultant psychotherapist who supervises the resident therapists' group and a senior psychoanalyst providing us with a monthly clinical seminar. We also rely on the local GP practice, NHS hospitals and even the police to be there when we reach our limits.

What happens in these well-defined but interlinked spaces within the crisis centre can be thought about in the light of Bion's theory of thinking (Bion 1970). The container/contained relationship, in which raw emotions and fears can be projected into the object, transformed and reintrojected as meaningful experiences, can provide a model to the therapeutic functioning of these spaces. The roles of container/contained fluctuate on the group level as much as in individual work. Another way of thinking about what we do in the centre follows the work of Michael Parsons, who develops Winnicott's idea of the centrality of play in psychoanalysis (Parsons 1999) and argues that what enables a serious, deep, exploratory and at times risky engagement between participants in an analytic relationship is the framework within which it is practised. In Parsons' view, the framework defines the activity as having a play element. The quality of play depends on maintaining a paradoxical position. The activity can be accepted as real, only if we know that it is not real. In other words, within the framework of therapy, the participants can engage in real experiences but without these carrying the meaning they would normally carry. This is possible only as long as the therapeutic frame is safe. Once the actual or psychological framework collapses, play is no longer possible, reality takes over and there is a risk of enactment. An enactment can have a therapeutic value, but only when, at a later stage, all participants can engage in re-establishing the framework.

One game that is played in the crisis centre forms part of its support for guests who want to reduce their medication. As an organisation, the crisis centre is philosophically and practically committed to the idea that use of medication may be harmful, addictive and can get in the way of feeling and of thinking. Here we are very much in tune with the findings of Mosher and his colleagues (Mosher et al. 1995) in the United States of America, and Armelius in the Netherlands (Armelius et al. 2002) in challenging the prevalent wisdom of pharmacological and hospital-dominated treatments. At the crisis centre, with the guidance of the centre's psychiatric consultant, we enable guests to reduce their medication gradually. However, giving up can produce anxiety in people who have been dependent on medication for a long time. Acknowledging these anxieties, the resident therapists may offer a sweet to replace a pill a guest has given up. Those sweets, which are kept, and given out with the medication, are provided by Joe Berke, the centre's founder and director and are known as JB's sweets. The use of Joe Berke's name in this game denotes both his paternal role as the director, but also the commitment to an ideology he represents. By choosing a 'JB', the guests reaffirm their own commitment to reducing their medication.

One evening when there was no medication for the guests because of a technical blunder, the resident therapists offered 'JBs' instead. But not everyone was pleased with this solution. A guest, Ms F, who in the past had been keen on dropping all her medication at once, was scathing. The game of which the sweets are part is based on an agreement that the sweets are not pills, but can stand for pills if people choose to drop their real pills. Choice is essential for sustaining this paradox but offering sweets in this case, in the absence of real pills, was not based on choice and the JB sweets became just 'stupid kiddies' things' as Ms F called them, a patronising trick to sweeten the guests and cover up a real failure.

An illustration of therapeutic work with a guest

This is a story of the therapeutic journey of one of our guests, which we believe, exemplifies the function and use of the holding structures described earlier.[3]

Ms O, a woman in her late 20s, was referred to the crisis centre by the ward team of a large psychiatric hospital. She had spent the best part of the preceding year as an inpatient, following an emergency psychiatric assessment, after she became seriously depressed and suicidal. This inpatient admission was the ninth in a psychiatric history that had spanned a period of 11 years. Ms O first came to the attention of the psychiatric services during her training in one of the healthcare professions. She had become depressed and taken an overdose. She terminated her training soon after that. In the years that followed, she was treated with antipsychotic, psychotropic medication and Lithium as well as several courses of electroconvulsive treatment. Diagnostic labels included depression, schizo-affective disorder and borderline personality. The symptoms included bingeing, excessive weight gain, repeated major overdoses, acts of deliberate self-harm such as swallowing of razor blades, cutting of wrists and dramatic and perilous attempts to kill herself by jumping in front of trains. Some psychological therapy had been provided. Family therapy sessions were taken up by the family without any follow-up and a referral to a well-known inpatient psychotherapy unit in the NHS was initially considered unsuitable. Later, when it seemed a possibility, Ms O refused this. A referral was later made to the outpatient psychotherapy department. However, it was felt that in her vulnerable psychiatric state there was a greater risk of self-harm and that she could not be held as an outpatient.

The voluminous notes accompanying the referral letter was enough for us at the crisis centre to anticipate a very difficult guest. It was not clear to us if the centre's therapeutic environment would be adequate in meeting her need for physical and psychological safety, after the kind of concrete environment of a psychiatric ward. It was also doubtful if she could make use of the symbolic nourishment and verbal interactions of the centre's milieu after the many years of her dependence on a variety of medications. Her psychiatrist stated in the letter of referral that she had been a constant user of the health service resources and it had become clear that all available psychiatric help had been exhausted. We were later to understand that the tone of exasperation and hopelessness expressed in that letter was what Ms O herself felt about her predicament.

What we knew of the early childhood and family history of this guest was as follows. Ms O was the oldest of three siblings. By the time she reached the age of 4, both her sisters had been born. The father had held a sensitive post in the armed forces, which necessitated the family's moving around various countries. This had a disruptive and fragmenting impact on the young family. The father was later involved in a major accident in which he became physically disabled. When Ms O was 12 years old, all the children were sent to boarding school. The following year the mother developed an interest in a career for herself and underwent training, and later gained employment, in the commercial sector. The father's slow recovery and early retirement led the parents to move to the country. Ms O's description of her father was of a cold and distant man. She regarded her mother as more tolerant and emotionally warm, but she had no memories of any intimacies with her mother. She had reported that physical affection was not shown in the family, either between the parents or between the children and parents. She did, however, state that her maternal grandparents were important to her and there was warmth and emotional closeness in her relationship to them. The parents were now in their 50s.

Ms O was seen for three consultation sessions at the centre and was accepted for a long stay of 6 months. When she attended the pre-stay meeting (a preliminary session which allows the guest, resident therapist, the team leader and, sometimes, a psychotherapy trainee on placement to meet together for the first time as a team), Ms O was uncommunicative at the beginning. She appeared very depressed and seemed to sink inside her immensely overweight body (her weight at the time was over 21 stones). She was heavily medicated and there was a marked psycho-motor retardation in her speech and bodily movements. Later, however, she spoke of her anxiety about the two nurses hovering outside the consulting room. They had escorted her from the hospital. Ms O said that she felt like killing herself just to get at the nurses. They were only there to make sure that they could get rid of her. Ms O said she was pleased to see that we were not in uniform and that she could talk to us.

It felt a significant moment of interaction when she asked the resident therapist if she was allowed to help herself to a cup of coffee or tea in the kitchen. When the resident therapist replied in the affirmative and pointed out that, if she accepted our offer of a stay, the centre would become her home. She was free to help herself at anytime to whatever she wanted in the kitchen. Ms O said that this house seemed an unusual place, unlike a hospital or a ward. She added that, in the hospital, she had become used to carrying her own thermos flask around. The nurses only allowed her in the ward kitchen at certain specified times. She then acknowledged that this freedom in the centre would be very difficult for her to cope with, although she told us know that she very much wanted to start her stay at the centre. During this meeting, in our countertransference, we felt intimidated by the presentation of her obesity, which seemed to concretise a ferocious internal opposition to life and the murderous rage she felt towards her objects. However, we also felt that we were able to make emotional contact with someone who was struggling to make sense of herself and seemed interested in forming relationships.

Initially, Ms O was often unable to speak about her depressive feelings and her urges for self-destructiveness. She was emotionally and verbally inarticulate (Berke 1995) and understanding her silence as communication seemed crucial (Khan 1965). However, in the months that followed, much hard work was done tolerating and working through in our countertransference feelings (Brenman-Pick 1985; Carpy 1989). The task of the team was to go on attempting to understand the apathy, depression, rage and resignation we felt in ourselves, while in team meeting after team meeting, Ms O sat silently looking at the floor, rejecting our attempts to make any contact with her.

Nevertheless, we noticed a change after some weeks. Ms O was beginning to form an attachment and some dependence on the resident therapist. The house meetings and the informal social spaces facilitated Ms O in relating to the resident therapist with more openness and warmth and lessened her paranoid anxieties and fears about contact. Ms O's competitiveness and rivalry with other guests in the house also became more apparent in her transactions. In the team meetings, by contrast, Ms O continued to be silent and tearful. Attempts to work with communication and meaning were met with her contempt and denial of any internal life. We then began to understand the extent to which split transference was beginning to emerge and we worked with this in the team. When important events and trans-actions happened in the house the resident therapist and sometimes, the trainee, brought these up directly as transference issues in the team. Otherwise, the team leader took on the interpretive focus and work on the transference while the resident therapist and the trainee retained active but silent listening roles. However, after the formal team meetings, they reverted their roles in helping Ms O to digest the team meetings. It felt necessary for a continuous shift between these two modes of teamwork and the structures of the house group and the team made such an alternation possible.

Although Ms O continued to make use of some of the team meetings in this way, and despite her depression seeming to lift, there were ominous signs of negative therapeutic effect. The more progress she seemed to make in gaining a capacity to talk and think about her feelings the more danger-ous she felt life became for her. Her paranoia about the growing levels of intimacy with the team leader and the resident therapist was counter-balanced with a sense of feeling lost and not cared for in the house. In the group meetings, she became full of apathy and hopeless. There was a sense of an oscillation between feeling outside and excluded and feeling inside and dangerously cramped (Hinshelwood 1998). Unsurprisingly, this inter-nal conflict came to be acted out in Ms O taking two major overdoses in quick succession. These resulted in her admission to hospital. When she returned to the crisis centre after the first overdose, she was unrepentant and in a state of rage about what she saw as a dangerously tantalising prospect of hope and life represented by the crisis centre. We, by way of contrast, felt that it was an important therapeutic event of her acting out her need to assassinate the person in her who had begun to feel hope and an inchoate sense of a new life. After some discussion, she and we decided that we could and should carry on with the therapeutic work.

Soon, however, the conflict between a temptation of life and a strong pull towards death was re-enacted in the second overdose, which was more serious and severe than the first. Ms O only survived this major assault on her life by the vigilant attention and quick responses by the resident therapist who was well aware of Ms O's vulnerability and arranged for the immediate admission to hospital. In a note left for the three resident therapists, Ms O stated that she was sorry about having done what she did in 'their home'. She added that she felt she had no options left open as her feelings were all churned up and that she felt sad, angry and lost.

During this difficult time, the Wednesday clinical meeting and team supervision meetings, as holding structures, played an important and vital role in helping the team's morale and attention to the therapeutic task. On one particular occasion, under an immense pressure of anxiety and guilt, the team leader called a colleague who was the team leader on call. When asked if he should visit Ms O in hospital as he feared that he might not see her alive again, her response was simple but highly effective. She pointed out that it was a matter of an important clinical judgment for him to understand that Ms O's real need was for him to survive the brutal and near fatal attacks on herself and the team as a whole. The team leader then felt able to sustain this profound sense of agony and await Ms O's return to the centre, without knowing if and when this would happen. In fact, Ms O was transferred to the psychiatric hospital from which she originally came to the centre. Then the conflicts and splits in Ms O became enacted in the relationship between the crisis centre and the psychiatric team at the hospital. They looked on the therapeutic milieu and ethos of the centre with suspicion. At times, their refusal to engage in a reasonable dialogue with us about Ms O's care reflected a paranoid attitude. A familiar struggle encountered by the Arbour's therapeutic team with the attitude of the established professionals towards Arbours (Coltart 1995).[4]

However, the impasse resolved following the enactment of Ms O's ambivalence in the conflict between the two teams. It allowed a major shift in her interest in life. She fought for and gained permission to continue to attend her team meetings, travelling from the hospital to the crisis centre and returning to the ward in the afternoons. Her persistence and our perseverance eventually facilitated her return to the crisis centre after a few weeks. Now there was a delicate, fragile but growing sense of hope and optimism in Ms O. She felt that she had reached an important stage in her life and her therapeutic stay at the centre. The team, of which she was a member, had survived her concrete and destructive attacks on life. The team's continued interest in and willingness to work in the service of her emotional and physical well-being had an immense impact on her. Now, she felt that she had a real involvement in her project for rebuilding her life. There was also a distinctive difference to her relationship to the resident therapist and the team leader, which now felt more emotional and real. She felt that we, as a therapeutic couple, could be allowed to work together while she maintained joint and separate relationships with us. What now seemed crucial to our work was the consistent 'gathering of the transference' (Meltzer 1968). All events, transactions and occurrences from the house meetings, art and movement therapy groups, informal social interactions in the kitchen and the garden needed to be brought together, into the therapeutic forum of the team meetings.

Furthermore, it was important openly to acknowledge, address and work with Ms O's capacity for splitting and projection. We began to talk with her about her as in two minds, two persons, in one body but in a state of irresolvable paralysis because they ferociously opposed each other (Sinason 1993).

Ms O successfully applied for funding, with the support of her psychiatric team, for a second stay of 6 months at the centre: a period that afforded her a number of important changes that were facilitated by the various 'holding structures'. Chief among these changes were the emerging issues of her identity and a sense of herself as a woman. With this, she began to think about her relationship to her body, an area of examination that became a rich source of self-discovery for her within the containing structures of her relationships to the resident therapist (who was a woman) and other female guests. Ms O began to talk about some of her early memories of her relationship with her mother. This also led to her exploring some of the difficulties she began to experience, as a teenager, in relation to her adolescent body when self-harm began. Ms O left the crisis centre after this second stay to live in a long-stay Arbours community. She was realistic about her continued need to be in a safe environment and setting where she could share her life with others who had similar difficulties to her own. Here is an excerpt from a letter she wrote to her psychiatrist in requesting the funding support for her application:

> When I first came here, although I wanted to come, I wanted to come to please other people and I came for the wrong reasons. Since my return I have realised that I am now here for myself which, although it doesn't make the work that is done here any easier, makes me more willing and receptive to change, work harder and feel happier in myself. The Arbours are teaching me lots of different things in ways that your team is unable to do because of your stretched resources and my specific needs for intensive therapy . . . The progress that I have made is difficult for me to see but I know it is there. I am learning to say what my feelings are and describe them instead of just being overwhelmed by feelings, which I could not put a name to never mind understand. I am learning that it is not wrong to say how you feel and that looking into my feelings and thinking about them will in the long term help me come to terms with always feeling suicidal and I am hoping that with

extra work I will be able to deal with my suicidal feelings in a different, healthier and more constructive way.

We believe this illustration of clinical work with a guest demonstrates the use of an applied psychoanalytical model and the function of the holding structures, which we highlighted in the earlier part of this chapter. It is this kind of work that underpins our therapeutic work at the Arbours Crisis Centre and makes it 'a thoughtful and a self-reflective place' which has pioneered 'an advanced and humane form of psychiatry' (Hinshelwood 2002).

Notes

1 For a discussion of these developments and their relation to the history of the Arbours Crisis Centre, see Berke et al. 2002, op. cit.
2 For a succinct summary of this, in relation to the ethos of the Crisis Centre, see Foreword by Hinshelwood, in Berke et al. 2002, op. cit. Also, see epilogue by Martindale.
3 For another discussion about our therapeutic work, see our recent article J.H. Berke, K. Navaratnem and T. Schonfield, Creative use of the countertransference, *British Journal of Psychotherapy* 22(3): 311–334, 2006.
4 For a discussion of similar institutional dynamics in relation to the crisis centre, see our article J.H. Berke, P. Williams, K. Navaratnem, L. Elliott and S. White, Crisis at the Arbours Crisis Centre, *Therapeutic Communities* 25(1): 73–80, 2004.

Bibliography

Armelius, B.-Å., Börjesson, J., Fogelstam, H., Granberg, Å., Hemphälä, M. and Jeanneau, M. (2002). *A Five-year Study of Patients and Staff at the Treatment Home Varpen 1993–1998.* Slutrapport nr 24 från Behandlingshemsprojektet. Umeå: Umeå University, Department of Psychology.

Berke, J.H. (1995). Conjoint therapy, in J.H. Berke, C. Masoliver and T. Ryan (eds) *Sanctuary: The Arbours experience of alternative community care.* London: Process Press.

Berke, J.H., Fagan, M., Mak-Pearce, G. and Pierides-Müller, S. (2002). *Beyond Madness: Psychosocial interventions in psychosis.* London: Jessica Kingsley.

Bion, W. (1970). *Attention and Interpretation.* London: Tavistock.

Brenman-Pick, I. (1985). Working through in the counter-transference, *International Journal of Psycho-Analysis* 66: 157–166.

Carpy, D.V. (1989). Tolerating the countertransference: a mutative process, *International Journal of Psycho-Analysis* 70: 287–294.

Coltart, N. (1995). Attention, in J.H. Berke, C. Masoliver and T. Ryan (eds) *Sanctuary: The Arbours experience of alternative community care.* London: Process Press.

Freud, S. (1904/1953). On psychotherapy, in *Complete Works Sigmund Freud,* Standard Edition XII: 264. London: Hogarth Press.

Hinshelwood, R.D. (1998). Paranoia, groups and enquiry, in J.H. Berke, S. Pierides,

A. Sabbadini and S. Schneider (eds) *Even Paranoids have Enemies*. London: Routledge.

Hinshelwood, R.D. (2002). Foreword, in J.H. Berke, M. Fagan, G. Mak-Pearce and S. Pierides-Müller (eds) *Beyond Madness: Psychosocial interventions in psychosis*. London: Jessica Kingsley.

Khan, M.M.R. (1965). Silence as communication, *Bulletin of the Menninger Clinic* 27: 300–317.

Meltzer, D. (1968). Terror, persecution, dread, *International Journal of Psycho-Analysis* 49: 396–400.

Mosher, I., Vallone, R. and Menn, A. (1995). The treatment of acute psychosis without neuroleptics: six-week psychopathology outcome data from the Soteria project, *International Journal of Social Psychiatry* 41(3): 157–173.

Parsons, M. (1999). The logic of play in psychoanalysis, *International Journal of Psycho-Analysis* 80: 871–884.

Sinason, M. (1993). Who is the mad voice inside?, *Psychoanalytic Psychotherapy* 7: 207–221.

Symington, N. (1986). *The analytic experience: Lectures from the Tavistock*. London: Free Association Books.

Winnicott, D.W. (1963/1990). Psychiatric disorder in terms of infantile maturational processes, in *The Maturational Processes and the Facilitating Environment*. London: Karnac Books.

Chapter 14

Psychological care in therapeutic communities

Marcel Sassolas

An objective: psychological care

When considering therapeutic communities, it is essential never to lose sight of their purpose. It is not only about helping patients with their day-to-day lives by providing a place to stay for long or short durations; it is not only about lessening their suffering through medication and encouraging social rehabilitation through activities within the project; it is about offering them psychological care (*le soin psychique*)[1].

The aim of psychological care is to extend the patient's mental functionality or, more precisely, to reduce the defences that limit it and render life painful. The people to whom such residential structures are proposed principally suffer from psychotic illnesses or borderline narcissistic personality disorders. These people see their psychological lives as a source of danger and pain. This unconscious perception is common in psychotic patients, who expend a lot of energy in denial or in psychotic projection. It is frequent in fragile, narcissistic personalities who, when excessively stimulated, are unable to limit this perception to a single mental register and react by altering their behaviour e.g. aggression, suicide attempts and social deviance.

In such cases, therapists are rarely able to access a patient's psyche as this constitutes a direct attack on the various defences mounted by patients to maintain distance between them and their own psychological lives. The use of artifice is necessary for patients to be able to create a relationship with their own psychological lives, via the inter-subjective relationship they experience with us – a method of mediation, if you will. Indeed, living in a therapeutic community is a particularly interesting mediation method.

Some criteria for defining a therapeutic community

Small numbers, a maximum of 10, allow a group existence to be maintained, also allowing caregivers to observe relationship dynamics. This is not possible when there are greater numbers of participants.

A banal existence avoids the social stigmatisation of those who live in the therapeutic community and softens the narcissistic wound associated with being identified as a patient. The community is first and foremost a place for people to live, thereafter a place of care. This kind of house has links with the social neighbourhood, which provides a means to fight against the desocialisation associated with mental illness.

A caring strategy that is low impact enough to make the active participation of patients necessary for their functionality an aspect of therapeutic communities which makes them radically different from structures like hospitals which operate according to the medical model, where patients' abilities are not investigated and are even considered to be superfluous. Patients participate in practical tasks e.g. cooking and house maintenance as well as participating in relational issues, which gives each person the opportunity either to act in a concerned manner or simply to refuse to participate. In both cases, the patient's involvement in material and relational issues results in the gradual expression of their psychological lives. However, by allowing patients to share real-life situations with us and by giving them the freedom to use these situations to express themselves via their actions rather than just verbally, we take the risk of making the situation confused and even sometimes chaotic. This risk can be removed by properly organising day-to-day life in the institution.

The designation of locations, periods and specific participants, and a statement of operational rules organise day-to-day life into a therapeutic framework. Within this organised existence, carers will be able to carry out their work, which includes managing the household, making particular efforts to avoid a drift towards confusion, which muddles the senses, and repetition, which deadens them; as well as acting as a carer.

Carers must be able to pay attention to two aspects of patients' lives: first, carers must ensure patients' psychological well-being and, second, carers must be aware of the day-to-day realities that patients experience within the therapeutic community. Within the context of a clinical analysis of relationships, this consists in identifying how a patient's psychological state may fluctuate as a result of events experienced within the institution or outside of it. It is necessary to look at the external day-to-day life and internal realities of each person in order to prevent the denial of one or the other, which is the most active defensive mechanism of such patients.

An occasionally long stay is measured in terms of months and sometimes in years. The therapeutic community represents a durable alternative to the old way of life, whether it was lived with parents, alone, on the streets or in a hospital.

Aims of the stay

Allowing patients to live in the project, while providing better support for the pain and problems resulting from their psychotic state of mind. This requires that the carer's presence be tailored to the type of patients living in the project: those who have a certain amount of autonomy can live in a community where there are no night staff and where it is up to them to organise their daily life; those whose competencies have been disabled through too many years spent with their parents or in hospital need a community where staff are present on a more permanent basis.

Not to aggravate the patient's illness, e.g. not encouraging psychotic defence mechanisms, and in particular not allowing denial. Two forms of denial can exist which, occasionally, co-exist in the same patient: denial of competencies and denial of the illness.

In the first case, the institution can become party to the denial of competencies if it accepts the discredited image a patient presents of himself at face value, responds with a number of temporary measures and gradually takes over the running of the patient's relational and social life. This is the risk which underlies all social rehabilitation measures when they do not take into account the defensive dimension of certain kinds of apparently deficient behaviour and fail to ask themselves what their meaning may be in the context of an individual patient history or what role the behaviour may play in their current relational universe.

In the second case, the therapeutic community can become party to the denial of the illness. It can do this in two ways. To avoid conflict, it can choose not to notice the behaviour of a patient in denial: abandonment of personal grooming or medical treatment, absence from arranged group meetings, defiance against the rules and framework. Conversely, the therapeutic community can choose to tackle this issue face on by setting up a framework of contracts and obligations, which transforms the caring relationship into a balance of power between the institution and the patient. In both cases, the response cannot be classified as a caring response, since it addresses the consequences of denial of the illness but does not address the underlying psychological conflict being overridden by denial. In a way, the institution is responding to denial with denial, denying the psychological suffering underlying this behaviour. What suffering? The failure of a patient's omniscience and their terror of being in a dependent relationship with people who have invested emotionally in themselves.

Encouraging patients to take an interest in what is happening inside them, giving them the opportunity to make connections between relational events experienced within the care institution and the way they react to them through withdrawal, escape into insane ideas or behavioural problems. The aim of familiarising patients with their own psychological life is modest, but essential: it is the first step a patient takes towards viewing events associated with their illness as an expression of their psychological life. Until that point, these events have been viewed by the patient as non-events, events that are not based in reality and are without meaning, rather like foreign parts of the self.

Reducing the patients' perception of danger in their psychological lives: in this way, patients will be better able to confront the content of their psychological lives and, therefore, will have less need to escape symptomatically. This journey is long. However, this way of addressing the illness is much less disheartening and discouraging than the medical approach. Thus placed in the active position of observing themselves, patients are able to take a narcissistic value-added from being in this position. As a result they are less disheartened, even when they present symptoms for an extended length of time.

In summary, what is proposed to patients is a kind of insight therapy where the emphasis is placed on them, their ways of reacting to the institutional framework and their way of living with the other patients and carers.

The therapeutic community: a place to live in, not just a place of care

Therapeutic communities provide psychological care to patients for variable lengths of time, occasionally months and sometimes years. They resemble real-life living situations and do not have the social characteristics of a hospital: as a result, they can be viewed not only as a place where care is given but also as a home where each person can practise living their life, e.g. experiencing separation, if coming from the family home, or experiencing invested interpersonal relationships, if previously living alone in an apartment or on the streets.

This possibility will induce modes of investment and defence in the patient. During psychotic functionality or in borderline narcissistic personalities, the greater the attraction of an object, the greater the resistance to investing in it because there is a threat associated with the object: the loss of the object if the patient were to invest himself in it. The object a patient chooses to invest himself in during a psychotic episode becomes one of the cornerstones of the subject's psyche; it is part of them. Its loss or withdrawal could cause the entire mental structure to collapse. Thus investing in an object does not simply involve accepting the painful risk of disappointment or loss, as is the case for each and every one of us; it also involves the risk of a real collapse of the psychological self – a narcissistic catastrophe. And it is this which creates the ambivalence that characterises psychotic behaviour; comings and goings, enthusiasm and withdrawal.

When patients move into a therapeutic community, they are induced to re-experience their former relational methods with their families or in their day-to-day lives in the present. If the institution carries out its work well, the patient will also be made to re-evaluate these former relational methods. Two clinical examples will allow us to better demonstrate how life in the therapeutic community puts carers at the heart of the unconscious scenario which governs the psychological life of a patient.

Case example

Sergio: anger and disappointment

Sergio is 40 years old and has already spent a lot of time in different institutions for his behavioural problems and episodes of insanity. In each institution, the scenario has been the same: he adapts very well for the first weeks and then the violent behaviour starts. Long periods of institutionalisation are therefore necessary to allow his real psychological problems to appear. His psychological issues are based on a relationship with an intrusive mother, with whom he has always lived and who can manipulate him like a puppet. When the case is examined in more detail, it becomes clear that carers were also manipulated by his mother, who has kept an upper hand on her son's life via interventions, interviews and commitment in various institutions.

His use of violence, which occurs within a few months of institutional life, is understandable: he is expressing a sense of intense disappointment at the fact that the alienating, dependent relationship he has with his mother is simply being re-enacted while in care. This disappointment involves both him and, above all, the carers, who are not able to prevent the re-enacting of this relationship. He sees them as forms of ancillary ego who prove to be as lacking in power as he is to elude the traps of his all-powerful mother. His inclusion in the community gives him the hope that change is possible, however each new contact between his mother, himself and his carers, shows him that the same relational method persists hence his despair, his anger and the reoccurrence of his problems.

Life in this community, which is an alternative to his life with his pathological mother, highlights not only the defective relationship but also particularly highlights his anger and anguish that he did not have the support of a father to help him deal with the relationship. However, the role of the community is not to replace the absent father and to do what he has not done: position itself as the third participant between him and the mother. The community's care role is to allow this anger against the failures of the father to be worked out little by little by working through his anger towards carers, in the hope that one day the anger may be overcome. This work can only be done during a long-term stay.

The aim is to allow patients to re-experience the episodes causing problems in their psychological lives via day-to-day interaction with institutional carers, rather than creating a mental representation of the issue as in the case of neurotic patients.

Case example

Lucia and her battle against the community investing in her

Here is another example. It involves Lucia, a patient who was twice abandoned during childhood – by her mother who died when she has 5 years old
and by her father who remarried immediately after the death of his first wife.
At 17, employed as a babysitter for a family, she attacked the child for whom
she was responsible. So began an itinerant lifestyle, with disastrous experiences: alcohol, drug addiction and prostitution, a relationship with a violent
man, abortions and prison. She is 40 years old and her psychiatric history
alternates between hospitalisation and attempts at living in a therapeutic
community.

The first time, she managed to stay in the same community for more than 2
years: this was a long-term situation, e.g. a reciprocal investment in the
situation by the patient and her carers. However, she did everything to
discourage carers, by repeatedly escaping and returning to life on the streets.
However, the carers did not give up. During her last escape, she was caught
by the police and gave them the telephone number of the community: for the
first time, she revealed the filial attachment she had with the community,
asking for help as one asks for help from one's family.

Lucia returned to the community, with a much less defensive attitude.
During a conversation with a carer she questioned her own behaviour, as this
dangerous behaviour, while it continued, resulted in her becoming unhappy.
Lucia herself created a psychotherapeutic atmosphere and it was therefore
possible to envisage the following therapy for her: to talk to her about her
behaviour, while resisting the temptation to suggest therapy to her within the
community. An unlimited stay in the care institution which became her home
permitted a succession of sequences which can be summarised thus:

In the beginning she viewed the care institution, which attempted to engage
her emotionally, as a good object. To protect herself against the risk of losing
it, she fought against investing in it, resulting in aberrant behaviour and
attempts to escape – proof not of a deficiency of investment or aggressive
rejection on her behalf, but rather her intense perception of danger associated with investing. We can hypothesise that the interrupted stays in previous
communities were the result of an erroneous interpretation of this defensive
behaviour.

Then, at the end of 1 year and once a reciprocal investment had been
acquired, Lucia's self-deprivation re-appeared: each outing became an opportunity to do herself harm. It was difficult for her to enjoy anything outside her
familial care environment without experiencing a sense of guilt and she

punished herself at every opportunity. From this moment on, the patient's deviant behaviour can be explained by transference: she deprived herself of happiness when outside the community to spare staff the pain of seeing her happy when she was away from them. She maintained her deviant behaviours to allow carers to remain good parents to her and so as not to abandon them.

The meaning behind this transference explains why the psychotherapy sessions took place with an outside therapist rather than with a psychotherapist from the institution. Therapy using a therapist from within the institution would have had an incestuous connotation and would not have helped this patient understand the complicated implications of her relationship with the community which today have become an obstacle to her psychological development.

Conclusion

Lucia's case is a good illustration of the two main difficulties faced in the psychological treatment of patients who need a long-term stay in a care institution. They do not occur at the same time points during the stay.

Being able to detect defences against investment

In the first instance, we must recognise that the care institution is in the process of assuming an essential role in the patient's psychological life: that of an object in which he/she has invested strongly. The patient views this nascent investment as a potential source of danger and defends himself against it by rejecting or attacking the relationship – this is the emotional expression of an unconscious fear of dependence. If carers do not perceive the defensive aspect of these attacks, instead interpreting them as proof of destructivity or viewing them as a negative reaction to institutional therapy, then this can lead to rupture of the care relationship. The solidity of the emotional and intellectual commitment of carers to the patient is put to the test here and needs to be supported by work sessions with an outside participant.

Then, watch out for narcissistic seduction

Once this investment has been acquired, staff must be aware of narcissistic seduction. Racamier's concept of narcissistic seduction describes a relationship between the psychotic patient and the care team where each of the two protagonists lives under the delusion that they are indispensable for the psychological and physical survival of the other (Racamier 1992). Narcissistic seduction is initiated by patients who discredit themselves, destroying their ability to function autonomously. As a result they cannot take responsibility for themselves and the institution is viewed as the only resource which can come to their aid. The only antidote to this process, which, Racamier rightly said, is inevitable but not untreatable, is the dual recognition of our own limitations as well as the competence of other professionals, recognition which must be clearly expressed during day-to-day life in the institution. Can this be achieved? The institution must refuse to answer to all the patient's relational needs, clearly expressing this refusal in two domains:

- The first is that of therapeutic responsibility: if a patient's personal psychiatrist who is responsible for medical prescriptions or psychotherapist is part of the care team, the community then functions as a family closed in on itself in a broad and incestuous relationship with the patients. This way of operating then assumes the same role as a patient's psychotic defences: it protects the patient from relational and psychological conflicts which is one of the conditions for accessing the situation of a subject. They maintain the fantasy of an all-powerful, indispensable and dangerous institution, rather like a Kleinian archaic mother (Klein 1978). By the same token, in refusing to take on all the roles, the care team shows its limits and authorises the patient to have invested relationships with other carers – rather like parents encouraging their child to lead their life independently.
- The second is that of social life: if the institution responds to all the needs or desires of the patient in the fields of recreation, training for employment and relationships it becomes party to the psychotic processes protecting patients from psychological stimuli from the outside world. If, contrariwise, the institution refuses to fulfil these social roles, instead supporting patient investment in situations external to the care institution, it disappoints patients and can even provoke their anger, however this may help patients to start living their own lives. The role of carers is to identify the way in which patients express this disappointment and help them live through it.

These precautions can ensure that a long-term stay within a care institution does not maintain dependency and chronicity. It is more productive to view the phenomena of dependence and chronicity as the avoidable result of an inadequate relationship between the patient and the institution, rather than the inevitable result of psychosis. An experiment that has been running for nearly 20 years allows an optimistic conclusion to be made: therapeutic communities are a relevant and effective tool in the psychological care of psychotic illness.

Editor's note

1 The French expression *le soin psychique* has been translated throughout as 'psychological care', rather than as 'psychic care' as in English the word psychic is almost always used merely as a synonym of psychological, mental or internal. This is true even in much psychoanalytic literature, where psychic is the more common usage, as in the expressions 'psychic determinism', 'psychic shield', 'psychic torture' or 'psychic reality'. However, it has been argued by Gomez (2005) that Freud used 'psychical' for a form of existence manifested in the psyche and its functioning, which he understood to be the unconscious ground of mental life. A ground which, she argues, is both subjective and embodied i.e. as a contrast with reality conceived in either purely mental or purely physical terms. Thus, Gomez proposes that the notion of 'psychical reality' in Freud lies somewhere between the physical and mental, the point at which physical and mental meet or the essence of the mental. Cf. Gomez, L. (2005), *The Freud Wars. An Introduction to the Philosophy of Psychoanalysis*. London: Routledge.

Bibliography

Klein, M. (1978). *Envie et gratitude et autre essaies*. Paris: Gallimard.

Kohut, H. (1974). *Le soi*. Paris: PUF.

Racamier, J.-P. (1992). *Le génie des origins: psychanalyse et psychoses*. Paris: Payot.

Sassolas, M. (1997). *La psychose à rebrousse poil*. Ramonville: ERES.

Searles, H. (1981). *Le contre-transfert* (trans. B. Bost). Paris: Gallimard.

Segal, H. (1987). *Délire et créativité* (trans. J. Vincent-Chambrier and C. Vincent). Paris: Des Femmes.

Winnicott, D.H. (1975). *Jeu et réalité* (trans. C. Monod and J.-B. Pontalis). Paris: Gallimard.

Chapter 15

Madness, persecution and transference

Diego Nin Pratt

The field of the psychoses is not homogeneous. So what should be included in this field? What are the inclusion–exclusion criteria? When referring to practices or methods of intervention, should they be of the same type for the different clinical realities (or disorders, as they are now called)? Moreover, how relevant are these questions when embracing the psychoanalytic approach, e.g. taking into account the uniqueness of each case. Bearing in mind this complex reality, I will not refer to clinical practice with the psychoses in their multiple variants or to any specific psychopathological or psychiatric condition, but rather to the psychoses in general and, in relation to the clinical intervention, I will only include the relationship with the so-called psychotic subject together with the central experience in the field of psychotic manifestations of delusional persecution or persecutory madness. I deliberately establish limits, leaving aside aspects that I believe are essential in any clinical intervention such as the work carried out with the family. I cannot think of the psychotic subject outside the family context, its network, history, actuality.

Feet on the ground: nobody has a panacea for psychoses

Our understanding and manner of approaching the psychoses should not be reduced to a single practice, discourse or theory. It is already significant that we are here being called to refer, prudently in my opinion, to the term practices. We are speaking neither of treatment nor of cure and I think this is most appropriate. We often find the a priori position according to which people take for granted the existence of a treatment and even a cure for the psychoses. Moreover, when these terms are used, their scope is not specified. Because one of the problems we face is the presence of an apparently serious literature, even psychoanalytical, that, unfortunately, sometimes comes close to the discourse of publicity for miracle cures. The analyst makes the most pertinent intervention or says something brilliant and everything seems to be transformed for good, madness is dissolved as if by magic. Too nice to be true. When we read these naive texts we begin to wonder why this does not occur in my practice, am I so inept? Without excluding this possibility, we must say that things do not happen in this manner in clinical practice.

Furthermore, a forceful speech circulates and builds on the illusion that a miracle drug will soon be discovered and both the patient and his family are told that they should only be more patient and wait for the advent of this saviour. We are in the field of palliatives that promise to stop being what they are. More often than not we find somebody who has been told that their only problem is the lack of a certain brain substance and that they must only wait until science manages to discover and synthesise it. We need not underline the desubjectifying effect of this type of response.

Thus, clinical practice is determined, in great measure, by our notions of the psychoses. What is a psychotic? What would it be to help him or her? Help in what manner, what for? This is linked with our theoretical views, but also with each of our personal expectations, be they conscious or not. What do we want to do with the so-called psychotic patient? What is the current status of these so-called psychotic manifestations? And, further-more, what sort of response should we attempt?

If we think that the psychoses may be reduced to neuronal disturbances or to problems at synaptic level and that symptoms and delusions are no more than their epiphenomena, then all our efforts will be turned, first and foremost in the direction of medication aiming to make every psychotic manifestation disappear, whatever the specificity of the case. They will all be treated equally, without caring for the function of their symptoms or the singular relationship each subject establishes with them. A tabula rasa policy. If this were really so, it would not ultimately make sense to establish a dialogue with the person declared psychotic: whatever he or she says will not entail a truth concerning anybody, not even him or herself.

A very particular relationship with the Other

If, contrariwise, we understand the psychotic's experience as entwined in his or her relationships with others, with whom he or she has structurally become a being in the world, if we are of the view that others are not absent or distant but very present, even unbearably present, so much so that when faced with the alienation in full daylight we must ask ourselves who is speaking, and finally see, as was the case for the 19th century alienists, the many forms of *folie à deux*, madness between two is also madness among many. If we realise that the psychotic person establishes a very particular relationship with the Other – *l'Autre*, according to Lacan's theory – (Lacan 1999) and that his or her symptoms, delusions and acts are inscribed within the circuit of this relationship that shapes and distracts him, if we under-stand that these manifestations are not mere neuronal processes but sub-jective elements that struggle to become inscribed, failed attempts addressed to solve a subjective catastrophe or perhaps an unbearable social tension, then, if we manage to realise all this and, correspondingly, do not exclude the so-called psychotic manifestations from the field of human significance, we will be able to conceptualise what can be done in a clinical practice of the word, in our case, a psychoanalytical clinical practice. Because these symptoms and delusions do serve a function for the subject and his or her family context, they are not there due to pure chance, even when the reason for this may not always be clear.

Acknowledgement

So, to start, I would like to briefly honour and acknowledge those who try to do something with psychoses in their everyday practice, beyond the circuit of medication and hospital admissions. I do not wish to minimise the importance of these places that try to support the psychoses. Although I know there are others, I would like to mention the therapeutic community and rehabilitation centre, Centro Psicosocial Sur-Palermo, as it was my pleasure to work there for 10 years. I can bear witness to its social function, as a last resort.[1] By this I mean that, bearing in mind the personal and family drama of psychosis with the corresponding gradual loss of links and social roles, being able to relate to a physical place as a reference point, a place providing containment, an ultimate support for a person within the social network from which he or she has been excluded, is of great importance. Because, even many years after having left the institution, in the user/patient capacity, many continue to consider their stay there as a landmark. It is one of the challenges that all of us who form part of society must face: what to do with those who are different in general terms? What should we do with the person who suffers from what is named mental illness, or more specifically, madness? Will we be willing to accept that they have a place in society among us?

On the one hand, institutions really can mean a lot – and very little, on the other hand! – because the families initially have real expectations of cure and demand that the ill person be restored to them, but cured, that he or she return as before the first breakdown that has distorted all their personal and family lives. The challenge is great because this does not only concern the so-called mental health professionals, it concerns us all, because society is not an abstract and theoretical entity, not something I can exclude myself from in order to be able to observe it objectively; we all shape it in our everyday mode of relating, in our concrete and daily actions.

A personal path of work with another

So, let us step back from the observation that for some of those suffering from a psychosis, medication and the social–institutional–group support network are not enough. A personal path of work together with another is necessary and this will be very special. The idea is to attempt a clinical practice of speaking – Lacan says *parole* and later *dire-vrai* – (Lacan 1999). And for this it is necessary to start with the basics, e.g. posing the issue of the transference, the field of inscription in psychoanalysis. We all know that Freud denied the possibility of the analysis of psychotics because they did not establish transference relationships. At least, not in the same manner as the neurotics do. That was his way of stressing the specificity of the psychoses, the particular quality of relating to others exhibited by those suffering from psychosis. But it is also known that others after Freud treated this differently. Jean Allouch (1990), for example, parting from Lacan's teachings, has stated that, as opposed to what occurs in the neurotic who essentially transfers onto the analyst, psychotics pose things transferentially. They come to posit something regarding a transference that concerns them or her in a very particular manner. In other words, if they come to talk with us, they will do so as witnesses to a real experience in relation to what the other is doing to them. They talk to us about the other, of the persecution: the other knows about them, is against them, is constantly vigilant, sneers, signals, makes life impossible for them, directs their thoughts, they are being controlled, they talk to them through the voices, they are taken for someone they are not, the other schemes and plans their destruction and that of others and lets this be known to them. Furthermore, the persecutor enjoys what he or she is doing to them. The psychotic is the object, the support for the transference of the Other in the persecution. And this specificity entails a special erotic position, different from that in the neuroses, an erotic that compromises his or her in their body and their sex as witnessed by Schreber (Lacan 1999) who said he could not pass a stool in peace because he constantly had to satisfy God's voluptuosity. Or like Iris Cabezudo (who said she had discovered her mother's secret enjoyment, a destructive enjoyment that used her as its instrument (Capurro and Nin 2006)). She based all her delusional deductions and interpretations on her conviction of her mother's destructive enjoyment, 'her face distorted by a wild and base happiness', wrote Iris, lost, enclosed within the Vilardebó Hospital.

A special relationship with the Other's knowledge and enjoyment

The psychotic subject establishes a special relationship with the Other's knowledge and enjoyment. And this is what he comes to talk to us about. We will be able to help insofar as we manage to occupy a place that allows us to intervene specifically in the way the subject structurally relates with the knowledge and enjoyment of the Other.

What does he seek? In the first place he is looking for somebody reliable with whom to speak. For somebody suffering persecution, trust in the other is an absolutely key issue. He is searching for an ally, somebody to place on his side, on the side of the entirely good in order not to be alone to face the entirely bad. I said that he comes seeking, not that he will necessarily find.

In the second place, he comes looking for somebody who would supposedly know how to discern something about this complaint of his, somebody capable of counteracting the persecution, to help him to cope better with it. In other words, that there are times during which the presence of an interlocutor and the type of answer provided may be decisive for the psychotic subject. It is therefore clear that, although we do not believe in miracle cures, on occasions, that are true subjective watersheds, some answers may provide relief and facilitate, while others may be harmless and others unquestionably deleterious. What happens when the psychotic is strongly committed, with a subjective impulse, to make their experience known but an interlocutor, capable of holding him in that very same moment, does not appear? Iris Cabezudo (Capurro and Nin 1995), whom I have already mentioned and the different responses she managed to elicit is an interesting case in this regard. The response given in 1957 by the renowned psychiatrists Isidro Más de Ayala and Antonio Brito del Pino (Nin Pratt 1997) and the type of interlocutors they became – persecutory allies of her mother – was quite different from the answer given years later, albeit in different circumstances, by Elida Tuana when Iris found her, by accepting the game she proposed and holding that place while serving as an interlocutor, without attempting to cure her.

The interlocutor's position and the excess of meaning

What then is the position on the interlocutor's side? How should the psychotic discourse be received? How should we treat what they say? Let us start by answering in a negative way. It is not a matter of believing in what he or she tells us, or agreeing with all they say or, less still, sharing the delusion. We should not disqualify or devalue their words because it is a mad deviated speech that should be adjusted to reality by means of the subject's capacity for self-criticism. Rather, the idea is to receive their words as Lacan stated (Lacan 1999), at the limit of the effort of assent. Assenting is acknowledging the pertinence of what is said in relation to each subject's particular experience. What each says is valid as speech insofar as there is a truth that concerns them as subjects.

As for the manner of treatment these situations require, it is important that it be rather friendly, honest and open, without protracted silences or interpretative interventions intended to add meaning. The idea is to try to reduce meaning because it is in excess, the idea is to circumscribe, placate the mad machine of significations imposed on the subject. By contributing to put a brake on the automatic imposition of the letter when saturated with meaning in a signification punctuating, questioning, aiming to empty or at least unburden the experience of meaning.

For example, a man, a former union militant, is at home and has delusional ideas according to which he has lost his job due to a manoeuvre made by union workers who support another political party. At home he cooks for his family. One day he goes to the door and finds some flyers on the sidewalk announcing a meal service. The flyers have the colours of his political party. Together with the text the colours acquire a literal value but their meaning is loaded with an imposed signification. It is a message from his persecutors – he knows they mock him because his failed and depreci- ated condition is coded there: so-and-so, from such-and-such a party, does not work any longer and has to cook at home. The persecutors enjoy his disgrace. He becomes anxious, is not sure if this is really so, there is no certainty. He needs to talk this over with me because until now his house has been a safe place. In this case, there is no certainty, there are doubts and anxieties and he comes to me in an attempt to rescue himself from the imposition of a persecutory signification. The interlocutor punctuates, questions, showing scepticism, he paves the way to restore the significant dimension, i.e. something that does not signify anything and at the same time may signify infinite things. But it is the subject who must carry out this emptying operation. In other cases the subject is affirmed in a delusional certainty that systematically disowns the dimension of a possible truth at stake. The delusional certainty is not the truth, but its disavowal. Truth is more related with an experience of uncertainty and perplexity.

In other cases, the subject's capacity for apprehending the difference between the satisfied smile of a mother who has sabotaged a glimpse of personal independence and the excess of meaning that he himself adds, when interpreting that satisfaction as proof that she enjoys harming him, are all important nuances that may imply consequences. Because a mother that enjoys retaining her son at her side, who could thus maybe damage him, is quite different from one who enjoys harming him in a deliberate, intentional and planned manner. For the subject both options entail quali- tatively different positions. Being able to apprehend this small and essential nuance has many consequences.

In summary, we should not so much battle against all the delusional constructions but rather do something with this excess meaning, with those significations that have become coagulated and impose themselves on the subject; delimitate the excess knowledge and enjoyment in the Other. This is what may eventually relieve the persecution, not cure it but make it easier to live with because it allows a different positioning vis à vis the Other of the persecution, if only momentarily. On occasions this will imply very difficult times, as for example when the subject perceives that he cannot convince us of the reality of his experience and strengthens himself in this position, disowning the level of truth at stake; or, even worse, when we are included in the network of persecutors. If we pass to the place of the main persecutor things will become really complicated and will probably mean the end of the game. The art of being able to continue with the work is to avoid falling into the persecutor's place. The more circumscribed the persecutory field, the greater the possibility of intervening effectively. In contrast, a wider and more acute field will determine a more severe condition.

If the transference is what enables somebody to abandon a certain subjective stagnation, the support of this transference relationship, which we provide to the psychotic, may occasionally produce moments of subjectivity, that enables the awareness that the radically strange, foreign other, the other of persecution, is me. And when this occurs there are subjective consequences. However, here there are as many differences as there are specific cases and it is therefore not useful to propose this as an ideal curative goal towards which we must push every patient equally.

Another very important consequence of being able to hold this place of interlocutor in the movement to make known, is by increasing the distance from the possibility of a violent passage to action, normally linked with persecutory experiences. Indeed, if we manage to maintain the subject's subjective experience in the word circuit, it is less probable that the relationship with the other will become tense to the point of becoming unbearable and leaving them with the last desperate resort of a de facto solution. Many criminal acts occur following clear attempts to find an answer from the Other, or maybe warnings. Responses that underestimate or only offer silence or refusal are generally transformed into a confirmation or implicit confession of the persecutor's malice. This type of response, among which I include some compulsory hospital admissions, consolidate the Other occupying the place of knowledge and power and obscene enjoyment, therefore leaving no way out. Sometimes the persecution becomes so strong and the hazard so great that there is no choice and it is necessary to resort to the psychiatrist in his capacity as keeper of the social order or even to the police.

And so, acknowledging the many constraints of our approach, it is fair to add that maintaining that virtual place of interlocutor may play a undeniably valuable clinical role.

Therapeutic community

The therapeutic community milieu may function as a very useful tool to help patients who suffer from delusional persecution. The community serves as a reference, as a social bond, as a reliable system of human relationships, a protective area against persecution. Nevertheless, we must be well aware that persecutory ideas may also appear in relation to persons who form part of the community. Bearing in mind these two aspects of the community context, I believe it strategically important for the people with the power to approach these patients and play an active role in creating bonds of trust and security. It is vital for these patients to be able to experience this type of alliance because persecutory feelings tend to be placed on those who hold or seem to hold a certain degree of power. A very significant and important stage in their treatment occurs when the patient allows himself to talk about their persecutory ideas to persons beyond their most immediately trusted entourage. Although we want this to happen, we should not push it, it should come through the patient's own initiative. As this process advances, patients will manage to cope better with their persecutory ideas and thus with the world in general. In my view, if we help them appropriately, they will learn to cope much better with their self-referential and persecutory ideas.

The best approach within a therapeutic community is when each patient has more than one person acting as a reliable reference, capable of listening and understanding the subjective drama described earlier. They have a strong need for personal face-to-face care. At the same time, the whole community system must respect the time that each individual patient takes to communicate. If the therapeutic community is able to manage the persecution appropriately within its own milieu, it will have a better chance to help the patient with his or her manner of relating with persecutory ideas in general. With the support of the type of relationship we have just described it will be possible to help patients to mitigate the automatic imposition of the personal significations of persecution. However, and just before ending, I wish to highlight an essential aspect of our work within therapeutic communities. That is the need to work with the specific characteristics of each organisation proper and the organised system of human relationships. Organisations may also present disorders and therapeutic communities should function as spaces in which to relearn about human relationships and interactions.

Note

1 El Centro Psicosocial Sur Palermo in Montevideo works with both physically disabled people and the mentally ill.

Bibliography

Allouch, J. (1990). Du transfert psychotique, in *Marguerite ou l'Aimée de Lacan*. Paris: EPEL.

Capurro, R. and Nin, D. (1995). *Extraviada*. Buenos Aires: Edelp.

Capurro, R. and Nin, D. (2006). *Yo lo Maté nos dijo – es mi padre*. Montevideo: Epeele.

Lacan, J. (1999). *Écrits. A Selection* (trans. B. Fink). New York and London: W.W. Norton & Company.

Nin Pratt, D. (1997). El encuentro de Iris Cabezudo con Isidro Mas de Ayala. El nudo del saber en la locura persecutoria. http://www.querencia.psico.edu.uy/revista_nro1/diego_nin.htm

A community treatment programme for people suffering from schizophrenia in Krakow

Andrzej Cechnicki and Anna Bielańska

Introduction

An integrated community treatment programme (CTP) for people suffering from schizophrenia has been running for the last 30 years at the Psychiatry Department in Krakow. Three generations of psychiatrists, inspired by the thinking of Professor Antoni Kępiński, have built in Krakow a system of open psychiatry (a network of institutions) that is available – with no limitations – to every person who has had schizophrenia. The programme is implemented at various centres and places in Krakow by the same team under supervision, based on a common concept of the illness and philosophy of therapy.

Community psychiatry perspective

Community psychiatry views the illness and the help provided to patients in the light of their biographies and in a wider social context. Its objective is to provide help in the patient's place of residence and this help is offered by a number of people who are members of local communities. This approach refers to the idea of bond and solidarity. It creates comprehensive, integrated models of treatment and rehabilitation and supports the individual throughout the long years of living with the illness. It focuses on the severely, chronically ill, while keeping in sight those who are ill for shorter periods and not so severely. It reconciles medical and social aspects. It takes care of treatment, accommodation, work and leisure. It embraces various kinds of treatment and care, depending on various needs of patients. It increases the person's empowerment, so that patients, as much as possible, can help themselves.

Understanding schizophrenia

Bleuler in his essay on schizophrenia wrote that his basic experience was the recognition that the important influences that positively affect personality development in each of us and then, throughout lifetime, support the 'sense of the self' are those influences which prove helpful to people suffering from schizophrenia (Bleuler 1986). Tackling the problem in this way, Bleuler seems to advocate this tradition in thinking about schizophrenia that stresses whatever is common, and not what is specific. Such an understanding of schizophrenia is reflected in his therapeutic recommendations: Bleuler thinks that what is needed is:

1   a stable relation with another person, a relation neither overburdened with excessive emotion, nor coldly and logically planned
2   the inclusion of the patient in an active community that is accepted by him/her
3   constant activation of healthy powers in an ill person
4   the mobilisation of dormant development capabilities by a transformation of crises.

These are all actions that turn towards the essence of the illness since they affect 'the harmonisation of the internal splitting' (Bleuler 1986: 18). Those methods of exerting influence, says Bleuler, are efficient, that are active at puberty; for instance, they work with our children (Bleuler 1972, 1986).

One can say therefore that the task is rather clearly identified: it is enough to act in the spirit of Bleuler, as many social psychiatrists say nowadays. We admit this message is close to our thinking and we cannot find anything more valuable or sensible in our work with patients with schizophrenia.

Our task then is to introduce a person with schizophrenia into the 'common space'. Because our attention has shifted from the psychotic episode to the course of life in a person with schizophrenia and the course of life with schizophrenia has moved from institutions to the community, we inherited the task of shaping the therapeutic community with the patient in an institution in the period of acute psychosis, but also, above all, of shaping the common space throughout the years of common life outside the hospital.

Patients suffering schizophrenia tend not to inhabit the common space. While they do not satisfactorily participate in the life of the community, they are deprived of the social experience and of the social energy which we are accustomed to tap from contacts with other people. Gradually, the deficit of what is common becomes larger in them and the empty space and unlived life make them helpless in confrontation, rivalry and competition, depriving them of the values and benefits that stem from participation in a community.

That is why, step by step, the motivation to participate in community life becomes subdued since, as we suppose, a strong source of this motivation is exactly the sense of belonging to a group, one's interest in others and in the world, and social competence, which is needed to explore the world. People suffering from schizophrenia lack all these things and the phenomenon is reinforced by the illness as such, by the treatment and by the stigmatisation in the environment. While the appearances of communication are kept up, there exists an abyss between what is experienced internally and what is expressed externally. Long before the onset of the illness, the protective function of the self is stronger than its expressive function and the man withdraws like a snail into its shell.

The process of enabling patients to express themselves and to regain their own activity proceeds from the aroused interest through an increased competence to a growing sense of belonging to a group. Undoubtedly, there exists a world based on the patient's own motivation, however slight, when we gain the patient's cooperation or when we lose it. We can say that our philosophy of work is:

1 Understanding schizophrenia as a special kind of development.
2 Acting in the spirit of Bleuler, assuming that persons with schizophrenia are aided by anything that aids our own children to develop.
3 Endowing psychotic experiences with meaning.
4 Enriching the patient's social experience with reflection stemming from psychotherapy.
5 Integrating individual therapy and cooperation with the family in overcoming the illness, often throughout the patient's lifetime.
6 Supporting the patient's own motivation and his/her bond with the group.
7 Considering many dimensions of life and therapy: work, accommodation, leisure activities.
8 Integrating pharmacotherapy, psychotherapy and rehabilitation.
9 Integrating education and research into one programme.
10 Building up the therapeutic imprinting of the experience of being together on young team members.

Patient–therapist relationship

When the acute psychotic crisis is over, a variety of therapies are offered based on the patient–therapist relationship, which may protect the patient from the harms of the healthcare system and the excessive interference of the activating social field. Depending on individual needs, the relationship may last even a lifetime, throughout the years of living with the illness. The relationship does not automatically ensure autonomy in relationships, but, when the system of supervision is properly constructed, it may prove to be a safety valve. In such a case the essence of supervision is to continuously reflect on the feelings of the person suffering from schizophrenia in contact with the therapist. What feelings are they? First, the patient feels dependent and helpless, would like to resist but is afraid actually to resist, because the therapist has at his/her disposal all the clearly defined instruments of power. Second, the patient hopes, in spite of all the limitations under the circumstances, that he/she may be understood, accepted, loved and at the same time is afraid that this may be unattainable. This fear is connected with great expectations and finally, the patient experiences fear and anxiously defends himself/herself against the relationship, which may be too involving and in which one can lose the sense of one's independence, if one has managed to preserve it, one's limits, if they are still there, one's identity, if the sense of self has not been utterly destroyed.

This is by no means a complete description of the emotional content of the patient's experience. The patient may experience polyvalent feelings in the same period of time or one of the feelings may gain predominance in the course of treatment. Then from the phase of physical dependence, connected with action that is undertaken against the patient's will, through the phase of great expectations, he/she may enter the phase of emotional dependence.

Freedom or self-activity of the patient as an objective of therapy in the community programme

From the clinical perspective, which is our vantage point, a person suffering from schizophrenia, who has little chance to break all ties with healthcare institutions, should experience as much autonomy and independence as possible – in the relationship with the therapist, in contact with healthcare institutions and in contact with the social environment.

An opportunity to reach these objectives appears within such therapeutic programmes that value freedom or, using a less lofty term, self-activity of patients as much as health. So the patient's freedom must be one of the objectives of therapy. In practice, every phase of therapy and every form of therapy can be and ought to be scrutinised from this point of view. In this way one achieves continuity: initially the patient is maximally dependent on the therapist/institutions/system as they take over almost all the functions of the patient's ego; then intermediate phases follow; and then the patient gains control over the functions of the ego and, adequately to the circumstances, a proper distance to therapists and healthcare institutions (Ciompi 1981).

So, in this case, the differentiating category, *differentia specifica*, amounts to looking at freedom and self-activity and at closeness and distance from the two merging perspectives: one of the patient and the other of the therapist. Patients suffering schizophrenia tend to discern or even find freedom in their schizophrenic world and break ties with their social environment and their previous life. When they are admitted to hospital, at the most basic level they experience dependence and a wish to resist it, which is usually unfulfilled as the therapist/institution/system has all the manifestly displayed instruments of power. With time, an uninvolved viewer may get an impression that patients no longer care for freedom and surrender to the mercy of the environment. That happens in the phase of post-psychotic balance or in chronic schizophrenic states.

The problem of freedom is omitted both from those therapeutic programmes that are targeted at removing symptoms, e.g. in biological treatment programs, as well as from psychosocial programmes chiefly based on a behavioural and educational approach, which focus on social training, correction of behaviour and adaptation. We opt for a third solution, where freedom, self-activity of the I, also belongs to the objectives of therapy. From this perspective we can describe the therapeutic system that is implemented by the Community Psychiatry Unit in the Medical College of the Jagiellonian University, by the Psychiatry Clinic in the University Hospital and by the Association for the Development of Community Psychiatry and Care in Krakow.

Community treatment programme (CTP)

An integrated community treatment programme (CTP) for people suffering from schizophrenia and their families in Krakow has been conducted with the aim to integrate treatment, psychotherapy and rehabilitation for patients and their families and to reach improvement in psychopathology, psychological and social competence.

The subsequent elements of the system are interlinked to form a continuity, starting with the maximum dependence of patients from institutions, through intermediate phases to a phase in which the patient achieves relative independence from institutions and therapists and starts to be active and self-reliant to the greatest possible extent. The program is implemented within the network of community centres (NCC), run by one team, which assures the continuity of care for each individual and allows 'person-oriented' therapy to be encompassed by one programme. The rise of such a system is a result of concerted cooperation of many institutions and associations in our city (see Figure 16.1).

A significant part in the development of the programme was played by independent non-governmental associations, both family and patients' organisations, which with our assistance conduct their own self-help and educational programmes.

The NCC consists of the Community Psychiatry Unit at the Chair of Psychiatry, with research and educational tasks, the day treatment centre, of a psychotherapeutic profile, the day rehabilitation centre, the outpatient clinic, the family unit, the therapeutic hostel, occupational therapy workshops, the day care centre and social firms (see Figure 16.2).

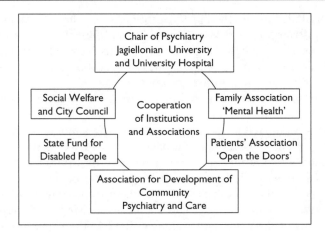

Figure 16.1 Cooperation of Cracovian institutions and associations

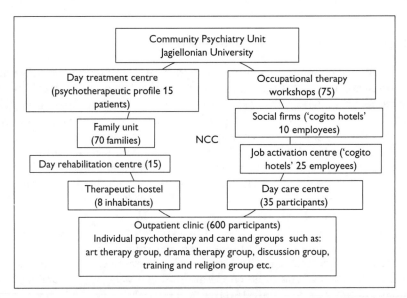

Figure 16.2 Network of community centres (NCC)

The subsequent components of the system correspond with various kinds of therapy, from psychotherapy and rehabilitation to self-aid and employment on the free labour market. The degree of autonomy is reflected in the language. And so in outpatient treatment we have 'patients'; in occupational therapy 'workshops', community self-help homes and therapeutic camps, 'participants'; in the therapeutic hostel, 'residents'; in the therapeutic theatre Psyche, 'actors'; in the organization of former patients Open the Doors, 'members of the association' and 'educators'; in the magazine *Dla nas* (*For Us*), which voices the opinions of patients and professionals, 'editors'; in the special workplaces for the mentally ill to become professionally active and in the social firm, e.g. the hotel and restaurant U Pana Cogito, 'employees'. The variety of roles is inscribed in the treatment programme.

The entire process of therapy, starting with the inpatient ward to the social firms U Pana Cogito, can be perceived as a process of a gradual increase in the activity of the I by using the social field that is the group and the emotional assimilation of the experience. In other words, therapists, therapeutic institutions and systems can either stimulate and support the process or block and hinder it. The same process can be described as a passage from the passive therapeutic environment, which is mainly to protect and support, to the active therapeutic environment, where significant therapeutic factors are the structure, inclusion and creation of active therapeutic fields and negotiations (Gunderson 1978; Gunderson and Carroll 1985).

Role of the group

Our treatment programme is based on working in small groups and on forming bonds within the group. The first group a patient meets is a group in the hospital ward. It is a place where bonds with the whole community of the ward are formed, with other patients and therapists. It is also a place where the first deeper relationship is formed with the therapist managing the case; this relationship may survive many years and serves as a basis for all the therapeutic measures and the patient's activity.

Therefore in the day ward (15 patients) we have a family-like atmosphere. Every day the therapeutic community meets to identify the problems and discuss them. The meetings of the therapeutic community build up a culture of open communication and personal responsibility, called by Penelope Campling a 'culture of enquiry' (Campling 2001: 365), which values things that are held in common, mutual interest and help and opportunities for partner-like dialogue.

The treatment programme applied at various points in the system, from inpatient treatment in a hospital ward to outpatient treatment, refers to the framework provided by the notion of therapeutic community. Our understanding of therapeutic community is as follows: on the one hand, it is a structure comprising defined roles, ways of communication and a system of values; on the other hand, it is a process that mirrors the group dynamics, from the stage of dependence to the stage of relative autonomy. One of the leading ideas of the therapeutic community is to favour horizontal rather than vertical hierarchical structures, democracy, smaller distance between professionals and patients and more and more responsibility taken over by patients. Therapists are engaged in genuine and meaningful dialogue with patients, but do not neglect their consciously performed professional role.

Permanent elements of the programme are negotiations concerning pharmacotherapy, the patients' own initiatives as to individually planned treatment steps and activity undertaken within the patients' board. Since patients are from the very beginning involved in the process of treatment, they gain a sense of being able to control both their therapy and the organisational matters in the hospital wards. The therapists' intention is that common meetings should foster the development of a good community and provide, in an active therapeutic field, successful corrective emotional experience and social competence (Campling 2001; Washburn and Conrad 1979).

Considering the phase of treatment (following a psychotic crisis or preventing it), this is a relatively strong field of group relationships. The support of individual therapists is required as well as their close cooperation with family therapists. The family unit has the same location as the day ward. Family therapists and individual therapists from the day ward together visit the patients at home, conduct educational or diagnostic sessions and for 25 years have run a conjoint group for a few families with the patients. Family therapists devote one whole day to their work in the day ward and hold all the meetings under the motto 'My family today and tomorrow'. The family and the cooperation with the family play a pivotal role in living a life with schizophrenia and affect the course of the illness. In Poland, after the onset of the illness, nearly 80% of patients live with their generational or procreational family.

For a patient, a group, as a form of outpatient therapy and an occupation, may become the main reference point in life. We suppose there are such situations and such forms of activity which add to the poetic density of the common space. Especially, they spur the motivation and activity or they create room (space) for expression. One example here is psychotherapeutic camps (Cechnicki et al. 1999), which we have been running for 25 years now or working in the therapeutic theatre (Bielańska et al. 1991) or shared activities such as spreading the idea of open psychiatry in education and TV films, preparing and coordinating for the whole of Poland the Schizophrenia – Open the Doors programme and organising the Day of Solidarity with People Suffering from Schizophrenia. All these efforts are undertaken together with self-help organisations of the patients and their families and are intended to reintegrate the patient into professional life, without which he/she cannot be fully reintegrated into social life. A special part here is played by the social firms, the restaurants and hotels U Pana Cogito (Figure 16.3).

So, common goals are achieved in various contexts. Generally our strategy consists of an appropriate, dynamic assessment of the illness and the treatment process: a good diagnosis should take into account that the illness progresses in phases and to evaluate what and in which form should be beneficial for whom and at which moment of treatment. The goal must be identified in a common discussion and the participants should be aware

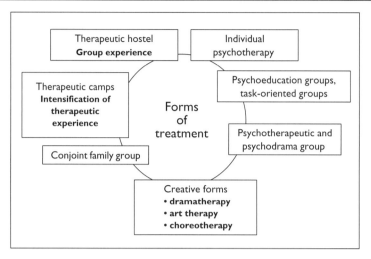

Figure 16.3 Forms of treatment

of the therapeutic process. The involvement and participation of the patient are indispensable. One should also consider the patient's expectations and demystify the treatment process because treatment is to be done with the patient and not for the patient.

Employment and education and their role in our anti-stigma programme

The main difficulty that resulted from the changes of the political system in Poland was the exclusion of mentally ill people from the labour market. Before the system changes, 80% of mentally ill people were employed. At present only 20% are employed.

The enterprise Cogito Hotels is an undertaking based on models of European social firms that are managed by people who have undergone mental crises. The assumption behind such a form of activity is to act against stigmatisation of mentally ill people, giving them equal opportunities to participate in social life. The hotels provide services for tourists and organise training courses and meetings for institutions and individual clients. The hotels are a model project of cooperation between non-governmental, local initiatives and governmental organisations.

Cogito Hotels are two pretty buildings with 14 rooms, a restaurant and a conference room, known for their friendly atmosphere. They are located close to the Wawel Castle and the Market Square. The social firm here started as one of the many hotels in Krakow and a part of the local hotel infrastructure. Now it employs 25 people suffering from schizophrenia and seven healthy ones. In 2005 Cogito Hotels received over 2000 guests from 23 countries from all over the world as well as 2000 inhabitants of Krakow who celebrated various family events in the restaurant. Cogito Hotels became valuable for the local community both as a social firm as well as a centre of education. We try to evaluate and propagate the benefits derived from this project by employees and other people who are educated about mentally ill people and their problems in an invisible way and in an organised way. Education in an invisible way is connected with contacts with neighbours, hotels managers and tourist who spend days in our hotel. Cogito Hotels, with their conference centre, developed a wide educational programme for medical students, social workers, family doctors, journalists, teachers and local authorities. We run vocational training for 160 clients in such areas as the hotel business, catering, bicycle mechanics (within the EQUAL project). Training courses for family members concentrate on solving problems, self-aid groups and support in managing NGOs.

During workshops, conferences and presentations, our clients and the hotel employees share their experience of illness and work. They participate in media campaigns, speaking about their subjective experience of illness and stigma, about coping, hope and the potential for personal development.

Cogito Hotels are a social firm, but at the same time they symbolise the patients' empowerment and the dialogue between the community and individual-oriented psychiatry as challenges for the future. This is a dialogue that stems from schizophrenia but overcomes the illness and social exclusion. In this way Cogito Hotels are included in a nationwide programme, which, in turn, constitutes a part of a worldwide programme against stigma, called 'Schizophrenia – Open the Doors'. The Anti-Stigma Global Programme is a project of the World Psychiatric Association and is run in cooperation with the main board of the Polish Psychiatric Association under the patronage of the Polish Ministry of Health and the Ministry of Labour and Social Welfare. A significant part of that programme is the Day of Solidarity with People Suffering from Schizophrenia, held in Krakow and all over Poland (Cechnicki and Bielańska 2002).

Day of Solidarity with People Suffering from Schizophrenia in Poland

This event is celebrated in every big town all over Poland and organised in cooperation with the local community. During the Day of Solidarity with People Suffering from Schizophrenia the elements of ritual are the events that are held in every town, for example people who go through symbolic doors at the same time in all the towns involved. Solidarity is a symbol that appeals to all Poles. The main consolidating idea was that of a good community. The event is a festival of the local community. It is celebrated on a popular street in the town centre. The cafés and restaurants house exhibitions of works by patients and artists and invite participants to poetry-reading sessions in the evening. The idea of solidarity is deeply rooted in the experience of Poles; it evokes images of attachment and bond. The experience of solidarity was the most important experience of the Polish nation: Solidarity proved victorious and opened up vistas of hope.

Cracovian prospective schizophrenia study

The Cracovian study on the course of schizophrenia is a prospective, real-time study. Its general aim is to observe 80 people who have been diagnosed with schizophrenia, following the DSM criteria, from the first episode through the years of living with the illness and to assess the results of the treatment and the prognostic factors. The study started in the years 1985–1988; the 3-, 7- and 12-year follow-ups were made and we now are processing the 20-year follow-up. One half of the group, treated in the inpatient ward after the first psychotic episode, took part in the individual treatment programme (ITP) and the other half in the community treatment programme (CTP). The latter involved hospitalisation in the inpatient ward after the first episode, therapeutic work with the family and group work during the first 3 years of the illness. After 3 years, those participating in the ITP could also take advantage of the services provided under the CTP.

The aim of the study was

1   to examine the course of schizophrenia
2   to assess the results of the treatment in the clinical and social aspect in different follow-up years
3   to differentiate between those patients who participated in the individual treatment programme (ITP) and the community treatment programme (CTP).

In the 12-year follow-up, the study group included 72 patients (e.g. 90% of the preliminary group n = 80), who took part in a direct clinical follow-up examination. Their average age was 39.2. Among others, the follow-up chart, BPRS, NSA scales and Lehman's quality-of-life questionnaire were used. Selected results of the treatment are as follows: general, clinical and social. In the 12-year follow-up, the results show the benefits of psycho-social (CTP) approach: 97% of the patients who took part in the CTP (community treatment programme) lived in the community; the programme effectively reduces the risk of suicide in schizophrenia (1.5%). Relapses become more frequent in the subsequent years of the follow-up period and amounted, after 12 years, to 69% in CTP against 89% in ITP (20% difference after many years). In the 12-year period, 42% CTP patients against 25% ITP patients did not undergo a second hospitalisation (17% difference). Throughout the 12 years, the average period of inpatient treatment was shorter in the community programme (ITP – 25 weeks as opposed to

CTP – 19 weeks; Mann-Whitney test p = .00). After 12 years, 33% of the patients displayed no symptoms; 51% of the patients were married (ITP – 58% against CTP – 45%), 72% of the patients received social security benefits. After 12 years, a reduced group of the patients remained active on the labour market (CTP – 39% as opposed to ITP – 25%).

Conclusion

Therapists who work with patients suffering from schizophrenia must be able to adopt two perspectives. On the one hand, they have to be able to immerse themselves in the inner world, to accompany the patient in the illness, to accept the existent situation and to attempt to understand it, to make sense of experiences, to order the inner chaos, only by their presence that is not characterised by quick action and by their care that has nothing to do with the whole machinery of social engineering. On the other hand, they have to be sensitive to those phenomena that constitute the real experience of our patients and their families. They are: homelessness, suffer unemployment, the empty day, loneliness, poverty in the world of consumerism, mercenary attitudes, social niches destroyed by the ever present market, lack or deterioration of social and family bonds, or even hostility and rejection, the stigma, the common lack of knowledge about the illness and treatment, the burden on and the tiredness of the family, burnt-out therapeutic teams and families that take up the task of daily care for the patient. We encounter these phenomena in our community therapy every day. The outcome of the struggle with the illness depends on the skill of particular therapists, therapeutic teams and institutions and on the extent to which they can integrate these two perspectives in coherent action in the spirit of Bleuler when they, let me repeat, create a common space. And this is what we consider crucial in psychosocial treatment of schizophrenia.

Bibliography

Bielańska, A., Cechnicki, A. and Budzyna-Dawidowski, P. (1991). Drama therapy as means of rehabilitation for schizophrenic patients: our impressions, *American Journal of Psychotherapy* XLV(4): 566–575.

Bleuler, M. (1972). *Die schizophrenen Geistesstörungen im Lichte langjähriger Kranken- und Familiengeschichten*. Stuttgart: Thieme.

Bleuler, M. (1986). Schizophrenie als besondere Entwicklung, in K. Dorner (ed.) *Neue Praxis braucht neue Theorie*. Guttersloh: Verlag Jakob van Hoddis.

Campling, P. (2001). Advances in psychiatric treatment, *Therapeutic Communities* 7: 365–372.

Cechnicki, A. and Bielańska, A. (2002). Schizophrenia – Open the Doors. Programme against stigma and discrimination of people suffering from schizophrenia, in J. Bomba and B. de Barbaro (eds) *Schizophrenia, Different Context, Different Therapies*. Kracow: Library of Polish Psychiatry.

Cechnicki, A., Bielańska, A. and Walczewski, K. (1999). Therapeutic camp as a part of an integrated community programme for schizophrenic patients, *Therapeutic Communities* 20(2): 103-1117.

Ciompi, L. (1981). Wie können wir die Schizophrenen besser behandeln? Eine Synthese neuer Krankheits- und Therapiekonzepte, *Der Nervenarzt* 52: 506–515.

Gunderson, J.G. (1978). *Functions of milieu therapy. Psychotherapy of Schizophrenia*. Proceedings of the 6th International Symposium on the Psychotherapy of Schizophrenia, Lausanne.

Gunderson, J.G. and Carroll, A. (1985). Klinische probleme im Lichte empirischer Forschung, in H. Stierlin, L.C. Wynne and M. Wirsching (eds) *Psychotherapie und Sozialtherapie der Schizophrenie*. Berlin: Springer-Verlag.

Washburn, S. and Conrad, M. (1979). Organization of the therapeutic milieu in the partial hospital, in R.F. Luber (ed.) *Partial Hospitalization. A Current Perspective*. New York: Plenum Press.

Part 3

Alternative therapies and extended applications

He whom I enclose with my name is weeping in this dungeon.
I am ever busy building this wall all around; and as this wall goes
up into the sky day by day I lose sight of my true being in its dark
shadow.

I take pride in this great wall, and I plaster it with dust and sand
lest a least hole should be left in this name;
and for all the care I take I lose sight of my true being.

Rabindranath Tagore

Chapter 17

Surrealism, psychosis and the therapeutic community: a window onto the mental landscape[1]

Beatriz Sánchez España, John Gale and María Sánchez Suárez

According to the Lacanian formula the unconscious is structured like a language (Lacan 1999). The premise of this chapter is that as every community is formed by the word, language is the primary focus for the therapeutic community, as it is for psychoanalysis (Lacan 1960). Thus the task of the therapeutic community can be summarised as one that leads the patient to articulate the truth of his being (Heidegger 1990; Lacan 2006).[2] This truth of being embraces the truth about his desire and it is the community which enables him to name his desire, and thus to bring it into existence (Lacan 1977). As art also functions linguistically it has the potential to access unconscious desire and as a result can be an important instrument in a therapeutic community, bringing into consciousness, in a contained way, those deep layers of irrationality that we find in psychosis but which are not limited to the psychoses (Cullberg 2006):

> [T]he question of truth conditions the phenomenon of madness in its very essence, and . . . by trying to avoid this question, one castrates this phenomenon of the signification by virtue of which I think I can now show you that it is tied to man's very being.
>
> (Lacan 2006: 125)

To suggest that works of art function like a language is to say that they have a structure, like verbal language with their own semantics and that they have meaning (Fer 1993a). Irrationality is the path that psychotic thinking takes in tracing out desire (Lacan 2006). Within the various artistic schools, dada and more especially surrealism hold a special place in relation to the broadly psychoanalytic project of articulation, in the form we find it in therapeutic communities for psychosis. There are a number of reasons for this. First, because surrealism focused on psychosis (Fer 1993a). Second, because it intentionally espoused a linguistic approach to art (Fer 1993a). In fact, unlike most other movements in art the unifying factor in surrealism lay, not so much in a common visual style but in the beliefs and ideas of the group. It was a group dominated by writers rather than painters and their *opera* included not only the plastic arts but also poetry, philosophy, sociology and psychoanalysis (Pappenheim 1953). Third, because of its stress on communalism. One of the slogans of the movement – 'poetry is made by all, not by one' – stressed the value of egalitarianism, collective action and group membership. The emphasis within surrealism of undertaking common activities was developed specifically in order to counter the tendency to explore private realms of the unconscious. To be a surrealist it was necessary to join a group, to be an initiate (Ades 1978). And fourth, because it understood artistic expression as a form of permissiveness, as the liberation of unconscious desire (Schmitt 1980).

Art and psychosis

During the 19th century works of art produced by the mentally ill caught the attention of the psychiatric community. They seemed to open a window into the psychotic mind (Pappenheim and Kris 1946). At the same time the place that irrationality held within art began to interest both artists and the general public and the term psychotic art came into vogue. It was used to describe an artistic trend characterised by a chaotic composition, full of facial distortion (Figure 17.1) and repeated forms (Figure 17.2).

Psychotic art was considered a paradigm of creativity. Paintings by some psychotic patients became known, for example, through an exhibition of

Figure 17.1 Art and psychosis: facial distortion

Figure 17.2 Art and psychosis: repeated forms

Adolf Wölfli, (1864–1930), a prolific Swiss artist and one of the foremost painters in the Art Brut movement. Wölfi had spend 35 years in an asylum. Aloïse Corbaz (1886–1964) lived in a mental institution from the age of 32 until her death. During this time she painted and wrote prolifically. Her paintings are filled with flowers, kings and queens, parties and dream cities and form a created world. Antonin Artaud (1896–1948) was another famous schizophrenic artist and for a brief time a member of the surrealist movement. He drew in order to protect himself from a fear of being assassinated (Lozano et al. 2004).

In 1919 Hanz Prinzhorn[3] extended an earlier collection of art, started by Emil Kraepelin, which had been created by the mentally ill in Heidleberg (Brand-Claussen, 1996).[4] Kraepelin observed that mental illness 'could set free powers which otherwise are constrained by all kinds of inhibition and that under certain circumstances artistic creativity could be enhanced by the euphoria and increased sensory acuity associated with it' (Brand-Claussen 1996: 42; see also Avenarius 1979). Most of the artists who contributed to this collection suffered from psychosis. Prinzhorn became aware of the similarities between expressionist art and the art of the mentally ill and was interested in the origins of the artistic impulse. He collected more than 5000 works and in 1922 published *Bildnerei der Geisteskranken – Ein Beitrag zur Psychologie und Psychopathologie der Gestaltung*. The volume was richly illustrated with works by the patients and here he discussed the relationship between psychiatry and art. His was one of the first attempts to analyse the work of the mentally ill.[5]

Surrealism and the unconscious

Therapeutic communities and surrealism share a common history. Both developed from the treatment of shellshocked soldiers (what we would now call post-traumatic stress disorder (PTSD) resulting from war and both sprung from a psychoanalytic foundation. The writers André Breton and Louis Aragon, founders, among others, of the periodical *Littérature*, which marked the beginning of the surrealist movement in 1919, met while studying medicine at L'Hôpital Val-de-Grâce in Paris, that treated patients suffering from battle fatigue during World War 1 (Gascoyne 2000). Here, Freudian techniques, specifically free association and dream analysis, were used (Montagu 2002). Both men took a keen interest in Freud, particularly in his *Interpretations of Dreams* (SE IV, V) (Freud 1953a) and *Three Essays on the Theory of Sexuality* (SE VII: 125) (Freud 1953b). Breton recorded the battle fatigued patients' hallucinations and delusional experiences and tried to interpret them along psychoanalytic lines (Davis 1973). To a certain extent the surrealists were descendents of psychoanalysis and considered Freud their mentor. Indeed, Breton dedicated his *Les Vases communicants* to Freud and in 1932 sent him a dedicatory copy. In this seminal text, Breton evoked the effect of bringing together two very different objects and the sexual energy of this meeting.

Freud himself did not reciprocate the surrealists' warm feelings and a close reading of three extant letters from Freud to Breton from 1932 shows Freud keen to keep a distance from Breton (Davis 1973; Fer 1993b).[6] Lacan, however, was to become far less cautious. Through the review *Littérature* he had become familiar with both dadaism and surrealism. In fact, he had met André Breton and Philippe Soupault sometime before he discovered Freud in 1923 and the first number of *Surréalisme au service de la Révolution*, which was published in 1930, had a profound effect on his re-reading of Freud particularly with regard to psychosis (Roundinesco 1997). In an article entitled *L'Ane pourri* Salvador Dalí argued that paranoia functioned in the same way as hallucination and amounted to a delusional interpretation of reality. This challenged both the received psychiatric view that paranoia was an error of judgment, or reason gone mad, as well as Freud's view that paranoia was a defence against homosexuality. As a result Lacan met Dalí and developed his own theory of paranoia which formed the basis of his doctoral thesis *De la psychose paranoïaque dans ses rapports avec la personnalité* which appeared in the winter of 1932 (Alexandrian 1976; Roundinesco 1997; Schmitt 1980). Here, Lacan linked concepts from psychiatry and psychoanalysis with surrealism.

In the EROS exhibition (*Exposition international du surréalisme*) in 1959, the surrealists proclaimed the freedom of artistic expression, intentionally including the work of mentally ill artists such as Aloïse Corbaz, in order demonstrate their solidarity with the outsider in society and with irrationality. Surrealism, like psychoanalysis, valued the unconscious and the place of desire in the development of the individual and of civilisation as a whole (Breton 1972; Gascoyne 2000). Freud's writings confirmed, for the surrealists, the existence of a reservoir of unknown energy within the psyche and its close association with sexuality. They also took from Freud the notion that techniques could be used to reduce conscious control in an attempt to access a person's inner world (Ades 1978). Poetry was synonymous with the dream and from this stemmed the techniques of collage and frottage. With their interest in the erotic it is unlikely that the sexual connotations of the latter term went unnoticed.[7]

> . . . the encounter, as a cornerstone of surrealist erotic experience, is mediated through ambiguity and distance . . . the effect of bringing together two very different objects, and the energy that their meeting could produce: 'two different bodies, rubbed one against the other, attain, by their spark, their supreme unity in fire'. The potential of such random combinations was famously inspired by a passage in Lautréamont's *Maldoror* (1868–70), which describes a charged urban encounter between the protagonist and a handsome young English boy . . . [his] beauty is compared to, among other things, the beauty of 'the chance encounter of a sewing machine and an umbrella on a dissecting table' . . . Breton picked up on the sexual implications of this pairing of the sewing machine and umbrella, identifying them as female and male, and imagining them as engaged in mechanical intercourse.
>
> (Kelly 2002: 80)

The surrealists held the view that man is a creature of desire and that this desire is the authentic voice of his innermost self.[8] They wanted to free desire from the social barriers which restricted it and to proclaim the pervasiveness of its influence (Mundy 2002). To this end they developed so-called automatic techniques, which were the artistic equivalent of free association. They also used surrealist objects, which were objects that represented the realisation of irrationality either originating in daytime fantasy or in dreams. In surrealist painting, as in dreams, images are condensed. For example, Man Ray, Brassaï and other surrealists, often used the female form in a fetishistic way, as a symbol that represented the absent phallus or symbolic phallus (Knafo 2003; Sayag and Lionel-Marie 2000). This had a protective function in that it diminished castration anxiety. The images of women are thus manipulated in a way in which they turn into a semi-penile form representing projections of male anxieties (Mundy 2002).

> From . . . [the] ideas of chance, or hazard (which really began in the days of Dada, with the production of poems by extracting words at random from a hat) to the paranoiac system introduced by Dalí, the development is much the same as that followed by Freud from his *Interpretation of Dreams* to *The Psychopathology of Everyday Life*, in which he advances the theory that accidents are very largely predetermined by psychic necessity.
>
> (Gascoyne 2000)

Permissiveness or freeing desire

The therapeutic community, under the rubric of permissiveness, allows space for the expression of the irrational within a context of containment (Haigh 1999; Rapoport 1960). Permissiveness amounts to the toleration of a wide degree of behaviour that might seem deviant by ordinary standards and is sometimes distressing. At times it may even be seen as preferable to a defensive attitude (Kennard 1998) as the patient's symptoms are seen as a manifestation of a deeper truth, as something primordial to which we must pay attention so as to discover desire and being. More specifically in psychotic phenomenon we find the emergence in reality of a meaning that concerns the subject (Lacan 1994). Hence the language that psychotic individuals use, even if they mean nothing to us at first, is not arbitrary (Sanchez 2004). For in psychosis the primordial signifier has not been assimilated and repressed as in neurosis, but has been foreclosed. The signifying chain, therefore, does not have the same anchor points that it has in neurosis and thus psychotic speech seems incomprehensible. The therapeutic community encourages this disordered language to be expressed and works towards understanding through dialogue. Paying attention to the signifiers and identifying full speech are the primary tasks of the community. In this way therapeutic community treatment aims at leading the psychotic patient to articulate his own truth, the truth of his desire and by naming it, bring it into existence (Lacan 1977). This truth about desire is ontic truth (Heidegger 1990; Lacan 1994).

Art and the therapeutic community

In the 1930s Margaret Naumburg, working in the United States, started using art in psychoanalytic psychotherapy sessions and described how the unconscious could be released by means of spontaneous art expressions that were comparable to free associations. She considered that all human beings have the latent capacity to project their internal conflicts onto visual works of art and that this could unblock the patient's inability to communicate (Naumburg 1950). Once transference developed, Naumburg would encourage her patients to interpret the images, believing that they were a symbolic form of speech. At the same time Adrian Hill was developing an art therapy approach in the UK. Hill had recognised the therapeutic benefit of painting and drawing, while recovering from tuberculosis during World War 2. Thereafter, art therapy started being used with increasing frequency in hospitals (Edwards 2004).

In the early days of the therapeutic community Laurence Bradbury, an occupational therapist who later became a professor of art and lecturer at the Tate Gallery, moved into one of the Nissen huts at Northfield Hospital and conducted a painting group that gave patients the opportunity to express themselves freely. It was seen as an opportunity for experimentation and a release, in which infantile conflicts could be expressed and explored. Cunningham Dax, a psychiatrist from Netherne Hospital in Surrey, visited Bradbury on several occasions and was impressed by the work he was doing and this led him to introduce an art group to Netherne Hospital (Harrison 2000). Edward Adamson carried on his work for many years afterwards and became one of the pioneer art therapists to work with psychotic patients in the UK (Schaverien 1997). This, together with the Northfield experiments, was to influence psychiatry significantly over the next few decades (Harrison 1999; Killick 1993, 1997; Shepard 2002).

In the early 1950s Irene Champernowne, a Jungian analyst, founded the Withymead Centre, a therapeutic community in Devon. She believed that psychotherapists and artists could work together and benefit each other and invited musicians, painters and sculptors like Rupert Cracknell and Michael Edwards to join the community. Champernowne and these two artists were also to become central figures in the development of art therapy in the UK (Killick 1997). During the 1960s the psychiatrist Leo Navratil worked in 'Die Künstler aus Guggin' in Austria and several exhibitions of work by his patients were made around the world. In 1972 Navratil began to develop the idea that psychosis can awaken certain creative abilities and that a schizophrenic patient during a psychotic episode is more expressive and more energetic than in his asymptomatic period. According to Navratil a bridge exists between creativity and mental illness, and psychosis has a fundamental part to play in artistic creativity (Navratil 1972), as art is always an allegory (Heidegger 1990). That which is made manifest is always something other than itself. The colours in paintings, the stones in architecture, the sounds in music and so on, are a substructure on which the art is built and what makes it a work of art is that it reveals the truth of being (Heidegger 1990; Lacan 2006).

Art and truth

Following Heidegger, Gadamer discussed art not in relation to beauty but in relation to truth. For Heidegger, poetry has precedence over all other art forms, 'as the letting happen of the event of the truth of beings' (cited in Phillips 2005: 155), first, because of it discloses truth. It is in its relation to ontic truth and not in its creativity that poetry is 'the essence of art' (Phillips 2005: 155–156). Second, because poetry is language it constitutes the internal condition for the possibility of all other art forms:

> [All art], in as much as it is language, reveals beings as such and thus reveals them in their Being. Revealing them not merely in the presence of their apprehensibility, it reveals them in their truth. The essence of all art is poetry, because poetry, in its turn, is defined, for Heidegger, by language's foundation of world. In comparison with its foundation of world, all other characteristics of language are inessential. Insofar as it founds a world, the work of art is language.
>
> (Phillips 2005: 156)

Thus art is a form of truth about the world and 'not a heightened state of individual feeling' (Lawn 2006: 87). It is not, therefore, a diversion or amusement but a crucial point of access 'to fundamental truths about the world and what it is to be human' (ibid.). This view of art as revealer of truth and being relies heavily on the Platonic insistence that there can be no distinction between ethics and aesthetics. That is a later distinction (Jaeger 1973).

Works of art function linguistically because they always reflect a community's shared understanding. It is an understanding of how truth unfolds in a given culture. Freud was more interested in the content rather than the form of works of art and was concerned with the manifestation of the unconscious conflicts and phantasies that were expressed there and by the artist's ability to create a world in which unconscious phantasies can be fulfilled. He identified sublimation as the process that underlies all artistic achievement (Levey 1939) and believed that the artist has an intuitive and unconscious knowledge that is manifested in the work of art without the artist being aware of it (Segal 1991). Previously repressed desires are exposed to the spectator and can have a deep impact because they touch on something universal yet hidden. For example, Picasso's *Guernica* may evoke universal emotions associated with war, not just the Spanish civil war, as well as the spectator's unconscious conflicts – the horse's big teeth awakening early phantasies of oral sadism and the experience of being both an aggressor and a victim of aggression (ibid.).

Surrealism and art groups in a therapeutic community

Art as mirror and container

In the environment of a therapeutic community clear boundaries are set in place in order to recreate a mirror of the body in which good and bad feelings and needs are contained. Here the community functions as a mirror:

> [T]he child not only needs to create a unified body image but it also has to create a body image that performs the role of container and contained (Lacan, Seminar I, 104) . . . For a human being, the body image as container needs to have a place for needs, feelings, faeces, urine, food, and even pain. The baby's task of creating a body image as container requires the skilled help of the maternal figure.
>
> (De Waelhens and Ver Eecke 2001: 75)

In psychosis, the subject has not been able to distinguish himself from the first love object, the mother, during the mirror stage. Psychosis is not just a failure of the symbolic system but also a failure of the imaginary construction of a libidinal body. The subject has never been recognised as an independent subject who desires (De Waelhens and Ver Eecke 2001). In the mirror stage (Lacan 2006) the individual begins to form a sense of himself and separate from the Other. Here there is an illusive sense of being a whole as he begins to separate from symbiotic relationships. Paintings produced by psychotic patients often have the same effect as the mirror, during the mirror stage and thus may function in a reparative way (Killick 1997). Works of art can also be used as transitional objects, in which the psychotic's fears are expressed and contained (Winnicott 1953). 'The picture, as a third element in the area in between client and therapist, offers a means of externalizing otherwise inexpressible thoughts and feelings . . . here they might be contained until the artist feels ready to acknowledge and own them' (Schaverien 1997: 14). This transitional function allows impulses that are intolerable to the patient to be contained within the painting. When patients are experiencing hallucinations and delusions, the pieces of art they produce can reduce their psychic distress. By defining their experience within a painting or other artifact they reveal their inner world with its distressing and persecutory objects to the community and find containment for their emotions within the group (Bion 1970; Ward et al. 2003). This is illustrated in Figure 17.3. It was painted in an art group in a therapeutic community by a patient diagnosed with schizophrenia.

For psychotic patients, art can be used as a path to explore their experience of the absence of identity, as well as an opportunity to construct an identity (Addington and Addington 2006; Kohut 1977). The art that psychotic patients produce often reflects either their hallucinatory world, with strong persecutory elements and delusions or is made up of symbolic paintings related to identifying dimensions of delusion (Lozano et al. 2004).

Figure 17.3 Inner world and containment of emotions

Painting as a window: communalism

Art groups often constitute an essential part of the therapeutic programme in therapeutic communities, as they can be an alternative way for patients to articulate the unconscious and to become part of a community. 'What is lacking in psychosis is the experience of self as a member of a community' (Schaverien 1997: 16). The images they produce are a window opening onto a mental landscape, an interior world.[9] At the same time, the images can be an attempt to communicate with the Other (ibid). They can help to enhance the capacity of patients to share and communicate ideas and feelings, and act as a medium to transmit experience, no matter how dramatic this may be. Images can create clarity in the expression of some aspects of life that are difficult to talk about. To symbolise feelings and experiences through images can constitute a more powerful way of expression and communication than verbal descriptions, and at the same time may be experienced as less threatening (Vassiliadou 2001). Consequently, patients often find it easier to start talking about themselves when there is a tangible piece of art that expresses something unconscious and hitherto unspoken, in front of them. Thus the work of art has the function of a bridge into speech, which implies relationships and community. And it enables the patient to begin to take part in the interpretation of his own unconscious material in relationship with others. This can powerfully change the dynamics within the group. Art also enables self-criticism and challenging to take place in the group, in order to resolve conflicts between the individual and the community. In this way, community members foster the revelation of some truth that will have an effect in the community (Heidegger 1990). This may help the group to deal with some disturbance and reinforce the sense of group identity. The communal element in the production and interpretation of works of art is considered a key therapeutic element in the process.

Permissiveness and artistic expression

In the same way that the surrealists used different techniques to provoke inspiration and produce creative process free of conscious control, art in the therapeutic community can be seen as an aspect of permissiveness. In other words, it can be used as a form of free association, as in the case of frottage, which circumvents consciousness to some extent, revealing unpredictable images. These images mirror the dislocation found in psychosis. At a later stage, as the patient becomes engaged with the group, in the organisation of the final piece, he puts himself at the centre of the therapeutic process by recovering and ordering the fractured part-images into a coherent whole.

Notes

1 All the illustrations in this chapter are taken from the work of patients at two therapeutic communities run by Community Housing and Therapy.
2 Following Heidegger's notion of truth as something which is disclosed or revealed, Lacan described psychoanalysis as a process of uncovering truth. Heidegger's concept was based on his view of Socrates acting as a midwife at the birth of truth. Ernst described his role as an artist in a similar way. He was, he said, a spectator at the birth of his works cf. Adnes op. cit.
3 Hans Prinzhorn appears, by all accounts, to have been an eccentric and attractive character. After a doctorate in the history of art and an abortive attempt to train as a singer, he turned to medicine. Eventually he settled as an assistant at the psychiatric clinic at Heidelberg university. Cf. W. Geinitz, Zur Biographie Hans Prinzhorns, *Kulturelle Psychiatrie und Psychologie* (ed. W. Pöldinger), Karlsruhe, 1992. Binswanger, who visited the collection in 1920, described him, in a letter to Freud of 15 August 1921, as an artist by nature with an independent personality, strongly opposed to all authority, cf. Sigmund Freud and Ludwig Binswanger, *Briefwechsel 1908–1938*, Frankfurt, 1992.
4 Emil Kraepelin was in charge of the Heidelberg clinic from 1890 to 1903 and it was while in post here, in 1898, that he first presented his concept of *dementia praecox*, Brand-Claussen, 1996 op. cit. For a review of Kraepelin's ideas cf. Cullberg, 2006, op. cit.: 127ff.

5 Douglas notes that 'John Haslam, apothecary at the Bethlem Hospital may have been the first to reproduce patient drawings, in his *Illustrations of Madness* in 1810. Haslam's interest was in the diagnostic value of the work of his patient, James Tilly Matthews.' Matthews suffered from schizophrenia and thought he was being persecuted by an 'influencing machine' which he called an 'air-loom', C. Douglas, Precious and Splendid Fossils, *Beyond Reason*, op. cit.: 36–37 and 46 n.5.

6 Freud had little understanding or consideration for surrealism and the use to which they were putting his ideas. His reaction was polite but sceptical! B. Frederick and M.D. Davis, Three letters from Sigmund Freud to André Breton, *Journal of the American Psychoanalytic Association* 21 (1973): 127–134. Cf. B. Fer, Surrealism, Myth and Psychoanalysis op. cit.

7 The word frottage, from the French for rubbing or polishing, is used in psychology to describe a form of paraphilia in which erotic stimulation and on occasion orgasm is derived by the act of rubbing up against others, without engaging in sexual intercourse, especially in crowded places where the *frotteur* is surrounded by strangers. In surrealism this term is used for the provocative feel of fur, feathers, fabrics etc. and suggests a state of arousal without real fulfilment.

8 The term *désir* is used in French to translate Freud's *Wunsch*. But while *Wunsch* is generally translated as wish by the English translators of Freud, Lacan's term *désir* is usually translated as desire in English because it conveys, like the French, the 'implication of a continuous force' (Evans, op. cit.: 35–39). The English word desire, as the French, also carries with it a resonance of Hegel's *Begierde*.

9 The phrase is that of André Breton from his 1921 preface to the collages of Max Ernst. See Ades op. cit.

Bibliography

Addington, J. and Addington, D. (2006). Phase-specific group treatment for recovery in an early psychosis programme, in J.O. Johannessen, B.V. Martindale and J. Cullberg (eds) *Evolving Psychosis*. London and New York: Routledge.

Ades, D. (1978). *An Outline of Dada and Surrealism*. The Arts Council of Great Britain. Published in association with the Hayward Gallery. London: Westerham Press.

Alexandrian, S. (1976). *Le surréalisme et le rêve*. Paris: Gallimard.

Avenarius, R. (1979). Emil Kraepelin, seine Persönlichkeit und seine Konzeption, in W. Janzarik (ed.) *Psychopathologie als Grundlagenwissenschaft*. Stuttgart: Enke Verlag.

Bion, W.R. (1970). *Attention and Interpretation*. London: Tavistock.

Brand-Claussen, B. (1996). The collection of works of art in the psychiatric clinic, Heidelberg – from the beginnings until 1945, in *Beyond Reason – Art and Psychosis, Works from the Prinzhorn Collection 7–23*. London: Hayward Gallery.

Breton, A. (1972). *El Surrealismo: Puntos de vista y manifestos*. Barcelona: Barral Editores.

Cullberg, J. (2006). *Psychoses*. London and New York: Routledge.

Davis, F.B. (1973). Three letters from Sigmund Freud to André Breton, *Journal of the American Psychoanalytic Association* 21: 127–134.

De Waelhens, A. and Ver Eecke, W. (2001). *Phenomenology and Lacan on Schizophrenia, after the Decade of the Brain*. Leuven: Leuven University Press.

Edwards, D. (2004). *Art Therapy: Creative therapies in practice*. London: Sage.

Fer, B. (1993a). Surrealism, myth and psychoanalysis, in B. Fer, D. Batchelor and P. Wood (eds) *Realism, Rationalism, Surrealism*. New Haven and London: Yale University Press.

Fer, B. (1993b). The language of construction, in B. Fer, D. Batchelor and P. Wood (eds) *Realism, Rationalism, Surrealism*. New Haven and London: Yale University Press.

Freud, S. (1953a). *The Interpretation of Dreams*, Standard Edition IV–V. London: Hogarth Press.

Freud, S. (1953b). *Three Essays on the Theory of Sexuality*, Standard Edition VII. London: Hogarth Press.

Gascoyne, D. (2000). *A Short Survey of Surrealism*. London: Enitharmon Press.

Haigh, R. (1999). The quintessence of a therapeutic environment, five universal qualities, in P. Campling and R. Haigh (eds) *Therapeutic Communities: Past, present and future*. London: Jessica Kingsley.

Harrison, T. (1999). A momentous experiment. Strange meetings at Northfield, in P. Campling and R. Haigh (eds) *Therapeutic Communities: Past, present and future*. London: Jessica Kingsley.

Harrison, T. (2000). *Bion, Rickman, Foulkes and the Northfield Experiments: Advancing on a different front*. London: Jessica Kingsley.

Heidegger, M. (1990). *Being and Time* (trans. J. Macquarrie and E. Robinson). Oxford: Basil Blackwell.

Jaeger, W. (1973). *Paideia: The ideals of Greek culture* (Vol. I) (trans. G. Highet). New York and Oxford: Oxford University Press.

Kelly, J. (2002). '*Prière de Frôler*': the touch in surrealism, in *Surrealism, Desire Unbound*. London: Tate Publishing.

Kennard, D. (1998). *An Introduction to Therapeutic Communities*. London: Jessica Kingsley.

Killick, K. (1993). Working with psychotic processes in art therapy, *Psychoanalytic Psychotherapy* 7(1): 25–38.

Killick, K. (1997). *Art, Psychotherapy and Psychosis*. London: Routledge.

Knafo, D. (2003). What does a man want?: Reflections on *Surrealism: Desire Unbound*, *Studies in Gender and Sexuality* 4: 287–307.

Kohut, H. (1977). *The Restoration of the Self*. New York: International Universities Press.

Lacan, J. (1960). *The Seminar of Jacques Lacan Book VIII* (trans. C. Gallagher from unedited French MSS).

Lacan, J. (1977). *The Four Fundamental Concepts of Psychoanalysis*, The Seminar of Jacques Lacan Book IX (trans. Alan Sheridan). London: Hogarth Press and the Institute of Psycho-Analysis.

Lacan, J. (1994). *El seminario IV: La Relación de Objeto* (trans. E. Berenguer). Buenos Aires: Editorial Paidós.

Lacan, J. (1999). *The Ethics of Psychoanalysis*. The Seminar of Jacques Lacan Book VII (ed. J.-A. Miller). London: Routledge.

Lacan, J. (2006). *Écrits* (trans. B. Fink). New York and London: W.W. Norton & Company.

Lawn, C. (2006). *Gadamer. A Guide for the Perplexed*. London and New York: Continuum.

Levey, H.B. (1939). A critique of the theory of sublimation, *Psychiatry* 2: 239–270.

Lozano Suárez, M., Zabala Falcó, S. and Madoz Gúripide, A. (2004). *Arte y Psicopatología. Los dibujos de Paloma*. Barcelona: Ars Medica.

Montagu, J. (2002). *The Surrealists. Revolutionaries in Art and Writing 1919–35*. London: Tate Publishing.

Mundy, J. (2002). Letters of Desire, in *Surrealism: Desire unbound* (ed.) J. Mundy. London: Tate Publishing.

Naumburg, M., (1950). *Schizophrenic Art: Its meaning in psychotherapy*. New York: Grune & Stratton.

Navratil, L. (1972). *Esquizofrenia y Arte*. Barcelona: Seix Barral.

Pappenheim, E. (1953). A review of D. Wuss, Der Surrealismus. Eine Einführung und Surrealistischer Literatur und Malerei, *Psychoanalytic Quarterly* 22: 101–105.

Pappenheim, E. and Kris, E. (1946). The function of drawings and the meaning of the 'creative spell' in a schizophrenic artist, *Psychoanalytic Quarterly* 15: 6–31.

Phillips, J. (2005). *Heidegger's Volk*. Stanford, CA: Stanford University Press.

Rapoport, R.N. (1960). *Community as Doctor*. London: Tavistock.

Roundinesco, E. (1997). *Jacques Lacan* (trans. B. Bray). New York: Columbia University Press.

Sanchez, B. (2004). Understanding the psychotic mental structure from a Lacanian point of view and a dialogical treatment in a therapeutic community, *Therapeutic Communities* 25(4): 253–260.

Sayag, A. and Lionel-Marie, A. (eds) (2000). *Brassaï – 'No Ordinary Eyes'*. London: Thames & Hudson.

Schaverien, J. (1997). Transference and transactional objects in the treatment of psychosis, in K. Killick and J. Schaverien (eds) *Art, Psychotherapy and Psychosis*. London: Routledge.

Schmitt, P. (1980). Dali et Lacan dans leur rapports à la psychose paranoïaque, *Cahiers Confrontation* 129–135.

Segal, H. (1991). *Dream, Phantasy and Art*. London: Routledge.

Shepard, B. (2002). *A War of Nerves. Soldiers and Psychiatrists 1914–1994*. London: Pimlico.

Vassiliadou, M. (2001). La expresión plástica como alternativa de comunicación en pacientes esquizofrénicos: Ateterapia y Esquizofrenia. Doctoral thesis. Madrid: Universidad Complutense.

Ward, A., Kasinski, K., Pooley, J. and Worthington, A. (2003). *Therapeutic Communities for Children and Young People*. London: Jessica Kingsley.

Winnicott, D.W. (1953). Transitional objects and transitional phenomena – a study of the first not-me possession, *International Journal of Psycho-Analysis* 34: 89–97.

Chapter 18

The multifamily structured therapeutic community: reflections on the experience of the therapeutic community Tarsia, Italy

Andrea Naracci

For the past 8 years I have been working in a therapeutic community for psychotic patients[1] in which we have had mainly cases of schizophrenic or schizo-affective psychosis (80%), together with a smaller number of border-line patients (20%). The total number of patients treated in the therapeutic community was 47. The average length of stay of the patients in TC was 27 months. The average age of patients on entry was 28 years and 7 months.

Illusion and the clash with reality

The therapeutic community that we have succeeded in setting up has turned out to be very different from the one we had planned. First of all, we had it in mind to offer treatment to young psychiatric patients who had been through a first crisis, or even in the period following the first crisis. This did not happen. Contrariwise, we were sent patients who had already been widely treated both by the psychiatric departments of general hospitals (psychiatric services for diagnosis and treatment – SPDC), as well as by the centres for mental health who deal with ambulatory and home treatments. In fact, during the whole of the first phase, we were sent patients which these two kinds of institution had had the greatest difficulty in treating. All this confirmed how difficult it would be to break away from a type of intervention based on the idea that a psychiatric patient is sick, when he has a crisis with delusions and hallucinations and is well when the crisis is over. Therefore, once he has been discharged from hospital, all that is needed is pharmacological control and a support interview every 15 days to stop him from relapsing.

  This assumption has unfailingly proved to be wrong, yet patients continue to be treated in the same way until the families of sufferers get tired and some enlightened professional suggests sending the patient to a therapeutic community, if for no other reason than that of lowering the pressure exerted by the family who are dissatisfied with the services being offered. The problem is that sending a patient to a therapeutic community when he has already been treated for several years following the model mentioned earlier, means there will be a very reduced possibility for either achieving a cure or indeed, any significant results. Certainly a therapeutic community can be useful for all types of patients, including those who are over 50. However, it must be said quite clearly that the results that can be achieved are definitely inferior to those that it would be possible in other circumstances. On the contrary, if the families that a therapeutic community has to deal with come at the point of the initial psychiatric crisis, or when they were just beginning to notice the emergence of a psychosis in a family member, then there would certainly be a greater possibility of achieving more significant results. In this case, the therapeutic community could adopt an approach based on the notion that the patient begins to be sick a long time before having a crisis. As Bleuler (1967) said, a patient tends progressively to withdraw into himself and the crisis is a desperate attempt to break the organisation of a life in which he feels a prisoner. For this reason treatment must begin during the crisis by trying to decipher its meaning and must continue intensely and at length for as much time as is needed, and must include not only the patient but the whole context in which he lives. There is a hope that, in time, this type of intervention may be better understood and put into practice more widely in the departments of mental health, both through therapeutic communities and through the regional centres for mental health as far as long-term treatment is concerned; and through the use of the SPDCs in hospitals when management of the crisis is to be integrated with all the other interventions.

Everything is potentially therapeutic and rehabilitating

In the meantime, while we try to wage war to change attitudes, our community has tried to continue its work with the patients referred to us and with their family members (Kernberg 1999). We have rediscovered, through experience, what we had already observed in previous circumstances, that in a therapeutic community it is very hard to differentiate the moments that are more specifically therapeutic from those that are not. This, in the sense that a therapeutic function can be accomplished both by those interventions that are expected to be more therapeutic from the psychological viewpoint – such as groups with patients, individual discussions, family interviews and art therapy sessions – as well as by those concerned with the general conditions of living together, such as assemblies to decide questions of the general organisation of the community or meetings in small groups to plan activities linked to the everyday life of the therapeutic community e.g. food, cleaning, etc. or initiatives for reflection, entertainment, both individual and group.

We have seen how all these occasions in which discussions regarding the self, one's own way of participating in each different situation and so on have offered the opportunity to debate questions concerning one's own internal equilibrium and, as far as is possible, to remodel it. This has undoubted repercussions for each person's way of living in the world. It could be described as an obsessive transmission of information, or the creation of a culture of therapeutic community intervention, which is shared by all community members.

There is another point that I would like to emphasise and it regards the relationships between staff who have had different types of training and experience, but who have found themselves working together in the same place with the same patients. These differences could have given rise to the risk of situations in which the doctors and psychologists, who had had long years of working with seriously ill patients and were more prepared and with more experience behind them would find themselves the only ones qualified to understand and make decisions. The nursing staff, many of them newly hired and in any case without the necessary specific previous experience and the social work assistants could not have done anything except not understand or understand very little of what went on around them and carry out the orders of those who understood more and knew which choices to make. We tried to ignore this reasoning and to aim at the active participation of the nursing staff and the social assistants, who responded positively to this initiative.

Supported, never put in danger, sure that they could ask for help to understand and certain that this would not be held against them or lead to them to be excluded from discussions about what was happening in reality and from decisions about the organisation of therapeutic interventions, the nursing staff and the social assistants with time acquired the same skills as those who were more highly qualified. They, in their turn, had to have sufficient humility to learn to use in the therapeutic community those skills of which they were masters in other contexts, but had to re-adapt for the purpose. All this enabled the setting up of a culture of community intervention in which both those with and those without university degrees could participate. A situation was created in which every staff member could feel that they had the right to make decisions, consulting anyone who they considered useful at that moment and knowing that, afterwards, their decision and the consequent choices would be discussed if necessary, not in order to judge a person, but to evaluate whether they were in line or not, rightly or wrongly, with the guidelines that had been decided on for that particular patient or family member or for that specific situation. This enabled us to construct a situation in which the staff do not have the feeling that they must first refer everything to others who are more expert than themselves and that they can only take action after having the OK to do something that they had already thought to do by themselves, without referring to a precise order from someone higher up in the hierarchy. On the contrary, it seems to me that staff and patients are living in a situation where the capacity to gather information, to express an opinion about it and to make decisions that translate into action are not assigned to one person rather than another, but are co-managed by everyone together according to that shared logic of the culture of community intervention that I have already referred to.

Meeting with the multifamily group of Jorge Garcia Badaracco and its repercussions on our work

Shortly before the opening of the therapeutic community we wondered how we were going to handle the problem that other therapeutic communities before us had had, where the patients improved while in the community, but once they returned home, found the situation unaltered or, in any case, only slightly modified compared with when they had left (Badaracco 1997, 2003, 2005). Often they began to get worse, although less so than in the past, compared with the significant improvements they had made in the therapeutic community. In some ways, it seemed to us that this was the Achilles' heel of therapeutic communities. As far as everything else was concerned, we thought that therapeutic communities were the most useful institutions for the treatment of severe psychiatric illnesses, inasmuch as they allowed for an intense, prolonged intervention based on the use of a combination of psychotherapeutic, psychopharmacological and rehabilitative interventions for psychiatric patients that, in my opinion, still remains today the most effective for severe pathologies. However, only a few months before the opening of our community we discovered an alternative way of working that seemed to be specifically addressed to the problem in question, the need to introduce elements of change in all the members of the family nucleus to which the patient belonged, as well as in the patient himself (Basaglia 1982; Bateson 1976). Of course, family therapy already existed, but it is well known that, in general, it is not so easy to obtain satisfactory results in the treatment of family members who interact psychotically. Moreover, we knew that dealing with the family nuclei of patients staying in therapeutic communities, was also more difficult than usual, because of the competitiveness that tends to arise between family members and the staff. Parents may easily feel guilty of having been substituted in taking care of the sick child (Winnicott 1974, 1975).

The therapeutic context that Garcia Badaracco suggested we use was, at least for us, completely new. It was that we should gather together in one big group all the members of the family nuclei of the patients present in the therapeutic community, composed mainly of parents and children, as well as a certain number of therapeutic community staff. It was important that at least some of the staff should participate in the group in a stable manner and that they should have had a psychotherapeutic training and be used to working with groups; it was important and useful that, as well as these people, not only doctors and psychologists should participate, but also the social assistants and, above all, the nurses and those in training. When the community opened, we began the difficult task of comparing the opinions of patients, parents and staff on the nature of the problems that exist between the parents and the children. We soon found confirmation of all the psychoanalytic and systemic theories emphasising the importance of the parents' involvement in keeping alive the pathological processes regarding, preponderantly, the children and the children's involvement in keeping their own parents just as much in subjugation. We tried to learn about and recognise, on the spot, the pathological and pathogenic interdependences between parents and children and vice versa, that according to Badaracco are the basic pathological elements. He considers these processes to be like a cage that restricts the child and one or both of the parents, in a repetitive and mortiferous bond that prevents them from growing.

Once we had learned to recognise the pathological and pathogenic identifications (Rosenfeld 1973; Searles 1994), we tried to render them less able to induce children and parents to endlessly reproduce the same type of behaviour. This would allow them, in the first place, to start up the process of dis-identification from each other and subsequently to realise that they had a series of ego resources, that until that moment they did not know they possessed, that could work to promote changes in the way they conceived themselves and the other (Freud 1969) and more generally, put their own life into motion again. Through working in the multifamily group, it became possible to learn a new way of doing and thinking psychiatry. As soon as one becomes aware of the importance of the parents' behaviour in keeping alive the symptomatology of their children and also of how the children force their parents into the equally impossible position of not being able to free themselves from carrying out the function of nursing someone who does not want to be helped, one also begins to realise that psychiatry is much more complicated than is usually thought, but also that the patients and their parents are much more modifiable than is generally believed. The role of the parents of severely sick patients must be completely revised. After the reform of psychiatric practice in Italy in 1978, which resulted in the closure of mental hospitals, parents were blamed and stigmatised for having, in the past, had their children put in a mental hospital. The parents were seen as the persecutors of their children and the children as the victims. Subsequently, patients were glorified. They learned to make themselves respected and to be taken into consideration and became privileged interlocutors with psychiatrists, finding out what actually happened at home, as well as anything to do with proposed clinical strategies. Clearly, there is nothing wrong if, as citizens, patients intervene publicly in order to define their needs and those of their family and, as we have mentioned, the subsequent organization and functioning of the structures designed to respond to these needs. But, so far as the specific situations of which they are a part are concerned, we believe that the way in which they have been considered is wrong. They are neither persecutors nor victims, but co-authors of a pathological situation. Family members should be taken into consideration together with the patients because the way in which we deal with them has a considerable effect on the potential for patients to set in motion an effective therapeutic process. This holds true for the parents of all patients, whether they are in the therapeutic communities, in inpatient SPDCs, in the mental health centres, day care centres or in group homes.

The presence of 'psychiatric familiarity' in severe psychotic patients

In fact, at least one of the parents is affected by the same pathology as the child, inasmuch as he/she is imprisoned in the same cage formed by the reciprocal pathological and pathogenic identifications in which he/she is trapped together with the child; either they come out of the cage together or neither of them comes out. It is not difficult to explain to a sick child, during the periods between crises when it is possible to dialogue with him, how his behaviour influences the quality of life of his parents (Searles 1988). However, it is far less easy to create a therapeutic situation in which one can get a parent to consider that he/she also has considerable difficulties, e.g. severe psychic problems and that these disorders have had an influence on the way in which the child's pathology has developed.

By working with many parents at the same time, as well as with their children, it is possible to compare the respective family nuclei, one with the other. That is to say, through multifamily work a completely new situation is created in which a dialogue can be created between the different generations who, contemporaneously, form part of a group. It is therefore possible to use both the transformative potentials of family therapy, whether systemic or psychoanalytic, as well as those determined by the fact that the minds of all the participants in the group tend to function as parts of one great mind, the group mind or 'amplified mind' as Badaracco defines it. The components of every specific family nucleus can take part in the discussions in another family group and, finally, come to understand how the pathological situation is maintained in action depending on the behaviour of the children as well as on that of the parents (Lidz 1975). The observation, recognition and attempts to transform the mechanisms that tend to maintain the family pathology in action thus become the arguments on which the group concentrates; and everyone – patients, family members and staff – are called on to make their contribution in order to observe, recognise and try to transform what is keeping the family pathology alive. Because of its particular formation, the family group can make it possible to recognise those phenomena, belonging to the internal functioning of every pathological individual, in relation to which people tend to excessively expel from inside themselves conspicuous emotional–affective parts of the self. Above all, multifamily work seems able to promote the possibility of everyone to reverse this tendency and to take back into the self those parts of the self that had been expelled into the other, and to drive back into the other the parts of the other which he/she has absorbed.

A working hypothesis

While working with the multifamily group one begins to make hypotheses as to the way in which the present situation came about, in which the children inhabit the parents and the parents inhabit the children. That is, both are the object of massive, reciprocal projective identifications that keep the pathological process alive. My hypothesis is that during their development, the children, who then became pathological, were the object of massive projective identifications on the part of the parents, through which the parents displaced into the children a series of affective fluctuations that they could not keep within themselves.

The children for their part, because of the immaturity of their psychic apparatus, were not able to act as the necessary filter to discriminate between the projections that they have let in and those that they should not have allowed to overcome their own defensive barriers. Therefore, they have let everything in, functioning more like a sponge that absorbs all the water with which it comes into contact, rather than as a filter that selects. Afterwards, the children have learned from their parents to, in their turn, evacuate into the parents their own unbearable feelings, ending up by restoring to them the same treatment that they, the children, have undergone. How often do we find ourselves faced with a tyrannical attitude in the sick children towards their parents, who do not seem able to defend themselves from the abuses of which they are victims?

The result is that a situation arises in which the children can no longer distinguish what belongs to them from what does not come from them, until the point when this suffering explodes and results in depersonalisation (Bion 1970). This, according to Correale, is one of the bases for the beginning of every case of psychosis.[2] The experience of placing massive quotas of their own affective projections into their children, is due to the presence of severe psychic disorders in the parents, who have not been able to separate from the children and have continued to experience them as part of themselves. Frequently, they do not realise that by relocating their own affective world inside their children, they could have harmed them. It is not easy, but neither is it impossible. While this does not amount to a scientific demonstration, any staff member, as long as they have been trained in psychotherapy, can test the validity of what I have said, by participating in a multifamily group.

Revision of the concept of vulnerability

Seen from this point of view, it is easier to understand the concept of the vulnerability of the schizophrenic that, otherwise, to our eyes at least, risks remaining fairly indefinite and unspecific. It is not so much a question of propensity to be particularly struck by events that, for everyone else, are more or less routine, but rather, the result of being repeatedly exposed to a series of relational mechanisms, that make it impossible to maintain the capacity to correctly perceive the external world. Consequently, it is difficult for the patient to continue to relate to the world as everyone else does.

What I mean to say is that the vulnerability that we hear so much about does not derive from alterations in the cerebral tissue – whether genetic or as a result of trauma – as is often suggested today in order to explain the onset of schizophrenia and the psychoses in general, but from a progressive deterioration of those structures that integrate the capacity to manage the affective and cognitive functions. This is due to the perpetuation of invalidating relationships characterized by a tendency to continue inhabiting the other and by not allowing the patient to free himself from the symbiotic bond in which he is enveloped (Canestri 2001).[3] With time, this results in replacing affective functions with a system of pathological and pathogenic identifications in which parents and children are equally involved. In relation to the installation and perpetuation of these pathological relationships, there is then set up a situation of pathological stiffening in the personality that leads the patient to clash violently with things that those who are not vulnerable can deal with easily. Consequently, as we have already mentioned, those pathological situations such as depersonalisation are installed, that will give rise to even worse problems later on.

Conclusion

Our understanding of mental illness has progressed considerably in the west over the last two centuries. First, we saw the mentally ill expelled from civil society and banished into psychiatric asylums. Later, following the popularity of psychoanalysis, it was recognised that psychotic elements were a part of normal mental functioning. This re-integration of madness contributed to a complex process of reform and, in Italy, the closure of psychiatric hospitals altogether. It now seems right to focus inside the family, to plot the development of those relationships in which mental illness originates. But, in order to try to move beyond the concept of mental illness altogether, we have developed a system where families meet together and learn from each other to share their doubts, hesitations and anguish. The multifamily group encourages its members to feel part of a virtual village, which puts its energy into discovering how to tolerate contact with the mentally ill and through proximity with their suffering, learn how everyone can improve his or her own life.

Notes

1 The therapeutic community Tarsia is a part of the Italian national health service in the Lazio region near Rome.
2 For a review, see A. Coreale, Psicosi e area traumatica, *La comunità terapeutica: istruzioni per l'uso*, Rome: Biblink Editori, 2005.
3 Quotation taken from a personnal communication during supervision, J. Canestri at the TC Tarsia, 2001.

Bibliography

Badaracco, J.G. (1997). *La comunità terapeutica a struttura multifamiliare*. Milan: Franco Angeli.
Badaracco, J.G. (2003). *Psicoanalisi multifamiliare*. Torino: Boringhieri.
Badaracco, J.G. (2005). *Demonios de la mente, biographia de una ezquizofrenia*. Buenos Aires: Eudeba.
Basaglia, F. (1982). *Scritti*. Torino: Einaudi.
Bateson, G. (1976). *Verso un'ecologia della mente*. Milan: Adelphi.
Bleuler, E. (1967). *Trattato di Psichiatria*. Milan: Feltrinelli.
Bion, W.R. (1970). *Analisi degli schizofrenici e metodo psicoanalitico*. Rome: Armando.
Freud, A. (1969). *Normalità e patologia del bambino*. Milan: Feltrinelli.
Kernberg, O. (1999). *Le relazioni nei gruppi*. Milan: Cortina.
Lidz, T. (1975). *Famiglia e origine della schizofrenia*. Florence: Sansoni.
Rosenfeld, H. (1973). *Stati psicotici*. Rome: Armando.
Searles, H. (1988). *Il paziente borderline*. Torino: Boringhieri.
Searles, H. (1994). *Il controtransfert*. Torino: Boringhieri.
Winnicott, D. (1974). *Gioco e realtà*. Rome: Armando.
Winnicott, D. (1975). *Dalla pediatria alla psicoanalisi*. Florence: Martinelli.

Chapter 19

The Farm House, Farooqabad, Sheikhupura, Pakistan

Haroon Rashid Chaudhry, Saima Niaz and Tahir Suleman

Mental health services in Pakistan were at an elementary level in 1970. The rehabilitation centre situated at 37 Lower Mall, Lahore, Pakistan, is part of the Lahore Mental Health Association and was established in December 1970, by the late Professor Emeritus Dr Muhammad Rashid Chaudhry. The association is registered with the Directorate of Social Welfare, Government of Punjab, Pakistan. This is the biggest and only organisation of its kind in Pakistan that is set up to rehabilitate patients with severe and enduring psychiatric problems.

The Farm House has established its effectiveness as a therapeutic community and as a pioneering facility in psychiatric rehabilitation, using agro-therapy (Javed et al. 1993). It has given a sense of direction to the development of community-based psychiatric services and helped to achieve significant goals in the management of chronic psychiatric patients. It serves as an example of best practice in the field of rehabilitation both in Pakistan and elsewhere.

Association with Fountain House, Lahore

In 1971 John Beard, executive director of Fountain House, New York, visited Fountain House in Lahore in the role of consultant in social and rehabilitative services. The close relationship which developed between the two houses resulted in technical and cross-cultural collaboration and the adoption of the name Fountain House (Chaudhry and Beard 1979) (see Figure 19.1).

Fountain House has provided rehabilitation services to over 3500 chronic psychiatric patients so far. It also provides acute treatment for the mentally ill. In 1981 Chaudhry introduced the term 'house members' to describe the patients and since then they have been called simply 'members'. The aim was to avoid the phenomenon of reducing the person to a patient. Fountain House, Lahore is the parent organisation of the Farm House.

Figure 19.1 The Executive Director of Fountain House, New York, meets the Executive Director of Fountain House, Lahore

Establishment of the Farm House therapeutic community

Pakistan is an agricultural country and about 70% of its population lives in rural areas. Their earnings depends on agriculture or agro-based sources. In view of this Professor Chaudhry proposed to rehabilitate members of rural areas in a thoughtfully created environment that would have therapeutic effects on them, in an atmosphere they were familiar with. Central to this was the belief that people can change. In order to realise their potential as individuals and useful citizens, they require an environment that fosters personal growth.

The Farm House is a not-for-profit and non-governmental organisation (NGO) providing a 24 hours a day residential therapeutic community. It was only the second example in the world of a project in agro-therapy for this type of community. Before this, a similar kind of project in New Jersey had been established on 1450 acres of land. The Farm House is situated 65 kilometres west of Lahore, near the market town of Farooqabad and is spread over approximately 20 acres.

Philosophy and objectives

The philosophy of the Farm House is to restore the members' lives in accordance with their aptitude, capacity and capability (Campling 1999). Its basic objective is to rehabilitate psychiatric patients and involve them in different activities that can contribute to their rehabilitation. The Farm House helps their emotional and interpersonal problems by creating self awareness, awareness of interdependence, deep mutual respect and the assumption of personal responsibility. It promotes excellence in mental health through innovative therapeutic techniques, training, technical assistance, research and policy development.

Environment, facilities and staffing

The construction of the main building started in 1983 after Fountain House had taken possession of the land in 1982. One irrigation system was constructed in 1984 and another in 1986. A tractor was provided in 1985 and the District Council of Sheikhupura helped in constructing a link road. The construction of a fish pond was also completed in 1985. A poultry farm for 1500 chickens and a goat farm for 100 goats were completed in 1986. A project for growing eucalyptus and poplar trees was started in 1994, with the financial and technical assistance of the United Nations. A mini-zoo comprising peacocks, deer and ducks has recently been added to the Farm House.

A large number of fruit trees, such as oranges and lemons etc. have also been planted. A special area is set aside for the cultivation of vegetables and nursery plants. Other seasonal crops include wheat, sugar cane, maize and rice. The departments of agriculture, forestry, fisheries, livestock and wildlife have helped in the development of the Farm House. The Agricultural University of Faisalabad and the Agricultural Research Council in Islamabad have offered to develop other projects such as growing mushrooms and special varieties of fruit and vegetable.

This environment has proved useful in the rehabilitation of people suffering from severe and enduring mental illness, drug dependency and learning disabilities. There is a distinct communal atmosphere that is relatively informal, casual and safe with a clear structure of boundaries and expectations (see Figure 19.2).

The Farm House has the capacity to accommodate up to 100 residents and presently houses 84 members, 25 of these are almost rehabilitated and nearly in the position of rejoining their families. This is a drug-free and largely democratic community with a relatively flattened hierarchy. There is an air-conditioned guest room, a classroom, a meeting room, a dining area, a dispensary, a TV lounge, a recreation area and a kitchen. A shed is used for a variety of purposes. A mosque has been built near the Farm House and takes care of the spiritual needs of the members. Other facilities available at the Farm House consist of water coolers, room coolers, refrigerators, a

Figure 19.2 A view of the Farm House

freezer, washing machine, a telephone area and a small library. A strictly non-smoking policy for staff, visitors and members is observed.

The project is led by Professor Haroon Rashid Chaudhry. There is a multidisciplinary team of 18 staff members comprising a psychiatrist, a physician, psychologists, supervisors, social workers, instructors, kitchen workers, cleaners, guards, etc. They are appropriately trained and receive regular supervision from an appointed consultant psychiatrist based at Fountain House. Refresher training courses are organised both at the Farm and at Fountain House. Regular forums and meetings are organised to examine how this community deals with various events and issues. The performance of staff members is appraised annually.

Categories of resident and admissions criteria

This community comprises only male members. They are divided into three different diagnostic groups. They either suffer from severe and enduring psychotic disorders, typically schizophrenia (N = 56), have a history of substance abuse (13) or have learning disabilities (15).

The initial assessment and treatment is carried out at Fountain House. Members from these three categories, who are manageable and cooperative, belong to rural areas or those from urban areas with interest in agricultural-related activities are referred for ongoing assessment, treatment and rehabilitation at the Farm House. There is a probationary period of 3 months. Members' overall abilities, positive motivation to change and ability and willingness to follow the rules of the Farm House are main factors considered for admission. They are finally accepted as full members if they adjust to the environment. Assessments, care plans and progress is carefully recorded and supervisors monitor the members' involvement in each activity.

Rehabilitation of people with learning disabilities

The Farm House has a Vocational Training and Rehabilitation Centre (VTRC) for people with learning disabilities aged 15 to 40, so long as they are without any physical handicap. The project is designed to train them in agricultural and other related activities, so that they become useful members of society. Innovative teaching materials/equipment, flashcards, toys, puzzles, etc. are used. Each individual is given training according to his ability and needs. Emphasis is placed on a spiritual model providing members with family-like environment where they can experience being equal citizens with others who are not disabled. There is less formal therapy and most of the activities involve ordinary day-to-day tasks undertaken in a therapeutic environment.

Rehabilitation of drug addicts

A rehabilitation centre has been established by the Richmond Fellowship Society (Pakistan), at the Farm House with the financial contributions from philanthropists. This centre collaborates with the Free Psychiatric/Epilepsy Clinic at Ahbab Hospital, in Lahore and with other psychiatric facilities in the province. Psychiatric patients who have co-morbidity with substance misuse are admitted here after detoxification. The services are provided for family members as well as the clients to re-educate them on basic issues such as, the concept of disease, addiction-related damage, the social, physical and psychological complications of substance abuse, motivational interviewing, relapse prevention, overcoming personality deficits, learning skills to stay free of substances and the role the family members can play in the recovery process. There is a highly structured environment with a distinct hierarchy, including novices, and senior members who are given similar responsibilities to the staff. The emphasis is on self-help. Maladaptive behaviours are explicitly not tolerated and members are expected to live as if they are fully functioning, healthy citizens.

Programmes and services

The Farm House was conceived as a multipurpose project with a variety of activities connected with the agricultural industry. Occupational and aptitude assessments are carried out before deploying members in these activities. All these activities engage members in routine jobs like sowing,

Figure 19.3 Crop harvesting

ploughing, irrigating and harvesting the crops, fruits and vegetables (see Figure 19.3). Members also have some free time to spend following their personal interests.

A maintenance dose of psychiatric medication is required by members during their stay and is reduced gradually over a period of time. Staff and members working together set small realistic/achievable goals and progress is reviewed in a multidisciplinary team every 3 months. The different work units are assigned to members according to their interests and physical/ mental abilities. This aims to give them satisfaction, along with a sense of responsibility. The work units include: fish farm, bee farm, gardening, poultry farm, cattle farming, dairy farm, agriculture (various crops, fruits and vegetables), kitchen, canteen, mini-zoo, creative arts and occupational unit activities, such as class work activities, paper bag and envelope making, plaster of Paris work, pottery, woodwork, painting, candle making, sewing, electric works, flower making, making greeting cards, stained glass and fabric painting (see Figure 19.4). Rehabilitated members pay return visits to the Farm House for regular check-ups, depot medication and psychiatric consultations.

Marketing and visitors

Members are involved in the manufacturing of various products in occupational units. These are sold and are a source of income. Yield from

Figure 19.4 The bee farm

the Farm House is made available for onsite consumption and surplus is sold. National/international visitors are encouraged to observe activities at the Farm House and give their valuable feedback and a visitor's book is kept. Families are encouraged to have regular contacts with the members. Day trips are arranged for the members of the Farm House.

The Farm House is a charitable facility. About 30% manage to pay the full fees but the remaining 70% are poor and unable to pay their medical and residential fees. Apart from the income earned through fees and the sale of produce, all other income is provided through charitable donations. As it is an organisation in which people are valued and feel safe and eager to work, donors are proud to support it

Therapeutic programme at the Farm House

In conjunction with agro-therapy, various other therapies contribute to improve members' well-being, such as the milieu itself, occupational therapy, group therapy, music therapy, art therapy, psychodrama, cognitive-behavioural therapy and participation in prayers in the mosque, which improves hygiene, discipline and social interaction.

The daily schedule incorporates practical arrangements for maintaining and developing the community. Individual therapy or support is provided to those on work placements at a time that fits in with their daily schedule. All members are involved in the daily programme, which contributes both to the needs of individuals, as well as the community as a whole. Other varied formal and informal therapeutic activities and programmes are arranged, e.g. personal hygiene, house cleaning days, general discussions, sports days, medical checkups and psychological assessments, literary activities, movies, rest days etc.

A typical daily schedule for the members is as follows:

06:30–07:00	Walk
07:00–07:30	Community meeting
07:30–08:00	Breakfast
08:00–10:00	Work groups
10:00–11:00	Music therapy/literary activities
11:00–11:30	Personal hygiene
11:30–12:30	Large group therapy
12:30–13:30	Lunch
13:30–15:00	Rest
15:00–16:00	Small groups
16:00–17:30	Religious therapy
17:30–18:00	Games (indoor or outdoor)
18:00–20:00	Dinner
20:00–06:30	Retire

Guided change

The experience of mental illness, drug dependency or learning difficulties tends to reduce an individual's sense of personal worth and dignity (Haigh 2002a). Even their families rarely take them into their confidence, consider them as equals or trust them enough to give them responsibility (Haigh 1999). They become vulnerable and socially excluded and exhibit emotional and behavioural difficulties and occasionally offending behaviour (Xeniditis et al. 2001). Permissiveness is a fundamental principle that ensures that behaviour that is otherwise not tolerated in society can be expressed, then engaged and worked with therapeutically (Campling 2001). Staff members use formal and informal therapy as the basis to help members to develop healthy relationships, by using the past to inform the members' experiences and behaviour in the present, following psychodynamic principles. The following factors contribute to a gradual change among members.

Developing a sense of self-respect

Member status helps to develop a strong sense of community membership and belonging which contributes to the development of self-respect and self-reliance. Members are expected to take responsibility for themselves in terms of personal cleanliness, tidiness and appropriateness of behaviour.

Sharing of responsibilities in the running of the Farm House

The Farm House committee is elected by the members to work with staff in the efficient running of the community, including administrative and other tasks assigned by the whole community. Members organise weekly meet- ings to discuss various matters related to the running of the Farm House. Members and staff meet regularly to discuss relevant issues. Democratic principles are adopted in making decisions which affect members as well as in the management of various activities in the community, for example members joining or leaving (Byrne 2003).

Sharing of responsibilities for running the units

Every unit has a staff leader and a member leader. Gradually, more and more responsibility is shifted on to the member leader as he gains confidence.

Appointment as staff member

Members who prove themselves equal to the tasks they are assigned are promoted to staff members (Haigh 2000). They are valued, accepted and supported by those around them while taking a real responsibility for themselves, others and their environment. This goes a long way in bridging the gap between staff and the members (McWilliam et al. 2003) (see Figure 19.5).

Responsibilities regarding individual care and caring for others

New members are allocated an old member for orientation to the Farm House. Members who show signs of disturbance are put in the care of their associates who look after their personal needs including medication. They form relationships with others in an atmosphere of trust and security. Feedback from peers enables members to reflect on the way their conduct affects others. Members practise new behaviours and new ways of relating, and therefore begin to gain increased self-esteem and knowledge of themselves. This improves members' interpersonal functioning, first, within the therapeutic community and, ultimately, in society.

Inviting ex-members to social and cultural events

Ex-members, their family and friends are invited to various social/cultural events organised throughout the year, so that members have opportunities

Figure 19.5 Community members, promoted to staff members, working in the kitchen

to gain support and keep on sharing their experiences, memories and the activities of the Farm House, learning from each other.

Special services

Family counselling

As, in most cases, a history of family conflicts and problems is found as a predisposing, precipitating and/or maintaining factor in the illness of members (Rose 2007), psycho-education and counselling are provided to the families. Initially, these efforts are often resisted but gradually families start appreciating staff and regular contact with the families is established (Walker and Akister 2006).

Work and student placements

As the community membership grew, the job placement needs of the members increased. It was therefore decided to work intensively to change the attitudes of employers and the general public, and help/encourage the members to find employment on their own. A number of members have been able to compete in interviews and secure jobs. Some members have been able to take up university studies, after a break of several years.

Free medical camp

A free medical camp is organised every Saturday, to provide psychiatric services for patients in the surrounding villages. A consultant psychiatrist from Fountain House comes over to set up a clinic there.

Public education

The campaign for public education is organised by regular social and cultural gatherings and prominent citizens and government officials are invited to the Farm House so that they can be introduced to its philosophy and functioning. A programme has been devised for social and cultural gatherings, mostly consisting of an introduction to the Farm House and presentations by members. Products prepared by the members are displayed and offered for sale. These social gatherings provide the members with an opportunity to be in direct contact with prominent members of the wider community and the Farm House has gained a good deal of community and financial support as a result of these events. By setting up stalls at festivals and prominent conferences, a large number of people have come to know about the work of the Farm House.

Awareness programmes are organised in collaboration with various NGOs working in the field of mental health. These programmes target various groups like school and college students, villagers, slum dwellers, women, industrial workers, politicians, professionals including psychiatrists and physicians, community and religious leaders, teachers, the judiciary and police, families of patients and the media (Chaudhry and Iqbal 2002). The main aim is to give them general information about the signs and symptoms of mental illness, treatment procedure and the role of individuals, family and the community in handling such patients and related issues. A few of these NGOs are worth mentioning here: PEACE (a Project for Environmental protection Antinarcotics and Community Education), working for psychiatric patients and their families. FIND (Families in Distress), working for patients with schizophrenia and their families. FLAME (First Liberated Action Movement against Epilepsy), working for patients suffering from epilepsy and their families. HORIZON, working for drug addicts and their families.

Quality of care standards, research and audit

To ensure the quality of services and improve standards, constructive criticism is welcomed by the management and employees. The programme and services provided at the Farm House are continuously evaluated and thus go through a process of evolution, under the influence of various factors. This amounts to a process of learning from experience (Kennard 2004). Feedback from members, their families and friends and from relevant professionals is actively sought. The exchange of views with other NGOs can also contribute to changes in the programme or in the physical conditions at the Farm House.

Updating knowledge and keeping in step with the latest developments in the field of rehabilitation is also absolutely essential (Haigh 2002b). Research projects, based on the effectiveness of the Fountain House concept in general and agro-therapy services at the Farm House in particular, are run (Chaudhry 1983; Chaudhry and Beard 1979; Javed et al. 1993). An action research project about agro-therapy was initiated in February 1987, to find out the extent to which agro-therapy is effective in rehabilitation of schizophrenics (Davenport, 1997, 2000). Members are evaluated on the basis of work performance in various agro-based activities, daily living, social relations and participation in religious services, sports and recreational activities. Regular audits are conducted for service evaluation and quality improvement and staff members keep themselves abreast with the latest knowledge in rehabilitation psychiatry (Bennington-Davis 2007). Staff members' continuing professional/and personal development is strongly encouraged and rewarded.

Limitations and the future

There are a number of limitations at present, such as limited financial resources and the inability of most of the members to cover the residential fees, the absence of a social welfare network in the country, a lack of coordination between university psychiatry departments and public health delivery systems and a lack of robust research. The priorities which have been identified for future work are the development of an international supportive network of mental health facilities to share best practice and learning, the exchange of knowledge to achieve an improvement in the attitudes and superstition regarding mental illness in the wider community and expanding and improving the research evidence for the effectiveness of the service. Recently, in order to help achieve some of these targets the Farm House has become a member of the Community of Communities project at the Royal College of Psychiatrists, United Kingdom. The Community of Communities (C of C) is a standards-based quality improvement network which brings together therapeutic communities (TCs) in the UK and internationally (Haigh and Tucker 2004). It is a part of the Royal College of Psychiatrists' Centre for Quality Improvement. The collaboration of Farm House and C of C will provide a strong network of supportive relationships and promote best practice through shared learning and developing external links.

Bibliography

Association of Therapeutic Communities (2000). Development of a UK-wide quality network of therapeutic communities. http://www.therapeuticcommunities. org/quality-network-process.htm

Bennington-Davis, M. (2007). Enabling recovery: the principles and practice of rehabilitation psychiatry, in G. Roberts, S. Davenport, F. Holloway and T. Tattan (eds) *Psychiatric Services*. London: Royal College of Psychiatrists.

Byrne, P. (2003). Psychiatry and the media, *Advances in Psychiatric Treatment* 9: 135–143.

Campling, P. (1999). Boundaries: discussion of a difficult transition, in P. Campling and R. Haigh (eds) *Therapeutic Communities: Past, present and future*. London: Jessica Kingsley.

Campling, P. (2001), Therapeutic communities, *Advances in Psychiatric Treatment* 7: 365–372.

Chaudhry, M.R. and Beard, J.H. (1979). Rehabilitation of schizophrenics – a collaborative study between Fountain House, New York, and Fountain House, Lahore, *International Journal of Rehabilitation Research and Development* 4 (Supplement 2): 39–43.

Chaudhry, H.R. and Iqbal, M.M. (2002). Community Involvement in Psychiatric Care. *Proceedings of the International Conference on Mental Health and Psychiatry*, Colombo, Sri Lanka, (eds.) V. Basnayake, T. Munasinghe, S. Sujeevan and N. Mendis.

Chaudhry, M.R. and Mirza, L. (1983). Fountain House, Lahore – a unique experiment in cross-cultural collaboration, *Indian Journal of Psychiatry* 25(4): 322–327.

Davenport, S. (1997). Pathological interactions between psychosis and childhood sexual abuse in in-patient settings: their dynamics, consequences and management, in C. Mace and F. Margison (eds) *Psychotherapy of Psychosis*. London: Gaskell.

Davenport, S. (2000). Treatment development in psychodynamic-interpersonal psychotherapy (Hobson's 'conversational model') for chronic treatment-resistant schizophrenia: two single case studies, *British Journal of Psychotherapy* 16: 287–302.

Haigh, R. (1999). The quintessence of a therapeutic community, in P. Campling and R. Haigh (eds) *Therapeutic Communities: Past, present and future*. London: Jessica Kingsley.

Haigh, R. (2000). Support systems to staff sensitivity groups, *Advances in Psychiatric Treatment* 6: 312–319.

Haigh, R. (2002a). Acute wards: problems and solutions. Modern milieu: therapeutic community solutions to acute ward problems, *Psychiatric Bulletin* 26: 380–382.

Haigh, R. (2002b). Therapeutic community research: past, present and future, *Psychiatric Bulletin* 26: 65–68.

Haigh, R. and Tucker, S. (2004). Democratic development of standards: the Community of Communities – a quality network of therapeutic communities, *Psychiatric Quarterly* 75(3): 263–277.

Javed, M.A., Chaudhry, U.R., Suleman, T. and Chaudhry, M.R. (1993). Agro-therapy, a new concept of rehabilitation for chronic schizophrenics, *Journal of the Pakistan Medical Association* 43(12): 251–253.

Kennard, D. (2004). The therapeutic community as an adaptable treatment modality across different settings, *Psychiatric Quarterly* 75(3): 295–307.

McWilliam, C.L., Coleman, S., Melito, C., Sweetland, D., Saidak, J., Smit, J. et al. (2003). Building empowering partnerships for interprofessional care, *Journal of Interprofessional Care* 17(4): 363–376.

Rose, N. (2007). Advanced family work for schizophrenia. An evidence-based approach, *Psychiatric Bulletin* 31: 158.

Walker, S. and Akister, J. (2006). Applying family therapy – a guide for the caring professionals in the community, *Psychiatric Bulletin* 30: 278–279.

Xeniditis, K., Russell, A. and Murphy, D. (2001). Management of people with challenging behaviour, *Advances in Psychiatric Treatment* 7: 109–116.

Chapter 20

Drama therapy in a community treatment programme

Anna Bielańska and Andrzej Cechnicki

In the last 20 years there have appeared more and more reports on the use of what might be generally termed 'theatre' in healing, in helping personal development or overcoming specific problems. I mean here those theatrical techniques which, in contrast to psychodrama and playback theatre, are not based on personal experiences and stories of group members but rather on improvisation or ready-made scenarios. Drama therapy is a general label for all the various creative uses of drama, targeted at the accomplishment of these therapeutic goals (Blatner 1988; Fink 1985; Johnson, 1982).

At the day treatment centre of the Krakow psychiatry department, for 20 years now, there has been a working theatre group as one of the outpatient groups for those who suffered from a psychosis and were diagnosed mainly as having schizophrenia. The theatre group is an element of the community therapy programme which includes diversified therapeutic offers for the patient and his/her family (Bielańska et al. 1991).

Most often the first therapy phase in our programme is admission to the day treatment centre. The person who manages the therapy of the patient at that unit becomes his/her individual therapist for the years to come and integrates the entire therapy the patient undergoes. The whole programme rests on this longstanding relationship, on the one hand, and, on the other, on the relations formed in small groups such as the aforementioned theatre group, arts group, discussion group, etc.

The theatre group, as part of the treatment system, also functions on the basis of the ideas of the therapeutic community. It is a task-oriented group: its task is to create a performance and to act it in front of an audience. As to the theatrical aspect of the task, the professional guide is the director, but working together for about 3 years in order to prepare a play requires cooperation, negotiations and mutual help. The theatre group forms a therapeutic community which works on itself and for itself also outside the limits of time and space assigned for the meetings. During rehearsals, it is the director who is the key person, teaching the actors how to play and encouraging them to experiment. Drama therapy intensifies the processes that normally occur in any therapeutic community, because it involves the patient/actor in relationships with people at the level of cooperation with other fellow actors, and in relationships between actors as performers of roles and relationships of presented personages (Bielańska et al. 1991; Campling 2001). In this way, the feelings and behaviours of the group members are strongly intensified. The actors, in order to create a spectacle together, need a sense of safety and an ability to communicate openly. This space of intensified emotions is expressed and reflected on in the group (Campling 2001). The theatre group consists of about 25 people: patients diagnosed with schizophrenia and one or two therapists, who perform with the patients. The group is led by a professional director, recently accompanied by a dance therapist. The meetings take place once a week for about 3 hours. Before public performances, additional rehearsals are held at the weekends. The latest production is *Tristram and Iseult*. Earlier productions include *Hamlet* and *Romeo and Juliet* by Shakespeare, *Lysistrata* by Aristophanes and *Alcestis* by Euripides.

The breakdown of the self in the acute symptoms of schizophrenia may be extremely severe. In the therapeutic process, the entire effort of the patient and the therapist is aimed at the integration of the patient's thoughts, feelings and behaviours, at the recovery of the sense of the cohesive self and at the defeat of fear. 'The first years of the illness were very tough for me', wrote John. 'In every situation I was haunted by a very strong fear, which paralysed my body and disturbed my feelings. I could compare my experiences to the nightmare experienced by the prisoners of concentration camps, although obviously the dangers there were much more real.'

In the outpatient theatre group, where psychotherapy and rehabilitation work together to assist and to treat the disintegrated identity, the main tool of therapy is the actor's performance.

To be a patient

The role of a patient comprises the feeling of weakness, the realisation that 'I am ill', dependence, necessity to rely on others and passivity. It also encompasses patience, 'being patient'. Mentally ill people may play the role of a patient for years and then the aforementioned characteristics, typical of this role, will be reinforced. We are all well acquainted with the phenomenon of the so-called secondary benefits that are derived by ill people who continue to play the role of patients. The long-term performance of this role leaves one with a feeling of discomfort and low self-esteem and changes one's social status. One is no longer a student, a pupil or an employee, but just a patient, so one ceases to fulfil his/her role. John wrote: 'After the first psychosis, when I left the hospital, I went outdoors only to attend therapeutic meetings; I felt very lonely and abandoned and I didn't understand at all what was happening to me.'

To be an actor

The role of an actor comprises the act of creating a character, of making it up based on the text and on the actor's personality. This creative act does not occur in a vacuum, it is determined by social, historical and psychological factors. There are many connections between the actor's creation and the roles he or she performs in his or her life. This constellation of factors allows for the construction of the artistic role. Naturally it is rather difficult to trace the interrelations and interdependences between the two 'worlds' with their own sets of roles and that is not my purpose here. I wish to emphasise that there exists an intense and dense relation between who the actor is and how she or he functions in life and the way in which he or she creates a role on the stage. Of course, the influences operate in the opposite direction as well: the stage role, the character's features, experiences and relationships have an impact on the personality of the actor. These influences are discussed during the group meetings and in individual psychotherapy. It seems that the role of an actor stands in complete contrast to the role of a patient. Dependence, passivity and limitations are juxtaposed by creation, spontaneity and looking for ways of expressing one's feelings.

With the benefit of hindsight, it is precisely the tension between or the polarisation of the two roles that is the therapeutic factor. It is an enormous challenge and a risk that can be undertaken only in a very safe environment. When the patients are shown the aims of their therapy and rehabilitation through theatre, they are given hope since the assumption is they have an adequate potential to create something together and to stage a dramatic performance. The essence of psychotherapy offered to people suffering from schizophrenia consists in such a change that will allow patients to achieve a relatively stable inner harmony, that is to obtain the ability to integrate various feelings and impulses and to express them and to obtain such a reduction of primitive fears so as to be able to live and to function among others and with them. Let us return here to the observation that in therapeutic theatre playing a character may influence the actor's personality by providing opportunities to enrich his or her experience. The features, feelings and relationships of the performed character exert their impact on the personality of the actor and these factors come into focus in our therapeutic theatre. The therapists' work is targeted at the following: all that happens in the play as well as the performance of the roles should empower the patients; they should expand their world of feelings and achieve a better understanding of themselves and other people. The reinforcement of the structure of the self and personal development account for becoming rooted in one's identity and for expanding it, which in consequence may lead to greater inner harmony, fewer relapses of psychosis and better functioning in real life.

One of psychodram's theorists, David Kipper, claims that the fundamental factor responsible for keeping or quitting a role is motivation in the
sense of satisfaction. While one is fulfilling a satisfying role, one may go
through periods of dissatisfaction, but the prerequisite for performing this
role is the predominance of satisfaction with it. When the predominant
condition is dissatisfaction, one gives up or swaps the role. Those people
who are satisfied with what they are doing remain in a state of, as Kipper
puts it, fluid experience (Kipper 1988). This experience is a result of the
interaction between two factors: an opportunity to accept a challenge and
take a risk, and abilities. The interaction between the perceived seriousness
of the challenge and one's abilities may give a great deal of satisfaction
when the two factors are in balance and when the abilities are adequate to
expectations (Kipper 1988). This is of utmost importance with the actors
who are also patients, the theatrical project must be carried out gradually,
step by step. Playing roles in therapeutic theatre is one of the ways that are
expected to stimulate the patient's motivation to live. It stems from the idea
of looking for motivation outside – not in the inner life of the patient,
which may remain withdrawn, muffled, empty or delusional.

How can a patient, a person who underwent a psychotic crisis and suffers
from a variety of disorders, adopt a role and play it? The patients who join
the theatre group fall into two categories, those with a dominant, developed
negative syndrome, overcome by the sense of vacuousness and helplessness;
and those who maintain good contact with people and who are emotionally
alive but periodically experience intensified hallucinations and anxiety.
Either subgroup has the same needs in theatrical therapy: encouragement,
stimulation, inspiration and requirements posed to its members against the
background of a strong sense of safety. The director who leads our theatre
group works with the patients just as he would work with professional actors.
In this way, he invokes the patients' hidden capabilities and talents and
expresses his respect towards them; he does not give the poor patients
a lenient treatment. Such an approach changes their role from the role of a
patient into the role of an actor. The relation with the director, a professional
leading a group of patients/actors, is of vital importance in the therapeutic
process. This is also connected with a different function of the director, who
is a father figure, while the group traditionally fulfils motherly functions.

The next factor that allows the patients to strengthen their identities
during the meetings of the group is the reality of the staged play. The reality
of the spectacle is an intermediary reality in the sense that, within it, the
patients/actors can display their feelings and fears, they can experiment
with new behaviours, they speak about the feelings of the characters they
play and therefore, indirectly, about their own feelings. In this manner, they
learn about themselves and others (Emunah and Johnson 1983). And
during regular rehearsals they consolidate their knowledge. Sometimes they
can simply experience certain feelings for the first time. John wrote: 'I begin

to realise that only now, when I'm over 20, I start to live truly and to experience truly whatever is around me.' If we understand psychosis as a response towards the inability to pass on to the next phase of development, we see that the experience of theatre offers a chance of going through a given phase in the arbitrary reality of the stage.

John wrote: 'The fact that I played the role of Tristan contributed to the experience that I, with time, began to understand better my emotions and my behaviour in everyday life, off stage. I was able to name many feelings in which the play is rich. Previously I wouldn't have been able to do that, for sure.' I would like to stress once again that a role provides an opportunity to safely try out various feelings experienced by oneself and by other characters, and also to keep practising. The patients may take part in the meetings of the theatre group for at least 1 year, and some stay in the group for several years. Therefore the theatre group becomes an area of both psychotherapy and social training. It appears that such a combination produces more lasting results, which can subsequently be of use in everyday life.

We have often discussed the question how it is possible to bear the stress of, first, exposing oneself in front of the group and, second, performing in front of an audience. Fear, which constantly troubles the patients, emerges on various occasions as a many-headed hydra. In the theatre group, fear is alleviated by the strong bond that exists between the group members, by the attractiveness of the group and by what we call the group structure. Moreover, as the therapeutic community operates in accordance with certain rules, a special atmosphere is created, which makes it possible to overcome fear and to improve the ability to function in a group.

The bond existing between the group members manifests itself in many ways: the patients take care of each other during rehearsals, they celebrate their birthdays together or have New Year's Eve parties; they go to the theatre or hike in the mountains together; they cooperate on the stage and in the wings and support each other every day. John wrote: 'I wish to underline that I made a few friends in the theatre group and that these friendships are stable, I believe they can last for years. They are characterised by mutual trust, frankness, joy and a sense of humour. I had never expected I could make friends in my life. I had never believed it, I had always cried and said I had nobody close. So then I was greatly surprised.' Common effort, cooperation and deep emotions on the stage bring about such close relationships between the actors.

The structure of the group is composed of the script of the play, usually its abridged version, the permanence of the place where the rehearsals are held, the propositions of the director and the presence of the therapists. The structure provides clear limits in terms of time, space and personalities, within which the group can find safety and support. Another important value that is created in the spectacle and that is significant for the performers is the play's aesthetic, artistic value. The spectacles are staged professionally in the same way as are the requirements posed of the actors and for each play a stage set, costumes and light are designed. Here again, therapeutic theatre meets real theatre. The actors who perform in the play are elements of the work of art, of their common creation. It makes the group attractive for patients.

The strong 'ego' of the group and the distinct, professional leader who does not allude to the role of a patient but draws on the resources and energy of the actor will awaken the dormant and suppressed components of the self or, through rehearsing the role, will reinforce what has been unstable, uncertain or broken. By playing others, the actors make themselves stronger; they open up to the task and not to the illness. In our treatment system, the theatre group blends group psychotherapy with rehabilitation, more insightful psychological work, focused on emotional problems, conflicts and self-portraits, with the execution of particular tasks on the stage and in the group. The objectives of drama therapy in this sense are better communication and self-expression. It seems that it is significant to internalise the acting experience and incorporate it in the inner world of the patient/actor.

Having fulfilled its function in the conventional reality of the drama, therapeutic theatre should be transformed in the patient's life into real work, study and relationships with people off stage. This does not mean that further problems will not resurface. The patients who join the theatre group often suffer from chronic disorders and therefore many of them do not venture into real life outside mental health institutions. They often function in their community thanks to the support of the rehabilitation centre, they start to learn at school, sometimes take evening courses, and they find jobs in sheltered employment enterprises. We are deeply convinced that such results are very satisfactory.

Bibliography

Bielańska, A., Cechnicki, A. and Budzyna-Dawidowski, P. (1991). Drama therapy as a means of rehabilitation for schizophrenic patients: our impressions, *American Journal of Psychotherapy* XLV(4): October.

Blatner, A. (1988). *Acting-in. Practical Application of Psychodramatic Methods*. New York: Springer-Verlag.

Campling, P. (2001). Therapeutic communities, *Advances in Psychiatric Treatment* 7: 365–372.

Emunah, R. and Johnson, D.R. (1983). The impact of theatrical performances on the self-images of psychiatric patients, *The Arts in Psychotherapy* 10: 233–239.

Fink, P.J. (1985). Creative therapies, in *APA Commission on Psychiatric Therapies, Part II: The Psychosocial Therapies*. Washington, DC: APA.

Johnson, D.R. (1982). Principle and techniques of drama therapy, *The Arts in Psychotherapy* 9: 83–90.

Kipper, D.A., (1988). On the definition of P: another view, *Group Psychotherapy, Psychodrama & Sociometry* 41: 164–168.

Chapter 21

Psychodrama and the psychotic member

Kleopatra Psarraki

Introduction

Despite the enduring presence of therapeutic communities (TCs) (Kennard 1999) and the variety of psychotherapy schools suggesting alternative methods to medication or hospitalisation, the psychological treatment of the psychoses still remains a rather controversial subject. There are political variations across Europe and cultural dimensions to this as well. When it comes to demonstrating the evidence for the effectiveness of psychological treatment for psychosis, there is, unfortunately, still a considerable way to go. Added to this, there is a general fear of mad people. Yet it may well be the case that fear and despair are precisely what these people feel; and that those who are considered normal are in turn afraid to face their own psychotic side. Whatever the reason, treating mad people is a demanding and, at times, rather strenuous undertaking, while our expectations for its outcome go hand in hand with our notion of what cure might be.

People with psychosis come to therapeutic communities in search of allies in their battle against inner threats. Their ego is so fragile that they need to erect a protective wall in order to make them feel secure, which explains why they often seek hospitalisation; in other words, protection. This is precisely where a longstanding issue arises. This relates to those essential elements that are found in therapeutic communities and which improve the life quality of people with psychosis both during and after treatment (Campling and Haigh 2002).

Whether as residential units or as day centres, therapeutic communities are founded on the well-established notion that the milieu per se constitutes the most crucial therapeutic factor for psychotic people. Here, the coexistence of psychotherapeutic sessions with community meetings and informal group activities has a significant impact. Yet, the mere presence of these mechanisms is not enough to make for effective clinical outcomes. For argument's sake, one may find quite interesting and innovative group activities in a number of hospitals, but this does not make them therapeutic communities. The actual difference lies with the way in which the staff in therapeutic communities regard their clients, as well as the atmosphere created in the whole building. These elements do not magically appear just by calling a building a therapeutic community or by applying the therapeutic community principles unless those principles are understood and practised to the fullest.

It is our firm belief that, above all, those suffering from psychosis need humanity for this is what is lacking in themselves and their environment. It is also our belief that Bion's notion of containment (Bion 1962)[1] and Winnicott's term holding (Winnicott 1965) denote more or less the same idea. It is the holding and containing environment that can reverse the despair that these patients experience, by allowing real emotional engagement to express itself, however primitive the form that expression takes.

Being held by the community means being accepted and affirmed and this alone contrasts with previous experiences of being rejected and labelled insane by social environments. In everyday practice, this approach may manifest itself in various forms. Something as simple as a benign smile and/ or as complex as a well-thought-out interpretation, the regularity of meetings, the community rituals and respecting privacy and personal time, the expectation to open oneself up when ready, to encourage others, all contribute to the development of a relationship of trust with the community.

At the beginning of the treatment, the patient's connection with the community may be facilitated by containing the extremes of psychotic reactions and through powerful projections onto the community, either in a positive or in a negative way. The community matrix (Foulkes 1964)[2] will be soon felt as a womb, where rebirth can take place. Dependence may be very similar to the infant's need for the mother. Nevertheless, after a period of good mothering,[3] the gratification of omnipotent fantasies must be followed by disillusionment.[4] The working through process of the patient's projective identifications, which is a primitive defence mechanism, widely used by people with a psychosis, and their transformation into contents with meaning, where the emotions have a name, the actions can be explained, the attitude is interpreted, relieve the patient and show him or her a better way of communicating their feelings than symptoms (Berke et al. 2002).

A relevant indifference to the symptoms is also important at this stage. Patients are treated as whole persons that are full of creative potential and are invited to invest in the healthy part of their personality.[5] This contrasts with the idea psychotic patients often have of themselves as dispersed pieces or as suffering from an incurable illness that renders them incapable of completing tasks such as housework or shopping. Psychotherapeutic sessions complete the work of everyday tasks, by providing a safe place for analytic work.

For the psychopathology in question, we deem it important to provide a set of interventions, sociotherapeutic and psychotherapeutic. Last, but not least, to provide enough time and space for the staff to meet and, together, work out both the difficulties of the patients and the relationships between them. This chapter will focus on the psychotherapeutic technique of psychodrama and its use in the context of a therapeutic community for those with a psychotic illness. Psychodrama belongs to the family of expressive therapies, e.g. music therapy, art therapy, dance and movement therapy and drama therapy (Searle and Streng 2001). As such, it uses the art medium as a way of self-expression and revelation. Some of its therapeutic qualities are common to all expressive therapies. After a brief reference to these, we shall concentrate on the specific properties and advantages of psychodrama, always in correlation with the psychotic psychopathology.

Expressive art therapies

Since the early years of human civilisation art has been one of the natural ways human beings express themselves and communicate with their fellows. The healing quality of the arts is not a recent discovery. Nevertheless, their use as a therapeutic medium only occurred in the 20th century. The interest in arts is primarily based on their unique quality to allow the unfolding of the human psyche, with little or no interference from logic, conscious control and the censorship of psychic defences, which is present even in our dreams.

Art renders the psychotic world accessible to the therapist, while giving the patient the possibility to express their inner world in ways that do not threaten their fragile ego. The art medium operates very much like a transitional object, as Winnicott (1974) defined it.[6] Through the medium of art, psychic material finds shape and the psychotic world assumes a certain structure. Dispersed or split parts of the self become apparent and thus their integration into the self is gradually achieved.

The psychotherapeutic technique of psychodrama

Psychodrama was one of the first expressive therapies used in psychotherapy. It was initially utilised as a treatment methodology by Moreno in the 1920s (Marineau 1989). Moreno maintained that performing an interaction helps ideas and feelings about it become conscious rather than often being hidden when simply talking (Moreno 1972). The technique involves staging a life problem – past, present or imagined – as though it were a theatrical play. Consequently, many psychodramatic terms derive from the theatre itself: protagonist, director, stage and audience. The protagonist is the focal figure on stage. The director directs him and the auxiliaries (other members of the group assigned roles by the protagonist) on stage. The auxiliaries may represent figures in the protagonist's life or hidden parts of his psyche. The audience is formed by all those present in psychodrama that are not actively engaged in the drama. Moreno considered his method as an action approach in which someone is introduced through acting-in to new ways of expression that are almost neglected in our society: creativity, spontaneity, emotions, physical contact, imagination and so on. The notion of catharsis is also crucial to the technique in question.

In drama, the therapeutic expectation is identical to many group psycho-therapeutic approaches: to explore both the traumatic early experiences of the subject and their influence on their life in the here and now of the group. However, instead of employing analysis of dreams, free associations and verbal interactions in the group, the primal object relations are seen through their dramatic representation, according to a scenario suggested by one of the members. It is in this context that auxiliaries participate in the action. Each time, the situation unfolding on stage involves the protagon-ist's problems inscribed in his personal history and elements derived from previous therapy sessions.

The available time is divided into three parts and space needed is usually two rooms. The first part of the session is called warming up and concerns the gathering of the group and its loosening through exercises and inter-personal encounter. When members reach a sufficient level of spontaneity the protagonist of the given session emerges and the group makes ready for drama. Drama, the action, takes place on the stage, located in a room or space different than that of the warming-up process. This differentiation denotes and ensures the passage into the imaginary world of playing. In the third part, the sharing, members express feelings and thoughts regarding playing, whether they participated actively as auxiliaries or as audience. At this point, the protagonists remain silent. They have already revealed themselves on stage and now receive feedback from the group. Members' comments may take the form of emotional expression or memories of similar experiences. In many schools of psychodrama, sharing also com-prises working through of drama, in an analytical sense.

The psychopathology of psychotic patients

People with psychosis experience moments of depersonalisation, char-acterised by distressing feelings of losing their internal boundaries due to an external presence that threatens their ego. This is sometimes described as psychotic disintegration (Rosenfeld 1965). In such cases, someone with a psychosis may feel the urge to tackle this threat by breaking the continuum between the external and internal world through building a protective shield that excludes contact with the object. One of the most common defences relates to withdrawing from reality combined with creating a powerful projective identification, whereby the object is expected to respond in accordance with the fantasy.[7]

However, one can never withdraw completely from reality. In such cases one would be faced with one's own psychic death. The protective shield is not impermeable because bits of reality always intrude.[8] In this case, people with psychosis either withdraw from the external world by hiding behind autistic walls or use interfaces in communication, like delirium, the primary function of which is to assure psychotic reality. Any meaningful linkage, for instance the relationship with the therapist, any progress achieved thus far in therapy, even the mental apparatus itself become the targets of the psychotic's powerful attacks and, as a consequence, they are underestimated, devalued and despised.

The survival of the therapeutic framework, both at a literal and at a symbolic level, is crucial. A setting free of noxious objects, at an imaginary level, through these processes just mentioned and via the mechanism of projective identification leaves the subject with a feeling of irreparable loss, as though having irretrievably lost the objects. As the object is part of the psychotic self and not separate from it, losing the object is tantamount to losing oneself. Projective identification then takes an intrusive form.[9]

Bion (1962) attempted to explain psychotic attacks on the mental apparatus by formulating the following hypothesis. He associated the formation of thinking to what he called alpha functioning, the capacity of transforming sense impressions into elements, alpha elements, that can be represented or symbolised. This mechanism is connected to repression and thus to the distinction between the conscious and the unconscious. When alpha function is lacking, sense impressions do not integrate and cannot be repressed and symbolised. Bion has termed them beta elements (Bion 1967). Beta elements are not symbolised in dreams and the unconscious. The subject feels the need to expel them from the self and uses projective identification for this purpose.

The primal object, the breast, is the determinant for the development of alpha function. The device to think the thoughts emanates from the metabolism of beta elements into alpha elements. The infant is deprived of this capacity in the beginning. It can only express its inner tensions by projecting these onto his mother. If the mother is a reliable container, that is if she has developed her own alpha functioning, she then returns the infant's emotions to it in the form of symbolised contents. The infant gradually introjects this capacity of the mother and thus develops its own internal container. In the opposite case, the infant will be deprived of perceiving the internal tensions through the external ones.

The psychodramatic treatment of psychosis

As we mentioned earlier, the world of the psychotic person is as far isolated from the external real world as it can possibly be. Failing to handle the frustrations and threats that their emotions represent to the integrity of their ego, the psychotic person takes refuge in defences. In other words, the psychotic's ego tends to invent two virtual screens that disrupt the continuity between the outside and the inside. In the critical phases of psychosis, these screens fail to appear and the ego is compelled to try hard and reconstruct these in order to separate itself from the object or to neutralise the latter from within. Delirium is the means to reconstruct and maintain these screens.

The psychodrama allows the creation of a third space that temporarily replaces this protective void. But how can people with psychosis actually play? The first obvious conclusion is that they cannot. They cannot actually treat a piece of furniture as something different, e.g. a bed as though it was a chair. They cannot say 'you are God' because they are God and Satan at the same time. A dialogue cannot possibly exist; it is more a case of a perpetual soliloquy. This act cannot unfold in a reality different than what is inside their mind. The drama transfers into the time and space of another reality. Therefore, for those with a psychosis, the objective of the group is precisely this: to lead someone suffering from a psychosis smoothly into the drama and thereby, contain them. During playing, a certain distance is allowed. The fact that the psychodrama takes place in a different room or space suffices to denote that the sphere where playing occurs is utterly detached from the everyday world, whose absurdity forbids the psychotic any access. Psychodrama offers those with psychosis the opportunity to deliver them from their delirium which, however, in this way, is not a delirium any more. Acting the delirium allows the psychotic to access his own internal divisions; henceforth, he is not without speech anymore. It remains for him to integrate the psychodrama, which is a new field that has been constructed for him.

The participation of the body in the psychodrama enables a primitive and silent type of communication, consisting of gestures and expressions, mostly unconscious, that still have a more effective dynamic than words, to be brought out by the emotions. In this respect, those with a psychosis who find it difficult to express themselves in words can actually make up for this insufficiency in communication, through the body. At this point, it is essential for the therapist and the other members to employ symbolisation by deciphering the gestures and interpreting the emotions and defences. Certainly, these should not be made too specific, but adequate attention needs to be given to it.

The particular advantage of psychodrama is that it allows the internal world of the patients to express itself verbally through the drama. In this way, the words may eventually accompany the actions on stage. This dual possibility of expression allows psychodrama to establish a structured space where regression is restrained[10] by the task due to the words and to the participation of the other members in the drama. With the assistance of the psychodramatist, the protagonist constructs a scene including representative characters of all the people that played a significant role in the patient's childhood. The roles assigned to the auxiliary egos reflect the primary object relations of the object. The significance at this point lies with the manner in which the protagonist chooses to represent these relationships. For instance, it is meaningful to observe which childhood scenes are actually selected, which essential elements are left out of the various scenes or which points are underlined as important by the protagonist.

In fact, the protagonist acts subconsciously. His usual defences are diminished because drama does not take place in the everyday world and for this reason, he does not run the risk of being attacked by his fantasies. The active presence of others on stage reassures the protagonist that those parts of the psyche that are represented by the auxiliary egos will remain intact. In this way, he devotes himself to the drama and without even willing or controlling it, he delivers his psychic scene on the psychodramatic stage. The others will shortly see the various splits. At this point, the psychodramatist will have the option to continue the drama by constructing scenes that reflect the revealed splits. In other words, the psychodramatist will proceed with an analysis of split emotions on stage.[11]

Of course the psychodramatist's choice depends greatly on the psychic maturity of the protagonist. Usually a certain number of sessions are needed in order to reach an adequate level of representation and understanding. Additionally, certain psychodramatic techniques, such as doubling,[12] may allow the auxiliary egos a larger degree of spontaneity in relation to their intervention in the protagonist's playing. This is certainly very important for those with psychosis as their ability to express themselves is very limited, especially at the beginning of their treatment. Through doubling, the most horrifying emotions may be displayed while at the same time remaining a concealed part of the individual.

The fact that the psychodramatist does not hesitate to direct the roles assigned to the members, testifies to his capacity to restrain the horrifying emotions. His presence on stage creates an atmosphere of trust and the patient is relieved to know that he will act as a boundary to his crude impulses. Furthermore, in the third part of the session, the other members along with the therapist can demonstrate to the patient the coexistence of split parties. The patient finishes by seeing through his ambivalence and rediscovering the stable feeling of his existence. The discussion that follows the drama acts to clarify what it was about. The other members are present to explain their role selection or their way of re-enacting the familiar characters of the protagonist. Thus, any misunderstandings and confusions are resolved. The translation of acts into words by the therapist allows the transition to the symbolic level.

It is essential to underline the importance of the possibility to choose a fantastic scenario or certain psychodramatic action techniques (Ossorio and Fine 1959) including the whole group; particularly so, when the group includes many psychotic patients. This is because direct dramatisation of personal stories may prove, at the beginning, particularly damaging for certain patients. In my opinion, the therapist should decide to postpone the dramatisation of such stories until the time is appropriate. The protective aspect of the therapist's attitude is far more crucial for difficult patients. For certain classic psychodramatists, this narrows the spontaneity of psychodrama. However, a period of time is necessary before proceeding with performing real scenarios.

Additionally, one should underscore the necessity for a co-therapist or well trained members of staff to participate in the group and on stage, when the group contains only psychotic members. This is due to the need to include members with greater psychic maturity, so as to achieve better containment of both group and individual phenomena.

Psychodrama within a therapeutic community

Therapeutic communities are complex institutions, since they comprise an internal network of relations and activities and at the same time, they are parts of an external network of relations, broader therapeutic institutions and psychosocial services (Hinshelwood 2001). Therefore, they are influenced by phenomena taking place within the community's matrix, but also by the rules, laws and dynamics of the broader cultural and political institutions. Psychotherapeutic groups, like psychodrama, may be valuable places, where the elaboration of various events, both internal and external to the community, is fruitful.

Each member carries his own history, when he first enters the community. However, the community itself has a history, which is mirrored in the other members' behaviour, thus affecting his own behaviour and psychic reality. Moreover, the community's life is not static: there are farewells and new arrivals, changes in building, the staff members and the community's rules. The advantage of psychodrama, and of any other expressive therapy, is that it makes it possible to explore both personal and community issues and to gain a deep understanding of their impact on community members. In any case, whether in the form of a discussion before drama, or in drama itself, members bring their daily experiences, their relations and their conflicts. Therefore, it is usual to dramatise the interactions taking place in the community, although this may be expressed indirectly, through a personal story that is similar to the one in question. Furthermore, changes in the community are often worked through in drama. Scenarios may involve themes reflecting the members' struggle to regain a sense of security, like having a lunch together as friends, memories of the family gathered around the table or celebrating together. Farewells and new arrivals are also explored, directly and indirectly, e.g. memories of trips abroad, friends that left to go to another city etc. The same holds true for great events, affecting the present and future of the community itself.

Conclusion

In psychodrama, the subject may work through his emotions, his defences, his fears on two levels: the real space of the group and the imaginary space of the stage. As the latter is isolated from the real world it acts as a refuge where the psychotic can project his inner threats without the dread of destroying or being destroyed. At critical times, or when newly arrived in the community, this works as a safety net and simultaneously as a space where a form of elaboration takes place, no matter how primitive. The holding function of the stage is more easily accepted, at these times, than holding by other members of the community, even therapists. By the same token, the community needs structured spaces for working through the various experiences of community life.

In turn, the community is, in itself, a holding environment with clear boundaries and a place where relationships develop every hour and every day. This regularity reassures the person with psychosis and fastens the unfolding of the psyche in drama. Understanding, in such a context is achieved, through the synthesis of the every day experience of the other and his inner representation on stage.

Notes

1 Containment refers to accepting one's most painful and disturbing aspects through affective understanding.
2 Matrix refers to the network of communication among group/community members (staff included).
3 In this setting of extreme emotional dependence, the analyst must provide the facilitating environment that was absent in the patient's childhood. Winnicott states that in the extreme case the therapist would need to go to the patient and actively present good mothering (Winnicott 1965).
4 At first, the baby experiences the immediate satisfaction of his needs: he is hungry and his mother adapts herself and presents the breast to him. This is felt, by the baby, as if he had created the breast. He feels that the breast is under his omnipotent control. The breast is a subjective experience. Nevertheless, gradually, his needs are not so promptly satisfied. This is the period of disillusionment: the object is created by the baby, but it was there, waiting to be created and invested. The use of the object presupposes the development of a capacity to use objects through the perception of them as distinct elements of the self-not-me (Winnicott 1974).
5 Bion has argued that in all those with a psychosis there is a non-psychotic part of the personality, needing to be discovered and invested in therapy so as to face successfully the vicissitudes of the psychotic part. The coexistence of a psychotic with a non-psychotic part, in the personality, is a valid fact for all individuals cf. W.R. Bion, Differentiation of the psychotic from the non-psychotic part of the personality, *International Journal of Psychoanalysis* 38: 266–275, 1957.
6 Transitional objects belong to the period following omnipotent control (subjective objects) and before the perception of others as true objects. It represents an intermediary stage of experience, where fantasy and reality meet: the object is – and is not – subjective.

7 The projector believes that the recipient experiences their exact feelings. When the latter shows signs that they are aware of the projection (anger for instance), the projector feels secure that the material he evacuated is indeed received by the recipient. This is a crucial point, since therapists should show such signs (with diminished intensity) so as to reassure the patient that their psychic material is not lost. Contrariwise, if the recipient fails to recognise the projective identification, the patient will revive their early experiences with the mother as an unreliable container cf. H. Searles, *Collected Papers on Schizophrenia and Related Subjects*, New York, International Universities Press, 1965, and T.H. Ogden, *Projective Identification and Psychotherapeutic Technique*, London, Maresfield Library, 1979.

8 This is in fact the non-psychotic part of the self that remains in contact with the reality principle.

9 This is a fantasy of inhibiting another person and controlling them from within. According to this, ideas and feelings are concrete objects, capable of being removed and placed inside another person. Apart from assuming control of the object, projective identification of that sort reassures the subject that the projected parts are safe inside the other person.

10 According to P.F. Kellermann, *Focus on Psychodrama: The Therapeutic Aspects of Psychodrama*, London, Jessica Kingsley, 1992, psychodramatic enactment is regression in the service of the ego.

11 The drama unfolds according to the directions of the protagonist; however, as the psychodramatist is present, his directions/suggestions regarding the construction of the scenes and the participation of the auxiliary egos, reflect his perceptions of the protagonist's needs, projections and fantasies: in other words, he formulates his interpretations into dramatic action: action interpretations cf. D.A. Kipper, *Psychotherapy through Clinical Playing*, New York: Brunner/Mazel, 1986.

12 It is the invisible self of the protagonist, his alter ego, often hidden, repressed or unknown. The technique involves him in using an auxiliary in the specialised role of playing the protagonist's alter ego. A double may express the protagonist's thoughts and emotions with the intensity he feels them, he may encourage the protagonist to take more risks and enter the interaction more completely, or he may make suggestions and interpretations concerning the protagonist's emotional and psychological state cf. A. Blatner, *Acting-in. Practical Applications of Psychodramatic Methods*, London, Free Association Books, 1997.

Bibliography

Berke, J.H., Fagan, M., Mak-Pearce, G. and Pierides-Müller, S. (2002). *Beyond Madness: Psychosocial interventions in Psychosis*. London: Jessica Kingsley.

Bion, W.R. (1962). *Learning from Experience*. London: Karnac Books.

Bion, W.R. (1967). *Second Thoughts*. London: Karnac Books.

Campling, P. and Haigh, R. (2002). *Therapeutic Communities: Past, present and future*. London: Jessica Kingsley.

Foulkes, S.H. (1964). *Therapeutic Group Analysis*. London: Allen & Unwin.

Hinshelwood, R.D. (2001). *Thinking about Institutions: Milieu and madness*. London: Jessica Kingsley.

Kennard, D. (1999). *Introduction to Therapeutic Communities*. London: Jessica Kingsley.

Marineau, R.F. (1989). *Jacob Levi Moreno*. London: Routledge.

Moreno, J.L. (1972). *Psychodrama*. New York: Beacon House.

Ossorio, A.G. and Fine, L.J. (1959). Psychodrama as a catalyst for social change in a mental hospital, in J.L. Moreno (ed.) *Progress in Psychotherapy*. New York: Grune & Stratton.

Rosenfeld, H.A. (1965). *Psychotic States: A psycho-analytic approach*. London: Hogarth.

Searle, Y. and Streng, I. (eds) (2001). *Where Analysis Meets the Arts. The Integration of the Art Therapies with Psychoanalytic Practice*. London: Karnac Books.

Winnicott, D. (1965). *The Maturational Processes and the Facilitating Environment*. London: Hogarth.

Winnicott, D. (1974). *Playing and Reality*. London: Pelican.

Chapter 22

New visions in the long-term outpatient therapy of psychosis: the therapeutic community within the community

Andreas von Wallenberg Pachaly

I understand the approach outlined here as an essential adjunct or sometimes alternative to a neuroleptic-centred quick-fix treatment, that tends to neglect the interpersonal forces that did and do influence the individual patient. The latter is not able to provide him with a long-term holding and containing environment that facilitates psychological growth.

The treatment setting created by us (Wallenberg Pachaly, A. 1992; Wallenberg Pachaly, S. 1997) is based on the planned use of human group interrelationships as an agent of change. It makes use of such processes as binding, containing, holding, dependency, growth, change and separation.

The setting

Psychotic and schizophrenic patients, but also patients diagnosed with a diagnosis of borderline, personality disorder, depression or severe neuroses, are invited to live for a period of 3 to 5 years in one of our four sheltered flats, two of which are actually villas in downtown Düsseldorf, and to join a living–learning community that fosters integrative forces and strives to counteract fragmentation and splitting. The developmental work in the therapeutic community within the community rests on five pillars (see Figure 22.1).

Each patient has to participate in two different groups. One takes place in the flat and deals with the organisational aspects of living together and the other is carried out at the head office of the umbrella institution, which offers the institutional container of the therapeutic community within the community. This group dynamics session cares for the emotional needs of the residents. The group living in one flat is perceived as an interpersonal matrix and a continuing effort is made to clarify interpersonal relations, make the unconscious dynamics conscious, e.g. in what way individual members put on stage earlier childhood or adolescent scenarios. A constant monitoring of the position each patient takes in the flat is carried out.

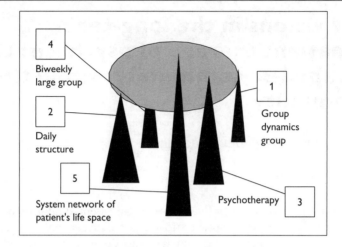

Figure 22.1 Therapeutic community within the community

Conflicts on all levels, primarily in the here and now, between patient and institution or the outside world are discussed and any violations of the rules are acknowledged and eventually resolved.

Each patient has to live according to a structured daily schedule, either work, school, a day clinic, sheltered work, etc. In the beginning it is frequently a hard task for the social workers to support the patients in structuring their time. An additional group is offered, where patients are helped to dare to explore future hopes and visions and are supported in their first steps to realise them. Each patient is required to undergo psychotherapy according to his needs, to enable him to work through the traumatising aspects of his previous life history. For many patients diagnosed as schizophrenic or psychotic, this is often their first chance to explore their lives in a psychotherapeutic way. There is a continuing exchange between the pool of psychotherapists who have developed an interest in cooperating with us and the social workers and psychologists that work within the community. Every other week patients from all flats, the staff members and the therapeutically trained board members (group analysts and family therapists), participate in a large group. A clear boundary is set between those inside and those outside the community. The function of the large group is to support the development of group boundaries and group identity. At the same time, it strengthens the group identity of the therapeutic community, within the community, as an institution and provides its member-patients with new strength to face the outside world, as well as their inner world. The integration and anti-fragmentation work with the system network which represents the individual patient's entire life space (see later).

The psychotic self – understanding the psychotic

Whereas the neurotic fends off only certain feelings the psychotic rejects feelings in themselves, especially anxiety and aggression, and projects them. The task of the therapist and the therapeutic community is to endure this and to digest the feelings, as a good mother does, so that the psychotic can re-introject them (Volkan 2004). In the process, it is however necessary to cross some hurdles because although the psychotic does constantly carry out attacks on the community's and his therapist's capacity to think (Bion 1959) and to relate, he tries to become not aware of himself and thus to avoid all the feelings that would be associated with self-awareness. The reason for his behaviour lies in the unbearable contradictions that result from the fragmented and split-off self and object images, and self-representations, as well as the corresponding overwhelming contradictory affective conditions. These contradictions lead to anxiety. This anxiety differs from the signal fear resulting from structural conflicts, since it is overwhelming and without specific signal character, and because it threatens totally the feeling of identity, even the feeling to exist and feel concerned. It only vanishes when integrated self- and object images have been developed. As I understand it, the probable origins for this lie in the lack of cohesive forces in the individual, as well as in the primary caretaker and the surrounding family group. I like to call this a lack of interpersonal glue. One reason for this may be that cumulative traumatic influences have weakened the cohesive forces of the individual and his holding group beyond a critical point. This hypothesis concurs with the research by Tienari and others from Finland on adoptive twins (Tienari et al. 1994). In the course of a normal development, aggressive emotions arising within the baby and toddler can be digested and integrated into his personality by himself, if he is embedded within a friendly, holding and benignly mirroring, digesting relationship and holding group environment (Winnicott 1972). If, however, these emotions are not contained and digested, unbearable aggressive emotions originate, and coagulate into an infantile psychotic self. This usually happens within a certain age span.

The therapeutic community, within the community, as a containing and holding environment

If the community succeeds in functioning as a container for the dreadful fears and feelings of the patient, projective identification can develop its communicative effect. This means that the community must be prepared to enter into an intensive relationship that demands to a high degree, the capacity to think and the capacity for active thinking (Wurmser 1999). Whereas the psychotic self gives up the relationship with reality and fuses with a fantasised world that counteracts feelings of impotence and fears to become annihilated and devoured the therapeutic community offers the psychotic and schizophrenic patient, several dimensions and qualities that encourage, support and enable his or her psychological development.

The group becomes a container for unbearable feelings. At times it will have to tolerate feelings of abandonment, isolation, agony, fear of annihilation, total loss of self and just sit and attend and be with the fellow patient. It takes over the role of demarcation between outer threats and inner threats from overwhelming feelings and it can mirror and digest feelings like a good mother who reflects with empathy. In a group which offers relationships, holding and containing, over a long period of time, it becomes possible for the patient to feel secure enough to reveal his psychotic kernel and a common exploration becomes possible. The community, as an empathic mirror, can then help the patient to find his post-psychotic personality, which will need to strive to integrate the experience of psychosis for the rest of his life. In this process, the limits are also felt most painfully. Therapy in many cases can only alleviate, not heal, least of all, undo for the container is broken and can be repaired only partially.

Case example

Jeff had been hospitalised twice with severe psychotic reactions. The second time he even tried to commit suicide by forcing a sharp key through his throat. His doctor had motivated him to contact a therapeutic community, within the community, because Jeff still lived with his mother and it was felt that he could profit from the growth facilitating environment. It took him about 4 months to decide to leave his mother and to move in into one of the flats. In the first phase of his stay he was very anxious and kind of tried to seduce half his female fellow residents into becoming his mother. At the same time it became obvious that his capacity to regulate distance and closeness was very limited. Almost like a borderline patient he succeeded in making two patients jealous over him. As he felt more secure, he dared to fall in love. He experienced a brief psychotic relapse in the face of his enduring, overwhelming feelings of guilt, because of his separation from mother, which, however, was contained within the community.

The therapeutic community as a transitional object

Case example

Anna's paranoid psychosis began 23 years ago, at a time when she could no longer contain her feelings of rage, aggression, hate and dissatisfaction. Severe parental control combined with a lack of support, which she had missed in her family and her denial of her own needs, in the face of her autistic brother, made her stick strictly to the rules, without being able to express her real emotions. She had given in to her severe superego, without being able to humanise it. In the course of her therapy the community, as a transitional object, became the carrier of the feelings that she was not able to tolerate, in her relationship with her therapist. By regulating distance from the relationship and closeness to it, she was able to tolerate these feelings and did not have to destroy her relationship with her therapist. The integration, through dialogue and supervision, between psychotherapy and the life in the therapeutic community, created the opportunity to understand the function of the therapeutic community as a transitional object and to work with it. The transitional object is part of a healthy development. It supports the growth in the capacity to be alone and to differentiate between the inner and outer world. Impairment in the development of a transitional object can have its roots in too long a separation between mother and child. In addition, inconsistent, unreliable contact, insufficient holding, insufficient responses to the spontaneous life expressions of the child, do not allow a differentiation between self and the other.

Thus the therapeutic community, within the community, as a transitional object, can help the patient survive separation from the therapist, and thus contain unbearable feelings that would otherwise be projected onto the therapist, which would result in the destruction of the therapeutic relationship. It helps to regulate closeness, intimacy and distance, which especially in the case of psychotically structured patients can also lead to a breakdown in the relationship. It can give comfort in cases of mourning and separation and it can support a narcissistic balance that prevents suicide. Transitional objects, like teddy bears, are loved and hated and thus help the child to endure the frustrations of life. The residential group in the sheltered flat also functions as a transitional object (Smith 1989) and, as well as the large group, can be loved and hated too. For example, Renate, in a separation situation from her therapist forced, through an attempted suicide, the transitional object/sheltered flat to behave towards her in a non-abandoning way; to visit her, to understand her, to accompany her. Through a displacement of those negative aspects of the therapeutic relationship that threaten to become overwhelming, onto the transitional object, the good therapeutic relationship will be allowed to survive.

Case example

I am reminded here of a patient, Siegfried, who denied all relationships in his sheltered flat. He strongly devalued his fellow residents and destroyed any

relationship in order to be able to experience himself as separate, autonomous, powerful and valuable. In his life, he experienced himself in
relationships as insufficient, worthless and, again and again, as inadequate. He
was only able to get involved in a meaningful, trusting relationship with his
analyst, within the context of the sheltered flat as a transitional object.
Gradually he could start sharing his feelings of extreme inferiority and how he
himself usually feels excluded. He no longer had to engage in a continuous
process of devaluating the therapist and later on the community.

The valuable therapeutic flexibility created by the therapeutic community, within the community, lies in the fact that the transitional object forms
a complex relationship matrix (Smith 1989), from the inner sheltered flat
and outer circle of the large group; can be held close or pushed away and its
quality can be changed from warm to cold, from friendly to hostile. It can
even be killed off and brought back to life again. A very important phase is
one in which the transitional object itself grows in the transition to become
a lively object. Winnicott discussed this in his later work, where he
differentiated between object-relatedness and the use of an object. In his
paper 'The use of an object' (1969: 13) he summarises:

> Object-relatedness can be grasped with a concept, how the subject
> experiences, a description of the use of the object necessitates a con-
> sideration of the nature of the object. I put the reasons to the discussion,
> why the capacity to use the object is more differentiated than the capacity
> to relate to the object. The object-relatedness can be directed toward a
> subjective object, but the use of the object implies that the object is part of
> the outer reality. The following course can be determined:

> 1. The subject relates to the object.
> 2. The object goes through a process by which it is found in the world
>   instead of being placed into the world by the subject.
> 3. The subject destroys the object.
> 4. The object survives the destruction.
> 5   The subject can use the object.

The study of this problem gives consideration to the positive value of
destruction. The destruction and the survival of the object moves this out of
the area that is occupied by the objects created by projective psychic
mechanisms. In this way, a world of common reality is created that the
subject can use and the other than me substance can lead back into the
subject (cf. Sugarman and Jaffe 1989).

The deduction from this hypothesis for our understanding of what
happens in the transference, is extremely interesting and manifold, because

it lends a new dimension to the experience of destruction in the entire atmosphere of the community. If the patient makes no contact and does not enter into a relationship, this is now no longer a negation of relating, but his attempt to progress from relating to the object, to using the community or his therapist as the object. So, the classic concept of transference that is regarded primarily as repetition, becomes far richer through the use of the community as well as the therapist as a transitional object.

In my understanding, it is essential to widen the availability of the transitional object in order to counteract chronification and petrification of the personality structure. This makes it possible to enter into and maintain a therapeutic relationship with very disturbed patients. Three vignettes may illustrate what I mean.

Case example

Oskar: Neglect, fragmentation and feelings of pointlessness are projected on the community and it is treated accordingly, unloved, neglected, considered tiresome, monopolising. This corresponds to how he feels treated himself.

Walter: Dangerous aspects are projected on the community, the good sides of the therapist can remain protected. The community is perceived as dangerous and as a cold, unloving place, that does not acknowledge his efforts but denies them, and consequently the therapist can be rescued as warm and friendly. The community is used as a transitional object and is created by the patient.

Ray: A young man, who always stood in the shadow of his strong mother and his weak father, over 5 years built a transitional object that gained qualities of intimacy and affirmed his own potency. Simultaneously, he could regulate closeness and distance with his therapist and could modulate his feelings. He thus could get involved in the community and live through his separation anxieties in the relationship with his therapist and with the community.

In the course of a lifetime transitional objects change from body parts to thing objects, to fantasies, to ideas, philosophies and even hopes and plans for the future that can be understood as a bridge that leads out from the present reality into a new reality, like Martin Luther King's 'I have a dream'. Transitional objects that become more and more abstract are important for the entire psychic development over the whole lifespan. They bridge the gap between inner and outer reality and they can serve, not only as comforters, but also as containers for aggressive feelings. Thus, developing a life plan, a vision serves as a transitional object, the patient finally may carry it with him when he leaves the community.

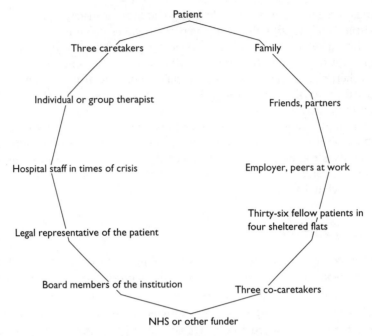

Patient

Three caretakers

Family

Individual or group therapist

Friends, partners

Hospital staff in times of crisis

Employer, peers at work

Thirty-six fellow patients in
four sheltered flats

Legal representative of the patient

Board members of the institution

Three co-caretakers

NHS or other funder

Figure 22.2 System network of 36 patients in four sheltered flats

The system network

The system network may include the patients' residential group, e.g. therapeutic community, family, partner and friends, the psychiatrist with medical responsibility for prescribing and monitoring medication, the individual and/or group therapists, the people at work or at his sheltered work place, family and friends and, during times of acute crisis and subsequent hospitalisation, the hospital staff, the representatives of the social welfare agency, which provides the financial support for the social work input and representatives of other bureaucratic institutions (see Figure 22.2).

Psychotic and schizophrenic patients, frequently, because of intermittent malfunctioning in reality are caught up in this fragmented network of helpers, legal authorities and administrative bureaucracy. However, if we succeed in conceptualizing (A. Wallenberg Pachaly 1997) this system network of significant others that represents the patient's life space, as a large group, which consciously and unconsciously relates, although it is not convened purposely and will almost never meet, we can work with it and understand disturbances in communication as a mirror of the psychic processes of the patient. Since the system network is, on the one hand, characterised by the fact that face-to-face communication is no longer possible, it easily arouses persecutory anxieties and reinforces the defence mechanisms of projection, projective identification, splitting and fragmentation (Kernberg 1985, 1993, 1995). It is, on the other hand, my understanding that the large group and even more the system network, is a means of getting in touch with the psychotic nucleus of groups as well as of individuals (de Marè 1974; de Marè et al. 1991).

From developmental, psycho-genetic and group genetic points of view, it is my understanding that feelings experienced in the large group, date back to an early developmental period in the life of the infant, where the differentiation between I and you, self and other, the inner self and the external world is at best blurred and certainly not yet fully established. The establishment of a mature sense of identity is in a *status nascendi* where feelings of omnipotence alternate with feelings of complete helplessness and impotence. Projective identification is a major means of maternal communication with the infant and persecutory anxieties alternate with feelings of oceanic well-being and ecstatic fusion. The formation of a group ego, described by Abraham (2006) as a co-self, precedes the development of a psychotic ego that is able to perceive moods and tensions in his group surroundings, and reacts to it without initially being able to gestalt them decisively. We can study this in group situations, where mothers bring their babies into the group therapeutic session. Here we see how sensitively the babies react to the surrounding group. It is already at this point where disturbance can occur and where development can become arrested. The conflict going along with this can later on be observed as it is put on stage in the scenario of the large group or the life system group. We then can perceive it, hold and contain it and interpret the resulting conflicts as well as interact with it in an interpretative way. This, in a favourable case will lead to the consequence that the large group, as well as the life system group, develops a culture which makes it possible for patients to become capable of dialogue; to observe themselves and their feelings and exchange freely about them; and to survive the fear of destruction or annihilation.

Case example

Beate, who had already lived for almost 2 years in the therapeutic community within the community, in the face of overwhelming feelings of guilt, had reacted psychotically. She had been hospitalised on a ward, whose chief psychiatrist was very opposed to any psychotherapy with patients diagnosed with schizophrenia and followed a strictly pharmacological regime. After 3 days the acute psychotic reaction had subsided and Beate became increasingly aware of the conflicting situation she was in. The situation deteriorated when Beate identified with the community and attacked the psychiatrist, who diagnosed this as a sign of another impending psychotic reaction. He urged her not to return to the community. Her psychotherapist, with whom Beate kept contact, informed the social worker in charge of the flat she lived in the community within the community. She asked for an appointment with the psychiatrist and succeeded in establishing a dialogue by outlining to him the personality growth process Beate had undergone, over the last 2 years. She also pointed out that the present situation, where Beate took one parent's side and nevertheless felt torn apart between different parents, resembled very much her infantile situation. Beate herself kept negotiating about the amount of medication she felt necessary for her condition, which was considerably lower e.g. 5mg instead of 20mg Zyprexa that her psychiatrist wanted to prescribe. She kept discussing with the members of the hospital the value of her experience with the therapeutic community within the community and with psychotherapy. In the end, with hindsight, this brief stay was very important for Beate on several levels. It increased her self-confidence, not to be completely powerless in the face of medical authorities but to be able to gestalt the relationship and was another step in the process of working through the trauma of her infantile situation, where she was torn between her quarreling parents.

The following hypothesis summarises my experience of working with patients with psychosis and schizophrenia in this setting:

1   That the large group dynamics and, even more so, the system network dynamics are prone to be experienced as threatening and persecutory, thus evoking projection, projective identification, splitting in the case of borderline personalities and fragmentation and fusion in the case of schizophrenically structured personalities.

2   We can observe parallel processes occurring within the large group and the system network dynamics and, within the psychotic, pre-Oedipal nucleus of the individual personality (Bleger 1972).

3   If, as influential members of the system network, we succeed in fostering a switch of the prevailing group dynamic towards one of a mutually holding relational matrix which fosters tolerance, respect, appreciation, communication and containment, then, as a result, split-off, fragmented feelings and aspects of personality become perceivable and discernible. They can then become contained, verbalized, worked through and integrated. A sense of security and a feeling of becoming master of one's own fate, of feeling able to survive and leave behind the catastrophe experienced by the self, grows within the patient. Some kind of glue comes into effect that bridges fragmentation and strengthens the container, which eventually is internalised by the patient.

4   This feeling, too, will grow in the other members of the system network. They will become more able to tolerate feelings of impotence and

helplessness in face of the landscapes of death (Benedetti 1992) of the patient's self. They will be less compelled to resort to managed care and instead become a facilitator of emotional growth, and accompany him on his developmental journey.

From our experiences we can recount that among those patients with whom we succeeded in this work of integration, we observed significant progress in subjective well-being, in emotional growth and in their capacity to relate, as well as in the decrease of their psychopathology, and their use of antipsychotic medicine. Also the quality of their social integration increased. That is, the degree to which they participated in the world of work and in social life in general. With residents who frequently had to be hospitalised for crisis interventions, the frequency and the length of these stays were reduce significantly to no more than 7 to 14 days.

Case example

Richard had been in four different hospitals more than 12 times. In the course of his therapy it became clearer when and why he reacted psychotically. A psychotic reaction – he has been diagnosed as having schizophrenia – was his way of regulating demands on him, distance and closeness. The fragmentation between the different services so far had not enabled him to integrate his different experiences and make sense of it, nor to survive psychosis without feeling fragmented.

Supervision

I understand the fragmented system network as a disintegrating mother, a broken container to whom life has to be inhaled and the capacity to respond to the patient's spontaneous expressions, otherwise chronification of the patient's symptoms and dissolution of his personality will occur, because he is fixed on the pathological symptoms and becomes more and more dependent on them as an as-if-personality.

Whereas a sufficiently good enough mother is able to make sense of the infantile expressions of omnipotence and gives him a feeling of being whole, the not sufficiently good enough mother will not be successful in answering his spontaneous gestures. Rather, she puts her own gestures in the place of a meaningful answer, which now in turn, only becomes meaningful through the compliance of the good child.

The community and the system network are confronted with the task of perceiving traces of spontaneous gestures and expressions of life as the patient's language (Montgomery 1989), however hidden they may be behind the vicious circle of symptoms,. The community, like a good enough mother, must answer the gesture of the patient, instead of replacing these with her own institutionalised gestures, to which the patient then gives sense through compliance. Initially, it is essential to welcome the omnipotent gestures, the healthy impulses and to filter them out from the many symptoms. A healing environment waits to grasp the spontaneous gestures and does not reward the pseudo-harmony of compliance. We feel regular, twice-weekly supervision is a necessary condition to achieve this.

Conclusion

The person with psychosis is an ultimate challenge to our capacity to understand and to endure emotions. Our task is to understand under which conditions these feelings can be experienced, endured and survived. However, ultimately we should not forget how Benedetti (1992) – that truly dedicated therapist of psychosis – saw things. For him when the therapist and, for that matter, when the surrounding community, endures the feeling of absolute impotence, powerless and helplessness in the face of the landscapes of death, when they are unable to change the horrible, that is the moment when the impotent and helpless patient no longer feels alone with his overwhelming feelings. In my experience it is this sharing of feelings that opens for the traumatised the way back to the humane part of mankind.

Bibliography

Abraham, A. (1999). The Coself, or Primary Syntheism, *Group Analysis* 32: 293–308.

Benedetti, G. (1992). *Psychotherapie als Existentielle Herausforderung*. Zürich: Vandenhoek & Rupprecht.

Bion, W.R. (1959). Attacks on linking, *International Journal of Psycho-Analysis* 40: 308–315.

Bleger, J. (1972). *Symbiosi y ambigüedad*. Buenos Aires: Paidos.

de Marè, P. (1974). The politics of large groups, in L. Kreeger (ed.) *The Large Group*. London: Karnac Books.

de Marè, P., Piper, R. and Thompson, S. (1991). *Koinonia. From Hate through Dialogue, to Culture in the Large Group*. London: Karnac Books.

Foulkes, S.H. (1948). *Introduction to Group-Analytic Psychotherapy*. London: Heinemann.

Hafers, A. (1996). Vom Inselhüpfen zum Festland, betreutes Wohnen als therapeutische Gemeinschaft, *Systema* 10(2).

Herman, J. (1992). Complex PTSD: a syndrome in survivors of prolonged and repeated trauma, *Journal of Traumatic Stress* 5: 377–391.

Kernberg, O. (1985). The couch at sea: psychoanalytic studies of group and organizational leadership, in A.D. Colman and M.H. Geller (eds) *Group Relations – Reader 2*. Washington, DC: A.K. Rice Institute.

Kernberg, O. (1993). Projective identification, countertransference, and hospital treatment, in A. Alexandris and G. Vaslamatzis (eds) *Countertransference: Theory, technique, teaching*. London: Karnac Books.

Kernberg, O. (1995). *Bureaucracy and Ideology as Social Defences against Paranoid Aggression*. Paper given at the Arbours Association 25th Anniversary Conference, London, 4–5 February.

Maslow, A. (1996). The Jonah complex: understanding our fear of growth, in E. Hoffmann (ed.) *The Unpublished Papers of Abraham Maslow*. London: Sage.

Milad, R., Quinn, B.T., Pitman, R.K., Orr, S.P., Fischl, B. and Rauch, S.L. (2005). Massachusetts General Hospital, Boston: PNAS, Online-prepublication, DOI: 10.1073/pnas.0502441102.

Montgomery, J.D. (1989). Chronic patienthood as an iatrogenic false self, in M.G. Fromm and B.L. Smith (eds) *The Facilitating Environment:* Clinical applications of *Winnicott's theory*. Madison, WI: International Universities Press.

Smith, B.L. (1989). The community as object, in M.G. Fromm and B.L. Smith (eds) *The Facilitating Environment:* Clinical applications of *Winnicott's theory*. Madison, WI: International Universities Press.

Sugarman, A. and Jaffe, L.S. (1989). A developmental line of transitional phenomena, in M.G. Fromm and B.L. Smith (eds) *The Facilitating Environment:* Clinical applications of *Winnicott's theory*. Madison, WI: International Universities Press.

Tienari, P. and Wynne, L.C. (1994). Adoption studies of schizophrenia, *Annals of Medicine* 26: 233–237.

Tienari, P., Wynne, L., Moring, J., Lahti, I., Naarala, M., Sorri, A. et al. (1994). The Finnish adoptive family study of schizophrenia: implications for family research, *British Journal of Psychiatry* 164 (Supplement 23): 20–26.

Van der Linden, P. (1994). *What We cannot Speak about*. Paper presented at the Annual Conference of the Association of Therapeutic Communities, Windsor.

Volkan, V.D. (1991). On chosen traumas, *Mind and Human Interaction* 3: 13.

Volkan, V.D. (2004). *Das infantile psychotische Selbst und seine weitere Entwicklung*. Göttingen: Vandenhoeck & Rupprecht.

von Wallenberg Pachaly, A. (1992). The time-limited psychoanalytic milieu-therapeutic community, *Therapeutic Communities* 13(4): 193–207.

von Wallenberg Pachaly, A. (1995a). A group-dynamic understanding of structural violence and group psychotherapy, *Free Associations* 5(2): 221–238.

von Wallenberg Pachaly, A. (1995b). The German marriage: intrapsychic, interpersonal, and international dimensions, in M. Ettin, J. Fidler and B. Cohen (eds) *Group Process and Political Dynamics*. Madison, WI: International Universities Press.

von Wallenberg Pachaly, A. (1996).*The Magic Mountain in the Community – A Paradigmatic Change from Sheltered Living in a Flat towards a Therapeutic Community within the Community*. Paper presented at the Annual Conference of the Association of Therapeutic Communities, Windsor.

von Wallenberg Pachaly, A. (1997). The large group and the large system group – coping with fusion, fragmentation, and splitting within the large group setting of the therapeutic community within the community, *Therapeutic Communities* 18(3): 223–239.

von Wallenberg Pachaly, A. (1999). *Community and Group as Transitional Object –*

A Developmental Space for Chronically Ill Patients. Paper presented at the Annual Conference of the Association of Therapeutic Communities, Windsor.

von Wallenberg Pachaly, A. (2000). Group psychotherapy for victims of political persecution and ethnic conflict, in R. Klein and V. Schermer (eds) *The Healing Circle: Group psychotherapy for psychological trauma.* New York: Guilford Press.

von Wallenberg Pachaly, A. and Griepenstroh, D. (1979). Das energetische Prinzip bei Freud und Ammon, in G. Ammon (ed.) *Handbuch der Dynamischen Psychiatrie (Vol. 1).* Munich: Ernst Reinhardt Verlag.

von Wallenberg Pachaly, S. (1997). The Odyssey of sheltered living in the therapeutic community within the community, *Therapeutic Communities* 18(2): 27–37.

Whiteley, S. (1980). A community study: the Henderson Hospital, *International Journal of Therapeutic Communities* 1(1): 38–58.

Winnicott, D.W. (1969). The use of an object, *International Journal of Psycho-Analysis* 50: 711–716.

Winnicott, D.W. (1972). *The Maturational Processes and the Facilitating Environment: Studies in the theory of emotional development.* London: Hogarth.

Wurmser L. (1999). *Magic Change Tragic Change.* Paper presented at the 5th Steprather Symposium on Visions in the Psychotherapy of Psychosis, Geldern-Walbeck, June.

Chapter 23

Evidence for the effectiveness of therapeutic community treatment of the psychoses

John Gale and Beatriz Sánchez España

Research into therapeutic communities

Lees et al. (2004) brought together a wide range of papers discussing all aspects of therapeutic community research. They consider which methods are most appropriate in the unique environment of therapeutic communities, as well as ethical questions. The volume includes several research studies undertaken in the UK. Other studies showing the effectiveness of therapeutic community treatment have also been published in the UK (Dolan et al. 1997; Griffiths 1997). Lees et al. (1999) undertook a systematic review of therapeutic community effectiveness in various settings in 1998, including a meta-analysis, of 29 studies.

The therapeutic community environment and effective use of group CBT

The therapeutic community modality of treatment represents a useful framework within which other treatment interventions can be applied. It fuses therapeutic approaches and practice from both psychodynamic and CBT traditions with rehabilitation, practical skills learning and retraining for work.

There is a growing body of evidence in the UK and elsewhere to suggest that group CBT can be effective with people with psychosis. Contemporary studies are shifting their focus from the treatment of individual positive symptoms – especially delusions and hallucinations – to therapy with people who present with complex and diverse difficulties. This is particularly relevant for therapeutic communities, as the group itself is an important component of the treatment. The group provides a forum for peer relating, safely experimenting with new behaviours and solidarity for bolstering self-regard through the challenging of negative social stereotypes. There is now convincing evidence from controlled trials for the effectiveness of group CBT at reducing symptoms and associated distress in people with medication resistant psychosis, acute episode and early psychosis. Important general studies include Barrowclough et al. 2006; Birchwood et al. 1998; Chadwick and Trower 1996; Fowler et al. 1995; Gledhill et al. 1998. Birchwood's findings (1988) were consistent with earlier studies, which had reviewed group treatment with people with schizophrenia and found benefits with interaction-oriented group approaches such as that discussed by Kanas (1986).

One of the central focuses of cognitive therapy for people suffering from psychosis is on identifying and questioning dysfunctional assumptions. A therapeutic community environment sets up the basics for this sort of intervention, in a culture of enquiry and reality confrontation. Perris (1989) analysed progress made by 30 patients when offered cognitive therapy in a therapeutic milieu context in a residential setting. Nine dropped out and the rest showed significant improvement in social functioning and maintained this for the following 3 years.

On the value of group cognitive therapy with people in acute episodes, Drury et al. (1996) report a trial that measured and confirmed the reduction of residual symptoms, hastening the resolution of positive symptoms when individual and group CBT was used in conjunction with pharmacotherapy and standard care for acute psychosis.

Effectiveness of therapeutic community treatment for schizophrenia

According to Werbart (1997) and Svensson (1999) residential homes, whether psychodynamically oriented or more centred on cognitive treatment, function well for those suffering from schizophrenia. There is a large body of very sophisticated research which demonstrates the effectiveness of therapeutic community treatment for a variety of diagnoses, including schizophrenia, in a number of different countries (Armelius et al. 2001). In the USA this had been led by the late Dr Loren Mosher and his colleagues who initiated and developed the Soteria Project in the 1970s and early 1980s, financed by the US National Institute of Mental Health. Mosher's team has published over 40 papers documenting the effectiveness of non-hospital-based therapeutic community treatment for schizophrenia (Mosher and Bola 2000, 2003).

Studies of the effectiveness of therapeutic community treatment in Switzerland and Sweden have also been published. Ciompi and his co-workers further developed the low drug milieu therapeutic approach for schizophrenia implemented by Mosher in 1984. Both support the hypothesis that therapeutic interventions could prevent the negative effect that basic emotional states on thinking and behaving play in schizophrenia, giving considerable weight to emotional factors in the disorder. They have worked towards implementing a psycho-social-biological treatment. Their studies have shown that similar or possibly better outcomes than those found in standard inpatient settings can be achieved in this way with significant lower doses of medication. Ciompi and Hoffmann (2004) identified therapeutic principles as practical guidelines: to create as normal as possible therapeutic settings, personalised being-with the patient, personal continuity, close collaboration and clear communication with relatives, other professionals and other patients, realistic goals and expectations and aftercare and relapse prevention (Ciompi et al. 1992). These accurately described some of the basic therapeutic community principles. This is in line with studies by Gunderson (1980), Ellsworth (1983), Carpenter et al. (1977) and Cullberg et al. (2002) that show that milieu therapy leads to a reduction in symptoms and social functioning.

Gottdiener and Haslam, from the University of Melbourne, conducted a meta-analysis on the efficacy of individual psychotherapy for people diagnosed with schizophrenia (Gottdiener and Haslam 2002). The findings of this meta-analysis are consistent with those of other studies (Mojtabai et al. 1998; Smith et al. 1980). These studies indicate that psychodynamic psychotherapy is associated with improved functioning in most patients diagnosed with schizophrenia. Although all forms of psychotherapy were associated with an improvement in functioning, the highest rates of improvement were associated with psychodynamic and cognitive-behavioural therapies. This is true especially with patients others consider incurable (Benedetti and Furlan 1993; Boyer and Giovacchini 1967; Karon and Vandenbos 1981; Kapur et al. 1997; Robins 1993).

A large-scale national project evaluating the treatment of 146 severely disturbed psychiatric patients living in 23 group homes in Sweden was undertaken by Armelius et al. (2001) over a 5-year timespan. The patients were mostly diagnosed with schizophrenia. Although the results showed relatively little change, as much as 19% of positive outcome was accounted for by the psychosocial climate at the homes.

Community Housing and Therapy

Community Housing and Therapy (CHT) is a national voluntary organisation and one of the few UK providers of therapeutic communities in the community for people suffering from psychosis. It runs nine therapeutic communities and brings together a concern for the underlying psychological causes of distress and disturbance, and a practical programme aimed at training and employment through partnership with other agencies. CHT provides psychological treatment in a therapeutic community setting in conjunction with pharmacological therapy. CHT is a leading member of the Association of Therapeutic Communities (ATC) and the International Society for the Psychological Treatment of the Schizophrenias and Other Psychoses (ISPS). CHT is committed to evaluation and research. It works closely with the Royal College of Psychiatrists Research Unit on monitoring standards and has been carrying out several quantitative and qualitative research programmes over the years. CHT's research team collect data periodically using routine clinical outcome measures recommended by the English National Service Framework for Mental Health, such as the Health of the Nation Outcomes Scales (HoNOS), which measures the health and social functioning of people with severe mental illness.

Research projects at Community Housing and Therapy (CHT)

Qualitative research

CHT commissioned Barbara Rawlings, a research fellow from Manchester University, to carry out a qualitative research in 2006. The project consisted of the design of a database and analysis of the collected data from the records of 100 former patients. The research describes how patients go through their placements in CHT and identifies what were considered to be evidence of progress and lack of progress, in a way that goes beyond the measurement of symptoms:

> As clients continued with their residencies, the signs of progress or lack of progress tended to be fairly specific to their particular situation. Thus, a client who had trouble cleaning or shopping would be seen as making progress if he took part in a cleaning group or accompanied another client to the shops. This would not be regarded as progress so clearly in a client who had always enjoyed these activities. One client who was in the habit of absconding when things got too stressful in the house learned instead to withdraw briefly to his room and calm himself down there. This was seen as progress, whereas in other clients such voluntary isolation could be seen as problem behaviour. The major measure of progress for all clients was the extent to which clients participated in and engaged in the therapeutic programme. Missing groups, meetings or key-working sessions were signs of trouble; attending and participating in these activities were signs of commitment at least, although it was possible to attend these activities but participate badly. To be making *progress* a client would generally need to do more than just attend and participate – they would need to *engage*. Engagement involves a number of things, such as actively listening to or confronting other clients and offering support to other clients, but above all it requires the client to talk about their own problems and to express their feelings about them. Thus it would be possible for a client to attend all groups, but behave in them in such a way that they would not be seen as making progress.

> (Rawlings 2007)

Research on clinical outcomes and therapeutic environment

CHT is currently carrying out a research project, under the direction of Dr Mark Freestone from Nottingham University, that focuses on designing and implementing a naturalistic analysis of the relationship between clinical outcomes in CHTs therapeutic communities and the therapeutic environment. The data collection measures are divided into four areas.

MEASURES OF THERAPEUTIC PROGRAMME AND ENVIRONMENT

The Residential Substance Abuse and Psychiatric Programmes Inventory (RESPPI) was developed by Timko (1994, 1995, 1996). It is a large, researcher-administered questionnaire that aims to capture all the salient features of the treatment environment, regime and service provision. It consists of five sections, each of which focuses on a separate aspect of the programme (physical, procedural, environmental, demographic and aesthetic).

The Community Oriented Programmes Environment Scale (COPES) is a part of RESPPI originally designed as the Ward Atmosphere Scale (WAS) but later adapted for community-based programmes.

The Good Milieu Index (GMI) is a quick checklist of items aimed at client members designed to catch perceptions of the quality of the social environment.

The Working Alliance Inventory (WAI) is a generic measure consisting of separate staff and patient questionnaires – or alternatively, as a single scale for observers – with 12-item scales reflecting the strength and nature of the therapeutic alliance (Horvath and Greenberg 1989; Tichenor and Hill 1989).

STATIC MEASURES OF PATIENT GROUP PSYCHOPATHOLOGY

The Structured Clinical Interview for DSM-IV Axis I (SCID I) is a structured, primarily clinical interview for ascertaining the presence of DSM Axis I disorders in client members (it also exists in an Axis II version – the SCID II). It must be completed by a trained researcher, ideally a clinician, and takes 1 or 2 hours.

The Borderline Syndrome Index (BoSI) is a 52-item self-report questionnaire that was originally designed in 1980 to provide an assessment of borderline traits. Subsequent research revealed that, although the questionnaire was at best only moderately good at catching actual borderline symptomatology, it was a good generic measure of psychopathological distress (Conte et al. 1980; Marlowe et al. 1996).

DYNAMIC MEASURES OF THERAPEUTIC CHANGE AND OUTCOMES

The Health of the Nation Outcome Scales (HoNOS) is a 12-item scale measuring mental health outcomes, developed by the Royal College of Psychiatrists Research Unit (CRU).

The Clinical Outcomes Routine Evaluation (CORE) is an outcome measure consisting of a 34-item self-report questionnaire (Evans et al. 2000).

The Borderline Syndrome Index (BoSI) is similar to the CORE but also used as a change measure.

ULTIMATE OUTCOMES

Length of stay data gathers information on the admission and discharge dates of patients to and from the therapeutic community that can be collated to give length of stay data relative to completion of self-report questionnaire packs during the study.

A Referral Questionnaire has been developed for discharged patients for structured information on their activities and experiences after leaving the community.

Psychoanalytically informed research on evidenced based practice in the context of social care

CHT operates in the hinterland between health and social care and is regulated by the Commission for Social Care Inspection (CSCI) and its clients are mostly funded by social service departments. This gives it a particular relationship to social work and, in fact, each year student social workers from a number of universities complete an internship with CHT, as part of their university course. Recently, the specific nature of evidence-based practice within social work has been discussed (Webb 2001). The Centre for Social Work Research (CSWR) at the University of East London (UEL) has been set up, in collaboration with the Tavistock Clinic, to offer a distinctive relationship-based approach to psychosocial interventions. CHT is in the process of setting up a long-term relationship with CSWR.

CSWR aims to make a significant contribution to the generation of knowledge in social work and to enhance research in the profession. The Centre's research is strongly influenced by the commitment in social work at UEL to psychosocial relationship-based practice, that explores the underlying processes of practice from a psychoanalytic and systemic perspective. The research which CHT is planning with CSWR aims to assess and evaluate the impact and effectiveness of therapeutic communities on clients with severe mental illness. Through developing a detailed, fine-grained understanding of the process of therapeutic interventions in the community, the study of outcomes will be closely linked to these processes. The research aims to demonstrate effectiveness of the therapeutic community approach and to assess, evaluate and understand the changes made by patients staying in the communities run by CHT. These changes or outcomes will be assessed in terms of psychosocial indicators and connected with the processes in the psychotherapeutic environment of the therapeutic community.

The National Institute for Health and Clinical Excellence (NICE) review of clinical guidelines on schizophrenia

In the UK, the National Institute for Health and Clinical Excellence (NICE) produced clinical guidelines for the treatment and management of schizophrenia in 2002. NICE is an independent organisation responsible for producing national guidance on the promotion of good health and the prevention and treatment of ill health.

Guidelines on public health, health technology and clinical practice are developed by a number of independent advisory groups made up of health professionals, those working in the National Health Service (NHS), patients, their carers and the public. In the 2002 *Guideline* psychological interventions were identified as a key element in promoting recovery in schizophrenia.

NICE is currently undertaking a review of the 2002 clinical guidelines on schizophrenia. As a stakeholder organisation, CHT has set up an advisory group with other stakeholder organisations, including ISPS UK, the Tavistock and Portman NHS Trust, the Association of Psychoanalytic Psychotherapy, Threshold and the Association of Therapeutic Communities (ATC). The advisory group is working to get a wide range of psychological interventions, including therapeutic communities recognised in these revised guidelines. Other interventions include psychodynamic psychotherapy, the treatment of anxiety and depression in schizophrenia, support to staff and carers. With CBT, which was already included in the 2002 *Guideline*, the group aims to have as wide a range of interventions as possible included not a single and specific psychological approach.

The members of the advisory group are conducting literature reviews on separate psychological interventions in order to be able to demonstrate effectiveness. NICE places research based on randomised control trials (RCT) at the top of the hierarchy of evidence. And this presents problems for therapeutic communities. But non-experimental, naturalistic studies or clinical experience are other ways of evaluating cost-effective treatments. The instruments currently used to evaluate effectiveness of treatments tent to focus on the measurement of symptoms and the advisory group recognises the importance of pointing out other ways of measuring effectiveness.

For example, finding out from users what factors they consider indicators of improvement in schizophrenia, whether sufferers are able to maintain social relationships or find and sustain employment.

Conclusion

Following their systematic international literature review, Lees et al. (1999) concluded that:

> [T]herapeutic communities have not produced the amount or quality of research literature that we might have expected, given the length of time they have been in existence and the quality of staff we know exists and has existed in therapeutic communities. This may be partly due to a lack of emphasis placed on research in the early days of therapeutic community development, and more recently to a lack of resources, in terms of finance, staff and adequate research methodologies, designs and instruments.
>
> (Lees et al. 1999: 3)

Although this study was commissioned to look at therapeutic communities for people with a personality disorder, undoubtedly the same could be said in the case of therapeutic communities for those with psychosis. The tide does, however, at last seem to have changed. First, with the work of Loren Mosher, followed by that of Luc Ciompi and later that of Raman Kapur and his colleagues at Threshold, Northern Ireland, therapeutic communities that treat psychoses are assembling a body of evidence to demonstrate their effectiveness. This chapter has endeavoured to show how a small organisation, CHT, is managing to incorporate research into its programmes by outsourcing the research function through partnerships and by bringing in research consultants. While still embryonic, this engagement with research has enabled CHT to participate as a stakeholder in the review of the NICE guidelines on schizophrenia and thus to play a small part in the formation of mental health policy at the national level. The next stage is likely to involve finding ways to include some forms of RCTs within therapeutic communities.

Bibliography

Armelius, B.-Å. (2001). *The Efficiency of Small Treatment Homes for Severely Disturbed Psychiatric Patients.* Paper presented at the Annual Meeting of the Society for Psychotherapy Research, Montevideo, Uruguay.

Armelius, B.-Å., Börjesson, J., Fogelstam, H., Granberg, Å., Hemphälä, M. and Jeanneau, M. (2001). *A Five-year Study of Patients and Staff at the Treatment*

Home Varpen 1993–1998. Slutrapport nr 24 från Behandlingshemsprojektet. Umeå: Umeå University, Department of Psychology.

Barrowclough, C., Haddock, G., Lobban, F., Jones, S., Siddle, R., Roberts, C. et al. (2006). Group CBT for schizophrenia, RCT, *British Journal of Psychiatry* 189: 527–532.

Benedetti, G. and Furlan, P. (eds) (1993). *The Psychotherapy of Schizophrenia*. Seattle, WA: Hogrefe & Huber.

Birchwood, B., Tood, P. and Jackson, C. (1998). Early intervention in psychosis, *British Journal of Psychiatry* 172 (Supplement 33): 53–59.

Boyer, L. and Giovacchini, P. (1967). *Psychoanalytic Treatment of Schizophrenic and Characterological Disorders*. New York: Science House.

Carpenter, W.T., McGlashan, T.H. and Strauss, J.S. (1977). The treatment of acute schizophrenia without drugs: an investigation of some current assumptions, *American Journal of Psychiatry* 134: 14–20.

Chadwick, P.D.J. and Trower, P. (1996). *Cognitive Therapy for Delusions, Voices and Paranoia*. Chichester: John Wiley & Sons.

Ciompi, L. and Hoffmann, H. (2004). Soteria Berne: an innovative milieu therapeutic approach to acute schizophrenia based on the concept of affect-logic, *World Psychiatry* 3(3). 140–146.

Ciompi, L., Dawaldes, M.P., Maier, C.H., Albi, W., Trfitzsch, K., Kupper, Z. et al. (1992). The pilot project: 'Soteria Berne': clinical experiences and results, *British Journal of Psychiatry* 161 (Supplement 18): 145–153.

Conte, H., Plutchik, R., Karasu, T. and Jerrett, I. (1980). A self-report borderline scale: discriminative validity and preliminary norms, *Journal of Nervous and Mental Disease* 168: 428–435.

Cullberg, J., Levander, S., Holmquist, R., Mattsoon, M. and Wieselgren, I.-M. (2002). One-year outcome in first episode psychosis patients in the Swedish Parachute project, *Acta Psychiatrica Scandinavica* 106: 276–285.

Dolan, B., Warren, F. and Norton, K. (1997). Change in borderline symptoms one year after therapeutic community treatment for severe personality disorder, *British Journal of Psychiatry* 171: 274–279.

Drury, V., Birchwood, B., Cochrane, R. and Macmillan, F. (1996). Cognitive therapy and recovery from acute psychosis: a controlled trial. Impact on psychotic symptoms, *British Journal of Psychiatry* 169: 593–601.

Ellsworth, R.B. (1983). Characteristics of effective treatment milieus, in J.G. Gunderson, O.A. Will and L.R. Mosher (eds) *The Principle and Practices of Milieu Therapy*. New York: Aronson.

Evans, C., Mellor-Clark, J., Margison, F., Barkham, K., Audin, J., Connell, G. et al. (2000). CORE: clinical outcomes in routine evaluation, *Journal of Mental Health* 9: 247–255.

Fowler, D., Garety, P.A. and Kuipers, E. (1995). *Cognitive Behavioural Therapy for Psychosis: Theory and practice*. Chichester: John Wiley & Sons.

Gledhill, A., Lobban, F. and Selwood, W. (1998). Group CBT for people with schizophrenia: a preliminary evaluation, *Behavioural and Cognitive Psychotherapy* 26: 63–75.

Gottdiener, W.H. and Haslam, N. (2002). The benefits of individual psychotherapy for people diagnosed with schizophrenia: a meta-analytic review, *Ethical Human Science and Services* 4.

Griffiths, P. (1997). *Psychosocial Practice within a Residential Setting*. London: Karnac Books.

Gunderson, J.G. (1980). A re-evaluation of milieu therapy for non chronic schizophrenic patients, *Schizophrenia Bulletin* 6: 64–69.

Horvath, A.O. and Greenberg, L.S. (1989). Development and validation of the working alliance inventory, *Journal of Counselling Psychology* 36: 223–233.

Kanas, N. (1986). Group therapy with schizophrenics: a review of controlled studies, *International Journal of Group Psychotherapy* 36: 339–351.

Kapur, R. et al. (1997). An evaluation of Threshold therapeutic communities in Northern Ireland, *Irish Journal of Psychological Medicine* 14: 65–68.

Karon, B. and Vandenbos, G. (1981). *Psychotherapy of Schizophrenia: The treatment of choice*. New York: Jason Aronson.

Lees, J., Manning, N., Menzies, D. and Morant, N. (2004). *A Culture of Enquiry – Research Evidence and the Therapeutic Community*. London and New York: Jessica Kingsley.

Lees, J., Manning, N. and Rawlings, B. (1999). *Therapeutic Community Effectiveness. A systematic international review of therapeutic community treatment for people with personality disorders and mentally disordered offenders*. CRD Report 17. York: NHS Centre for Reviews and Dissemination.

Marlowe, M.J., O'Neill-Byrne, K., Lowe-Ponsford, F. and Watson, J.P. (1996). The Borderline Syndrome Index: a validation study using the personality assessment schedule, *British Journal of Psychiatry* 168: 72–75.

Mojtabai, R., Nicholson, R.A. and Carpenter, B.N. (1998). Role of psychosocial treatments in management of schizophrenia: a meta-analytic review of controlled outcome studies, *Schizophrenia Bulletin* 24: 569–587.

Mosher, L. and Bola, J. (2000). The Soteria Project: twenty five years of swimming upriver, *Complexity and Change* 9(1): 68–74.

Mosher, L. and Bola, J. (2003). Treatment of acute psychosis without neuroleptics: two-year outcomes from the Soteria Project, *Journal of Nervous and Mental Disease* 191(4): 219–229.

Perris, C. (1989). *Cognitive Therapy for Patients with Schizophrenia*. New York: Cassell.

Rawlings, B. (2006). Paper submitted to *Therapeutic Communities*.

Robins, M. (1993). *Experiences of Schizophrenia*. New York: Guilford Press.

Smith, M.L., Glass, G.V. and Miller, T.I. (1980). *The Benefits of Psychotherapy*. Baltimore, MD: Johns Hopkins University Press.

Svensson, B. (1999). *Treatment Process and Outcome for Long-term Mentally Ill Patients in a Comprehensive Treatment Program Based on Cognitive Therapy*. Lunds University: Academic dissertation.

Tichenor, V. and Hill, C.E. (1989). A comparison of six measures of working alliance, *Psychotherapy* 26: 195–199

Timko, C. (1994). *The Quality of Psychiatric Treatment Programs*. Palo Alto, CA: Center for Health Care Evaluation, Department of Veterans Affairs Medical Center.

Timko, C. (1995). Policies and services in residential substance abuse programs: comparisons with psychiatric programs, *Journal of Substance Abuse* 7: 43–59.

Timko, C. (1996). Physical characteristics of residential psychiatric and substance abuse programs: organizational determinants and patients outcomes, *American Journal of Community Psychology* 24(1): 173–192.

Webb, S.A. (2001). Some considerations on the validity of evidenced-based practice in social work, *British Journal of Social Work* 31: 57–79.

Werbart, A. (1997). Separation, termination-process, and long-term outcome in psychotherapy with severely disturbed patients, *Bulletin of the Menninger Clinic* 61: 16–43.

Index